Josephine Community Libraries
Grants Pass, Oregon

D0438205

DATE DUE   4/18

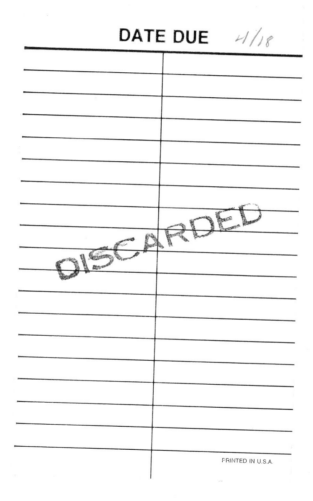

PRINTED IN U.S.A.

ALSO BY EDWARD TENNER

Our Own Devices:
How Technology Remakes Humanity

Why Things Bite Back:
Technology and the Revenge of Unintended Consequences

Tech Speak:
How to Talk High Tech

THE EFFICIENCY PARADOX

Josephine Community Libraries
Grants Pass, Oregon

THE EFFICIENCY PARADOX

WHAT BIG DATA CAN'T DO

EDWARD TENNER

Josephine Community Libraries
Grants Pass, Oregon

ALFRED A. KNOPF

NEW YORK

2018

THIS IS A BORZOI BOOK
PUBLISHED BY ALFRED A. KNOPF

Copyright © 2018 by Edward Tenner

All rights reserved. Published in the United States by Alfred A. Knopf,
a division of Penguin Random House LLC, New York,
and distributed in Canada by Random House of Canada,
a division of Penguin Random House Canada Limited, Toronto.

www.aaknopf.com

Knopf, Borzoi Books, and the colophon are registered
trademarks of Penguin Random House LLC.

Library of Congress Cataloging-in-Publication Data
Names: Tenner, Edward, author.
Title: The efficiency paradox : what big data can't do / Edward Tenner.
Description: First Edition. | New York : Knopf, 2018.
Identifiers: LCCN 2017032040 | ISBN 9781400041398 (hardcover) |
ISBN 9780525520306 (ebook)
Subjects: LCSH: Industrial efficiency. | Serendipity. | Artificial intelligence. | Big data. |
BISAC: BUSINESS & ECONOMICS / Knowledge Capital. | SOCIAL SCIENCE / Media Studies. |
SELF-HELP / Time Management.
Classification: LCC T58.8.T45 2018 | DDC 658.5/15—dc23 LC record available at
https://lccn.loc.gov/2017032040

Jacket design by Tyler Comrie

Manufactured in the United States of America
First Edition

To the memory of William H. McNeill

CONTENTS

THE SEVEN DEADLY SINS OF EFFICIENCY

WHY IT IS STILL A WORK IN PROGRESS

This book is a critique of something self-evidently desirable, even wonderful, until it isn't: efficiency. And it's also about an apparent oxymoron that seems absurd until we realize that it's also been essential: inspired inefficiency. Efficiency is mostly good but, like all good things, can be carried too far; even an excess of water can be lethal.

More than twenty years ago at the dawn of the web as we know it, when I wrote my first book on the unintended consequences of technology, *Why Things Bite Back*, published in 1996, the idea of efficiency itself as a threat hardly occurred to me. In fact, far from allying with the critics who called themselves neo-Luddites (a term now shared by their friends and foes), I was an early adopter and enthusiast. As a science book editor recruiting authors globally and affiliated with a university offering email, I had already been using it to correspond and set up appointments. As a researcher already using electronic databases, I found the new web browser and graphic interface a welcome improvement. As a writer always tinkering with my text, I had embraced word processing since the days of the TRS-80 in the early

Reagan era. Remembering the tedium of retyping and the mess of carbon paper, I felt (and feel) no nostalgia for my own typewriting, though I do find that the typewritten letter has a distinctive graphic personality through the "bite" of letters in the paper and the varying impressions created by carbon ribbons from saturated to faint.

I saw and wrote about the downside of new technology, the chronic back pain and carpal tunnel ailments resulting from the ever more sedentary office, and the comical fate of the paperless office. But I shared in much of the technological optimism of the later 1990s. The web at first appeared a godsend for newspapers and magazines. Whether or not electronic publication ever replaced print, their publishers reasoned, they held a priceless franchise in high-quality content that attracted an affluent readership coveted by advertisers. Technology itself was a profitable advertising focus into the early twenty-first century. I occasionally find the thick "Circuits" section of *The New York Times* among my clippings, well sponsored by hardware and software publishers and electronics retailers. The efficiency of the electronic newsroom helped make all this possible.

It seemed that society could have its cake and eat it, too. Amazon appeared, but it could coexist with still profitable chains of giant bookstores. It was hard to imagine that Amazon threatened Borders and Barnes & Noble, as these had decimated independent bookstores in the 1980s with crushing scale and an earlier generation of technology. The rise of robotics did not seem to threaten employment levels. Old-line business magazines shared still thriving newsstands with technology-oriented newcomers like *Wired* and *The Industry Standard*. Technological utopian authors spread the gospel of individual empowerment while corporate elites made more money than ever. If the 1960s were the go-go years, the 1990s were the win-win decade thanks to the efficiency of the web.

Beginning around 2005, the new hyperefficient world entered a different phase. With the introduction of the Apple iPhone in 2007, made possible by the rapid evolution of computer processing speed, electronic devices were gradually ceasing to be tools that people used and put away and becoming extensions of their selves and their personal and professional networks. At the same time, the exceptionally efficient search engine Google and the social networking site Facebook, together with Amazon, were transforming online commerce by adding a new level to the Internet, the platform, between the corporate website and the open web.

Since 2008, the dream of utopia through ever-increasing electronic efficiency has been dimmed. The recession that began that year had many origins, but was due in part to the technical ease with which bankers and securities industry professionals were able to manage risk. Meanwhile, the rate of increase of the number of transistors that can fit on a computer chip has been slowing down. It used to double every eighteen months or so, a rhythm described since 1965 as Moore's Law (after Gordon Moore, a founder of the dominant chip manufacturer Intel), but since 2005 has been stretched to two to three years. Further, the success of new platforms in attracting advertisers and marketers has come at the expense of the revenue of newspapers and magazines. (The all-time peak in advertising revenues did not occur until ten years after the advent of the web, in 2005, when it was $47.4 billion in print and $2 billion in digital; in 2014 these numbers were $16.4 billion and $3.5 billion, respectively.)[1]

There were, of course, many winners as well as losers in the new hyperefficient web, in which computer techniques—algorithms—were supplanting intuitive judgment. And there were benefits to web-savvy consumers from increased price competition. But for many economists, the hope was dimming that the benefits of more efficient production and distribution would lift the public's standard of living. Two noted economists, Tyler Cowen in *The Great Stagnation* (2011) and Robert J. Gordon in *The Rise and Fall of American Growth* (2016), even advanced the previously heretical idea that the twentieth century had seen the last of an era of "low-hanging fruit," transformative innovations that by today's standards were relatively cheap to develop. This is a sharp turn from the mood even at the beginning of the 2008 recession, when the computer scientist and futurist Ray Kurzweil repeated his prediction from 2000 that a computer with the hardware to emulate a human brain would be available for $1,000 by the year 2020.[2]

Not only some economists but many citizens of Western countries have lost faith in the ability of industrial and academic elites to deliver the benefits of technological efficiency to either the middle class or the poor. Unless the trend reverses, politics around the world are likely to remain unsettled for years to come, no matter which parties hold power. So it is time to consider whether too much efficiency is part of the problem. I will suggest that we need not abandon the idea of efficiency but cultivate inefficient behavior that in the long run will make technology not only more effective (getting more done) but more efficient (doing it with fewer resources).

First we need a definition of efficiency. Economists use the term technically in a way that I could not follow here without making this a different book. I would define it as producing goods, providing services or information, or processing transactions with a minimum of waste. The word came into wide use in the nineteenth century, when scientists and engineers extended to human labor the physical idea of efficiency as useful work per unit of energy. Social scientists from the 1890s through the 1920s in turn expanded this sense to all inputs and outputs in society, and indeed to an ideal of "social efficiency," the rational optimization of human welfare. Innocent as the phrase sounds today, at the turn of the century it was rooted as much in racism and xenophobia as in technological idealism. Its prophet, the sociologist Edward A. Ross, was forced to leave Stanford University for his anti-Asian pronouncements in 1900. In his book *Social Control*, published the following year, he combined admiration for "the restless, striving, doing Aryan, with his personal ambition, his lust for power, his longing to wreak [*sic*] himself, his willingness to turn the world upside down to get the fame, or the fortune or the woman he wants," with fear that this Faustian individualism would ruin society if left unchecked. As a nativist progressive, Ross looked to the schools to use the methods of industrial work rationalization to indoctrinate a new generation in the ethics of good government. That ideology of efficiency has long vanished, but the goal of achieving more with less effort still thrives. I would apply the word "efficiency" to all technology intended to reduce human time needed for a task, whether buying a product, learning a subject, planning a trip, or making a medical decision. The economist Robert Solow remarked over thirty years ago, in 1987, that computers had become ubiquitous everywhere but in productivity statistics; today we see the benefits of algorithmic efficiency everywhere except in real personal income statistics.[3]

I take no position on the future, whether we are doomed to stasis and growing inequality or whether some new superefficient technology will make today's concerns seem like the pessimism of many economists of the 1930s, when in reality the technological foundations of the postwar boom were laid in antibiotics, detergents, plastics, and ultimately personal computing itself. If any generalization is possible about technological forecasting, it is that many of the projected revolutions are stillborn, while other, often originally more obscure innovations transform society. Science fiction is no exception. Jules Verne's publisher considered his most accurate vision of the future, *Paris in the Twentieth Century*, unbelievable; Verne agreed, and it was not issued until the 1990s.[4]

There are many other caveats regarding efficiency that are not part of this book because others have noted them so ably. One is environmental. Conservative and libertarian economists questioning mandatory energy efficiency targets cite what is called a "rebound effect," in which the savings from a more efficient technology are offset or even completely annulled by increased consumption. This pattern was first noticed in British coal consumption in the 1860s by the economist William Stanley Jevons, and has reappeared with each new energy-saving innovation. Reduced energy costs often have led to purchase of sport utility vehicles and McMansions. More efficient air-conditioning technology has meant that units are installed in more rooms, or replaced by central whole-house air-conditioning systems. This effect is far from an iron law; even one of its leading proponents, Robert J. Michaels, acknowledges that mandatory efficiency standards for refrigerators have created no apparent rebound. But there is no doubt the effect is real. And the efficiency of technology from LED lighting to electric cars is also offset by environmental damage from rare earth mining to electronic waste.[5]

Next after energy are critiques of agricultural efficiency, usually from the left. In output per farmer and farm employer, mechanized conventional agriculture has been outstanding. Yet Swedish agricultural scientists, painstakingly adding up energy inputs and outputs, recently were able to show that a tractor needs 67 percent more energy than the feed required for a draft horse tilling the same field. The tractor is far more *effective* than the horse; it will produce almost two and a half times the food from the same area that the animal's ancestor did in the 1920s, but it needs thirteen times as much energy. And there are other objections to our conventional agriculture. Efficiency of breeding plants and animals for rapid harvesting and slaughter, respectively, has often damaged nutritional value and taste. Only recently has the heirloom tomato begun to make a comeback. Pigs and chickens raised for efficient production may suffer health problems; bovine growth hormone, while "natural" and safe for human consumption, induces a level of milk production that can be painful to cows. And the quest for efficiency can encourage a potentially disastrous monoculture, such as the lumper potato that dominated pre-Famine Irish agriculture. Since almost all potatoes in Ireland and much of the rest of Europe were genetically identical, a blight originating in the New World devastated the 1845 harvest. "Monoculture," as the writer Michael Pollan put it in *The Botany of Desire*, "is where the logic of nature collides with the logic of economics; which logic will ultimately prevail can never be in doubt."[6]

On a global level, true efficiency has always been difficult to calculate, especially since some means to efficiency (fertilizers and pesticides) can reduce the earth's overall productivity (by harming fish in runoff, and by endangering pollinators, respectively). In fact, our entire industrial civilization has been threatening its own efficiency through carbon emissions. If "efficiency" is defined broadly, a book on its paradoxes would become a study of everything. It would be returning to ecological economics of the Romanian American scholar Nicholas Georgescu-Roegen, who saw the decline of order in the world—the increase of entropy—as the inevitable consequence of human attempts to defy it. Climate change has helped to revive interest in Georgescu's ideas, but I leave assessments of their validity to others.

Even Silicon Valley culture, which rejects such theoretical limits and tends to regard space exploration as the solution to all earthly resource constraints, recognizes the environmental, health, cultural, and ethical costs of too much efficiency. For all their smart houses, web-connected appliances, and self-monitoring devices, the acolytes

of efficiency know how to draw the line. From organic heirloom produce to (as we will see in Chapter Three) technology-free Rudolf
Steiner elementary schools, the fruits of artisanal values attract
many otherwise high-tech families. Inefficiency in the form of labor-
intensive goods and services has a place in their society, as a signi-
fier of authenticity and privilege. This new upper stratum seems to
have little in common with the robber baron society described by
Thorstein Veblen in his 1899 tract, *The Theory of the Leisure Class*.
The patriarchal and often racist values of the Gilded Age plutocracy
may not have vanished entirely, but they are considered worse than
immoral now; they are unfashionable. So is the old ideal of cultivated
ease as embodied in palaces like the Frick Collection and the Morgan
Library, a pose already obsolete as early as 1970, when the economist
Staffan Linder published his pathbreaking *The Harried Leisure Class*.
Today's technology multimillionaires are more likely to be scout-
ing for the next start-up than to be enjoying the cash from their last
venture in early retirement. Yet as in Veblen's day, ostentatious inefficiency has its privileges. As the technology journalist Dave Rosenberg noted in 2013 on the *San Francisco Chronicle* website: "Luxury
goods, especially watches . . . are part of a subtle push in Silicon Valley toward 'quality crafted' tools, clothing and accessories. . . . While
the general population looks forward to the latest in futuristic status
symbols, tech's futurists are going retro." The same can be said of
other labor-intensive tools such as hand-forged chef's knives.[7]

The private traditionalism of technologists may be seen as admirable pragmatism and open-mindedness, and a force for more
employment amid growing automation. It can also be seen as a cyn-
ical endorsement of a two-tier society: mediocrity for the masses,
luxurious heritage for creative innovators. (There have always been
extremes, but the market for good middle-range products has declined. There is room for Bloomingdale's and Walmart, but the classic middle-class department store, Gimbel's, closed its doors in 1986
and its former rivals are struggling.) This points up yet another criticism of technological efficiency, a tendency (according to some economists) to amplify inequality and thus to endanger civic life and even
democracy itself. Arthur M. Okun's *Equality and Efficiency: The Big
Tradeoff* is still debated among economists forty years after its pub-

lication and was reissued by the Brookings Institution in 2015. It's possible to imagine a society that is both highly efficient and unstable. The Silicon Valley cult of disruption may have originally suggested turning power from oligarchs to the people. But now it can also mean the creation of a new oligarchy that appears even harder to dislodge. In Silicon Valley itself, the increase in house prices and apartment rent has borne out the analysis of the economist Fred Hirsch, who in the 1970s foresaw that even if efficiency and productivity continued to rise, there was a "positional economy" of goods that could never, like information technology products, become affordable to the masses, like good tickets to a hit play, or apartments in global economic hubs, both of which are what Hirsch called "positional goods."[8]

Even so, the rising importance of and frustration engendered by positional goods is not, I believe, the best argument against efficiency. Technological enthusiasts have countered that even if the gap grows and billionaires capture more of the world's output, the planet's people are still better off, and might not be if there were no incentive to take risks and fail, as most ventures do. Silicon Valley depends on an inefficient and wasteful start-up culture to create a more efficient society in the end, in this view.

Electronic efficiency has more serious problems. On a technical level, there is still no answer to the challenge of security and the threat of hacking. If fear of electronic transactions reaches a critical level, there may yet be a backlash against web commerce, but so far it has been so profitable for banks and credit card companies that they have been able to absorb at least some varieties of fraud as a cost of doing business. Likewise, the 1990s dream of participatory democracy has at least been stalled by fringe groups' ability to use websites and social media, but defenders of electronic democracy can always point to promising new initiatives. The technology critic Evgeny Morozov rightly observes that inefficiency can be good if it results from "deliberative commitment by a democratically run community" taking a stand against "the inhumanity of Taylorism [regimentation of work methods] and market fundamentalism." But that does not prevent market fundamentalists from securing *democratic* consent for hyperefficiency. Likewise, algorithms can both intentionally and unintentionally discriminate against individuals by gender, race, geography, or socioeconomic status—but defenders can reply that offending programs can be made fairer and thus even more efficient. Algorithms and the staggering data they gather on our spending, travel, investments, credit, and political views (or at least those of our friends) threaten the privacy of Americans every day, and some people have begun opting out of online life, but so far there has not been enough damage from either identity theft or intrusive marketing to change Americans' behavior radically.[9]

Yet another critique of the efficiency of mobile technology aims at its damage to human relationships, whether commercial or personal. But Americans at least have always been unsentimental about the first, forsaking local merchants for big box retailers even before the rise of electronic commerce. And while many people, especially parents of young children and teenagers, have reservations about the effects of social media on concentration and human relationships, abrasiveness remains a feature rather than a bug in much of Silicon Valley culture.[10]

To the enthusiasts of efficiency, in and out of Silicon Valley, such objections are only temporary issues for technical resolution in the next round of algorithms. Mass unemployment from robotics is still only a disputed hypothesis, and robotics advocates can point to the failure of previous doomsaying. Efficiency remains a core American value, and while Silicon Valley billionaires now face more skeptical scrutiny, they have not lost their mantle of being successors of Thomas Edison, John D. Rockefeller, and Henry Ford as builders of American culture. Steve Jobs, ruthless like all of them at times, still was widely mourned by millions who believed he had enhanced their lives.

This book offers a different critique of technological efficiency, one that accepts the goal of reducing waste in the use of human time and natural resources, but recognizes that a single-minded drive for a "friction-free" world, as Bill Gates and his coauthors put it in 1995, can actually reduce efficiency. Instead of examining all the social, political, and ethical challenges of information technology, it focuses on its long-term self-subversion. We know that the obsession with childhood hygiene, so popular since the early twentieth century, can weaken the immune system. We know that overprescription of antibiotics can foster superbugs, that liberal use of opioids can reduce their effectiveness and encourage addiction, and that habitual reliance on sleeping pills can worsen insomnia. Few of us renounce medicine or pharmaceuticals, but we have a new respect for natural equilibria.

Questioning efficiency must now go beyond the familiar distinction between efficiency and effectiveness. War is extremely inefficient when the number of bullets or shells needed to defeat the enemy is considered, but since defeat can be catastrophic, all that inefficiency can be effective. Conversely, "clean diesel" automotive engines are highly efficient in fuel consumption, but because their emissions are difficult to control, they can no longer be considered effective. Algorithms—the programming techniques that multiply the power of computer hardware—present a different set of problems. Most of the time they are highly effective as well as efficient. For example, public key cryptography takes advantage of the difficulty of factoring very large numbers to make electronic financial transactions secure and Internet communications generally secure, despite many successful attacks. But other algorithms may risk not only effectiveness but efficiency itself in the long run. That is, they can lead not just to undesirable consequences but to wasted efforts and missed opportunities. They fall into seven groups:

COUNTERSERENDIPITY. Most chance events are adverse or neutral. Efficiency makes the world more predictable. But if everything is as direct as possible, we are also deprived of the benefits of occasional randomization and of productive mistakes. Conventional algorithms reduce negative surprises at the high price of threatening positive ones. The two are inseparable.

HYPERFOCUS. Efficiency is often expressed as focus, which up to a point is excellent and necessary. But evolution has given us and other animals a second kind of sight, peripheral vision, which is less sensitive to details but allows us to see large patterns and motion. Early in the history of astronomy it was understood that faint objects could be seen better by looking slightly away, "averted vision." As Edgar Allan Poe wrote in "The Murders in the Rue Morgue": "To look at a star by glances—to view it in a side-long way, by turning toward it the exterior portions of the retina (more susceptible of feeble impressions of light than the interior), is to behold the star distinctly." Efficiency, indispensable in everyday operations, makes it harder to pull back for the big picture.

SELF-AMPLIFYING CASCADES. Intentionally or not, algorithms may fail to select the most optimal choice by amplifying initially small effects. Their early decisions can become self-fulfilling prophecies. This is a special risk in automated processes, from financial trading to self-driving vehicles, in which multiple algorithms, none of which can be flawless, are turned loose to interact, sometimes without the possibility of quick human intervention.

SKILL EROSION. Automated systems perform most tasks better than most people, most of the time. They are nearly always more efficient and consistent, which is why they have been so popular. And rightly so. The partnership of a skilled person and an electronic system in principle delivers better performance than either alone. But there can be severe problems when the robotic partner fails. If the human—whether physician, airline pilot, or everyday motorist—has not maintained skills, the result can be catastrophic for the efficiency of the whole system.

PERVERSE FEEDBACK. The interaction of automated systems becomes even more problematic when they are called upon not only to execute human goals but to provide incentives. It's possible to satisfy a criterion (like a test score) through means that frustrate the real desired outcome (actual understanding). In social science this is known as Campbell's Law.

DATA DELUGE. Huge data sets, when used by skilled people with a deep understanding of underlying processes, may increase efficiency. But their use can also threaten efficiency itself. The volume of automatically acquired data in many fields is increasing more rapidly than the per-terabyte cost of storage, increasing expenses. Big data can also suggest false positives and erroneous hypotheses that take expensive person-hours to evaluate and rule out, leading (especially in health care) to alarm and alert fatigue. The net result may be less real efficiency.

MONOCULTURE. Without careful design, an algorithm can multiply a successful formula to the point that a system becomes less

responsive to changing circumstances. Social psychologists acknowledge, for example, that some of their experiments cannot be replicated, not because of any error in the original design, analysis, or data
collection but because societies and their values change. Life scientists' mice are genetically standardized, but people live in a constantly
evolving technological environment and adjust their behavior constantly and often unconsciously.

To write about information technology is to shoot at a target that
appears to be not only moving but accelerating. And one of the greatest challenges is that there are so many other books addressing the
same issues. As I'll suggest in Chapter Two, far from killing the publication of printed books, network technology has helped strengthen
them. One of the favorite topics on the web is the web itself; in May
2017, a Wikipedia category article listed forty-nine pages of books
about the Internet, and a number of major new works had not yet
been included. Amazon.com listed over 24,000 books on "Internet
& Social Media" alone. It is a striking illustration of the information
abundance that will be discussed in that chapter.[11]

While many of these books are technical monographs or college
texts, and others are reports on primary research on economic and
social statistics, databases, or experiments with human subjects, others (like this one) are interpretations. There are so many that overlap-
ping studies citing similar evidence may appear in the same season;
parallel ideas and mutual influence are inevitable. This crowding is
hardly new. Literary theorists have long expounded on intertextual-
ity, while as early as 1898 the fiction writer Arnold Bennett, in his
autobiographical novel *A Man from the North*, more vividly portrayed
the majestic British Museum round reading room as a "cannibal feast
of the living upon the dead" served by attendants off rolling book
trucks.[12]

So it seems to be almost 125 years later. I thus should situate this
book. It is obviously not in the cornucopian genre of Kevin Kelly's
What Technology Wants or Ray Kurzweil's *The Singularity Is Near*. But
technological optimism is, on balance, a blessing. Given the dismal
failure rate of innovation, even unrealistic hopes help raise money for

potentially beneficial inventions. Hype can be good for society if not always for the average individual investor or consumer. At the other extreme are the works of technological Cassandras such as *Superintelligence*, by the Oxford philosopher Nick Bostrom. Joyful and fearful prophecies actually have much in common. They both foresee a transformed humanity and disagree only as to whether it will be paradise or inferno.[13]

The Efficiency Paradox is part of a great middle range by authors skeptical of technological utopianism but not necessarily alarmed by the likelihood of meltdown. A half dozen are especially worth discussing.

The most thoroughgoing nemesis of Silicon Valley is Evgeny Morozov, who combines polemical verve with impressive documentation. Morozov's early years in Soviet-era Belarus inform his rejection of planners' arrogance. Having grown up in an ideology-saturated society he has a keen eye for the cant of the Western information technology industry and its admirers as well. His book *To Save Everything, Click Here* is a critique of what he calls (adopting a concept from architecture critics) solutionism, the idea that human problems have purely technological remedies, a pursuit of efficiency that ignores serious social, political, and ethical consequences, and unjustifiably equates innovation with improvement. He might equally have called it neo-efficiency. "Inefficiency, ambiguity, and opacity—whether in politics or in everyday life—that the newly empowered geeks and solutionists are rallying against are not in any sense problematic," Morozov observes. "Quite the opposite: these vices are often virtues in disguise." In fact, he argues against the very existence of "the Internet" as opposed to the agendas of powerful organizations exploiting networked resources. At the same time, he scoffs at what he considers futile attempts by web critics like Eli Pariser (*The Filter Bubble*) and Ethan Zuckerman (*Rewire*) to promote their own progressive solutions. More efficient communication has not and will not resolve social, political, and ethical questions.[14]

In Morozov's terms I am probably a "technostructuralist," one less interested in the "direct, anticipated, and desirable consequences of innovation" and more interested in the "indirect, unanticipated, and undesirable ones." Yet I part ways with Morozov's "post-Internet"

viewpoint and cite what sociologists call the Thomas Theorem, proposed by William Isaac and Dorothy Swaine Thomas. If people
believe something is real, it becomes so in its consequences. To take
a mundane example, false news about gasoline shortages sometimes
creates real gasoline shortages as panicking drivers top up their fuel
tanks more often. "The Internet," as opposed to the maneuverings of
those who control influential websites, may be a myth, but if enough
people accept (for example) the neutrality of Google and Facebook
algorithms, it is a reality. Since web-based commerce and publishing
won't go away, and since they have had positive as well as negative
results, I believe in accepting this situation as a fact and finding new
ways to blend the intuitive and algorithmic, the analog and the digital.
That is obvious. To his credit, Morozov is not afraid of negativity, just
as I am not afraid of obviousness. I recall the lecture-hall remark of
one of my undergraduate teachers, the historian of science Charles C.
Gillispie: "There is nothing more embarrassing to the educated mind
than a true cliché."[15]

Like *To Save Everything*, Nicholas Carr's *The Glass Cage: How Our
Computers Are Changing Us* identifies efficiency as the core of both
its values and its strategy—"dogged, almost monomaniacal" in the
case of Google. It also correctly highlights the dangers of allowing
overreliance on algorithms to erode human skills, a theme that Carr
presented forcefully in his earlier book *The Shallows*. From similar
facts and studies, this book draws different conclusions. Carr is a disillusioned information technologist; I am a historian by background.
In the late 1970s and 1980s I found that first word processing and
then electronic library resources helped me to return to a writing
career that had been interrupted. Because I already had an excellent
education in research, information technology turned out to be a
multiplier. Pessimism about the effects of technology is a distraction
from the real need for education and self-education on the best way
to combine algorithms and intuition, digital and analog.[16]

The Glass Cage elaborates a point that I believe was first made by
the technology curator James Blackaby, that we lose something when
we shift from tool use (the premodern woodworker's shaving bench)
to tool management (the workbench, a nineteenth-century innovation). Blackaby showed how the slide rule required engineers to be
more directly involved in their calculations than did the electronic

devices that replaced it decades ago—a point also made more recently by the engineer and historian of technology Henry Petroski. Without calling for a return to eighteenth-century agriculture, Carr praises the unity of body and tool in the operation of the scythe, citing a sonnet of Robert Frost. Carr is not alone. Hand mowing is a flourishing niche hobby. Thanks to modern search engines the would-be mower can choose scythes from Austria, Italy, Denmark, and Australia. He or she can also find other literary evocations of hand tools, like the Tolstoy-quoting *New York Times* op-ed piece "The Russian Peasant's Workout," which makes one want to find a meadow and swing away. Inspired by this style of human-tool relationship, Carr scorns Morozov's allegedly simplistic idea of technology as a mere means to liberate us from toil. (Is that payback for Morozov's remark about Carr's "McLuhanesque medium-centrism"?) But I suspect it must have been much less satisfying to premodern peasants to be swinging (and sharpening) those blades for their livelihoods from dawn to dusk during harvest season than it was to more recent poets and novelists. Pieter Bruegel the Elder's paintings and prints, with their images of muscular prowess, fatigue, and thirst, are stylized but may also be more historically accurate. So I cannot agree that our age necessarily has more "aimlessness and gloom" than previous decades or centuries—or conversely find it one of joy and fulfillment just because it is easier to join a hand-mowing club. Instead, I agree with Norbert Wiener in believing that if properly used, information technology can spare us mind-numbing routine and free our time for more creative activity. There was an intimate relationship between tool, hand, and mind in the quill pen, and it may have enforced deliberate writing of so many literary classics, but I am glad I never needed to sharpen one.[17]

Cathy O'Neil's *Weapons of Math Destruction: How Big Data Increases Inequality and Threatens Democracy* offers another important caveat from an information technology professional; unlike most technology critics, O'Neil has been on the forefront of the systems that alarm her, the use of algorithms to target vulnerable people, whether in workplace "wellness" programs, in for-profit higher education sales, or in the justice system. The cynicism that she reveals makes her book the work on the ethics of big data and algorithms most widely reviewed online to date. But as in medicine, therapy is more challenging than diagnosis. Her proposal for audits of artificial intelligence systems raises questions. First, many other theorists and technical experts now believe that with machine learning, artificial intelligence can no longer be understood in the way that the source code of conventional programs can be studied. It is not clear that even if the initial code is freely available online, the ultimate behavior of the program after assimilating vast quantities of new data is humanly understandable. If these specialists are right, rationality carried far enough creates a black box machine impenetrable to human reason and thus to auditing. Second, even if the software and its implicit biases are understandable, financial auditing is a discouraging precedent. Who can forget the collapse of Arthur Andersen following the Enron scandal, and the failure of other giant accounting and bond rating firms to question the practices leading to the 2008 recession? Seeking objectivity, judges protect forensic science and sentencing software from disclosure and effective challenge. In such cases, potentially biased algorithms may annul the right to confront witnesses and rebut government evidence.[18]

The legal scholar Frank Pasquale's *The Black Box Society* preceded *Weapons of Math Destruction* and remains the best account of the challenges facing legislators and regulators from the power of secret algorithms. Pasquale recommends the European approach to regulating big data, and I agree that we can learn from it. But well-intentioned privacy laws are a two-edged sword. The "right to be forgotten" enshrined in European Union legislation may have been motivated by a desire to remove the shadow of youthful indiscretions from search engine results. But laws protecting the powerless may also shield the privileged. The London *Daily Telegraph* published summaries of stories deleted after objections brought by their subjects, including a physician, a military officer, and a cleric involved in sexual abuse cases. Of course, press reports may be unfair or inaccurate, but erasing published information is an alarming precedent. Pasquale's book and O'Neil's complement each other in demystifying Silicon Valley's claims. Their concern is with effects on society; O'Neil in particular is impressed with how well today's algorithms work, which makes them all the more dangerous. My own emphasis is on why the short-run efficiency of algorithms can impede rather than stimulate innovation.[19]

David Sax's *The Revenge of Analog* documents persuasively that older media and experiences, from chemical film to mechanical watches and retail stores, have been remarkably resilient, meeting human needs that digital life cannot fulfill. It's a vivid account of the continued relevance of tactile, concrete experience and of Silicon Valley's recognition of it, from the flourishing of Apple Stores since their introduction by Steve Jobs in 2001 to the revival of Moleskine notebooks. It is also one of the best expressions of the grounds for optimism about the coexistence of algorithms and human intuition, a theme that also underlies this book.[20]

But since the appearance of Apple Stores, clouds have returned to the horizon. For example, from the inauguration of the stores to spring 2017, employment in American department stores had shrunk by a third. There are still physical niche markets, but none of the historic major chains except Walmart has the resources to compete with Amazon; two great chains that had weathered over a century of recurring depressions and recessions, Sears and Macy's, were struggling in 2017. Amazon's own retail ventures are unlikely to match the tempting exhilaration of experimenting with rows of Apple devices, and of receiving personal support and repair service on the spot. New owners of Polaroid patents may have revived instant photography, and Kodak has announced it is bringing back Ektachrome color slide film, but Kodachrome is probably extinct forever. Production of 35mm motion picture film continues, yet it depends tenuously on the leverage that a small number of star directors wield with studios and exhibitors.[21]

Messy, by the economist and writer Tim Harford, arrived in 2016 as a welcome corrective to a business self-help genre dominated ever since Benjamin Franklin by organization and system and admonitions to methodical habits. No wonder a transatlantic public weary of management jargon rejoiced at the idea of sweet disorder. It makes an excellent case that disorganization can be creative, even if it falls into a countergenre of its own, including Kathryn Schultz's *Being Wrong* and Harford's earlier volume *Adapt*. Yet like most other business gurus, Harford undervalues luck. Drawing on a study by the Nobel Laureate economist Paul Samuelson from the 1980s and on more recent research on rewards for investments and management, the finance economist Moshe Levy has argued that most of the superior returns attributed to talent can be explained by luck. Narratives of success like Harford's reflect survivorship bias, the use of striking examples without consideration of how many other people sharing the same traits, experiences, or strategies were unsuccessful. As on Wall Street, a style performing brilliantly in one market environment may be a flop in another. When contemplating Silicon Valley's big winners—Amazon's CEO Jeff Bezos is featured in *Messy*—we can retrospectively find brilliant strategies. Yet we also find potentially fatal crises.[22]

"Messy" behavior that wins contests may be maladaptive in power; Harford was bold enough to praise Donald Trump's improvised oratorical style, yet what made Trump a successful campaigner appeared to be failing to win broad approval in the first year of his presidency. Of course, Bill Clinton, another notoriously disorganized chief executive, was reelected, survived scandal and impeachment, and is still remembered nostalgically by millions, so Harford may yet be right. Nevertheless, critics have also noted that messiness contributed to the mixed record of the Clinton presidency.[23]

At its best, *Messy* illustrates the principle the sociologist Charles Tilly called the Invisible Elbow, that apparently planned accomplishments are actually the products of a cascade of contingencies. But messiness falls short as a watchword. First, literal messiness is costly. There may not be a truly scientific estimate of the hours lost in looking for misplaced objects and documents—studies seem to be funded by companies selling solutions for tracking keys and business records—but most of us have found that messiness can take precious time from creativity. Second, at least one of the people Harford characterizes as messy, Charles Darwin, may have pursued multiple research projects at once. But Darwin was a careful and organized worker who ran his investigations as a family enterprise. In the Cambridge University natural history museum his labels are still highly regarded. Third, corporate management doesn't really believe in messiness for the great majority of employees. Conformity prevails. Efficient performance-monitoring software denies creative mistakes to most of the rank-and-file workforce, whether white- or blue-collar. Messiness may thus be just another status marker, a privilege of the post-leisure overclass. Elites, researchers have suggested, use nonconforming behavior like the Facebook CEO Mark Zuckerberg's hoodie to signal their immunity to the masses' norms, the so-called red sneakers effect. And no wonder, since Harford's employer, the London-based *Financial Times* newspaper, described its readership in May 2017 as "the world's most desirable audience, with the largest purchasing power and highest net worth." In other words, if you're not already in the one percent, don't try this at home.[24]

Two other books appeared as *The Efficiency Paradox* was about to go to press, *Move Fast and Break Things: How Facebook, Google, and Amazon Cornered Culture and Undermined Democracy*, by Jonathan Taplin, a media studies academic and former music tour manager and film producer; and the even more ominously titled *World Without Mind: The Existential Threat of Big Tech*, by Franklin Foer, a writer and former editor of *The New Republic*. I did not have a chance to read either carefully enough to deal with their arguments, though I agree (using similar statistics) that the platform economy has done economic damage to many writers, artists, composers, and musicians. I am one of them; *The Wilson Quarterly*, *American Heritage of Invention & Technology*, *Civilization*, and other magazines to which I contributed are no longer publishing. I also agree with what I have read of Foer's analysis of the harm that pursuit of digital efficiency and the pursuit of clicks can do to quality. The control of an increasing share of advertising by Facebook in particular is a serious problem. I can make only two preliminary comments now regarding both titles. First, the present book covers a greater range of professions than the media and the arts, and the positive as well as negative consequences of the rise of mobile computing, apps, and big data. Second, for all their hundreds of billions of dollars in assets and their theoretical influence on decision making, the moguls were unable in 2016 to prevent the election of a presidential candidate whose positions on climate change, immigration, diversity, and marriage equality, among other issues, most of them deplore. An essay on the pro-Trump site Breitbart has endorsed the breakup of Google. Democracy—or at least Electoral College majority—may be threatening Silicon Valley more than vice versa.[25]

The Efficiency Paradox links two eras of the pursuit of efficiency. The first began in the late eighteenth century and continued through most of the twentieth. It substituted continuous processes for discrete production and gave us the classic image of the wheels of industry: rolls of paper, spools of thread, ribbons of steel, the classic assembly line of films like Charlie Chaplin's *Modern Times*. Of course, such industries represented only part of even industrial nations' output, but the ideal of the continuous process inspired capitalists and socialists alike.

Continuous production may still be going strong—in fact, stronger than ever thanks to industrial robots—but it has lost the excitement of the early and middle twentieth century. The platform company, which uses software to bring together buyers and sellers of goods and services, represents a new kind of efficiency, based less on the organization of machines and human labor than on the gathering, analysis, and exchange of data.

The platform era that began in the late 1990s with Amazon.com entered a new phase in the twenty-first century with the rise of search engines, smartphones, social media, networked web-based software, and a revival of artificial intelligence from the doldrums of the early 1990s. I am looking at four sides of the new efficiency and asking why, for all its convenience, its benefits to most people have been elusive: media and culture, education, transportation, and medicine.

My conclusion is that we don't have to choose between big data, algorithms, and efficiency on one side, and intuition, skill, and experience on the other. We need the right blend. I will present a set of strategies for achieving it.

The problem of platform efficiency, I will suggest in the first chapter, is that it promotes what the originator of the concept of disruptive innovation, Clayton Christensen, calls business process innovation. It reduces transaction costs by matching buyers and sellers with automated software. The social benefits are real but limited; platform companies can promote competition and benefit consumers by holding inflation in check. The risks are also real and have been well documented by critics: loss of consumer privacy, sometimes unconscionable boilerplate in terms of service agreements (Ancestry.com's contract claims broad ownership rights to customers' DNA data), current oligopoly, and potential monopoly. Less commonly noted is another consequence of Wall Street's romance with platform-based efficiency. It has diverted capital and talent from riskier but ultimately more broadly beneficial market-creating innovation. Nineteenth-century continuous process innovations did not just reduce friction. In eliminating some jobs, they created many others, often more skilled and highly paid. Some economists believe that this phase of technology was a one-time event that will never be repeated. Yet there is reason to doubt any pronouncement about the future based on extrapolation from the recent record.[26]

The second chapter turns to the revolution made possible by the most powerful algorithm of all, Google's PageRank, and its roots in the analysis of influence and impact in the sciences. With the advent of the web and later of social media, this originally elitist technique was transformed for a populist environment. In journalism and the arts, far from promoting the "long tail" (the large number of works below the best-seller lists), a concept made famous by the former *Wired* editor Chris Anderson, it tends to multiply random initial advantages, a cascading effect. The rise of mobile computing, of social media, and of new and allegedly more precise advertising options has simultaneously threatened the efficiency of much of journalism by taking resources from the producing of news and opinion to optimizing it for the algorithms of social media.

The third chapter considers the efficiency movement in education. The computerization movement in higher education is almost a century old, dating back to Thomas Edison's dream of replacing what he considered "two-percent-efficient" textbooks with 100 percent efficient classroom films. Yet while computers have made impressive progress in educating themselves, there is little evidence in either test scores or popular culture that computers have done much for mass literacy or numeracy. In fact, they have been increasing rather than reducing inequality by multiplying the advantages of an early start.

The fourth chapter examines the revolution in geography created by digital maps and geographic information systems (GIS). It frames this in the context of wayfinding, the skills used by men and women in the absence of compasses and even maps. We have grown much more precise but less sophisticated. The electronic map, especially when displayed on a small-screen mobile device, is extremely efficient in providing information about a particular place but much less so in putting it in a broader context, a hyperfocus effect. There are many times when the direct routing of a smartphone Global Positioning System (GPS) is exactly what is needed, when detours are out of the question. But the fastest route is not necessarily the most efficient way to get the most out of a journey. GPS may be more efficient than human wayfinding most of the time, but it can weaken one of humanity's most valuable skills.

The fifth chapter, on medicine, considers the obstacles to efficient medicine created by programs for medical efficiency. Laboratory automation is one of the outstanding successes of computerization; the cost of sequencing a human genome is now within the reach of the middle class. The interpretation of genetic information has been much less straightforward so far. The electronic medical record once promised to relieve health care providers, especially physicians notorious for ambiguous handwriting, of many of the burdens of note taking. Instead, the need for both consistent and detailed medical records has increased the human burden, creating a new administrative specialty of code entry and a cottage industry of coaching providers on categorizing procedures for maximum fees: "upcoding." Even when it is working successfully, medical quantification will have limits because patients are not passive recipients of interventions. Their culture, values, and attitudes toward life and toward risk, and their relationships with doctors and other providers, can't be separated from outcomes. The ability of a professional to motivate healthier choices—an inefficient process of persuasion—often matters more than medications. Just as a book is a kind of place, just as a large-format map is more than the sum of its details but a territory that should be understood as a whole, so the patient's body and mind are a terrain, not just a set of notes and data points, helpful though those may be.[27]

The concluding chapter presents a heterodox view of efficiency and inefficiency. It is no surprise to psychologists that the extreme memory for details in which computerized knowledge excels can be detrimental to understanding. Drawing on the work of the sociologist Harry Collins in *Artificial Experts*, I will suggest that every human being has a vast store of tacit knowledge that could never be imparted to an artificial intelligence program in a lifetime. These intuitive understandings can inform our career decisions and purchases, our education, our experience of places, and our health. The consequence is that more algorithms should be optimally inefficient, taking more time for deeper analysis (as some search engine researchers have advocated), and providing what-if advice rather than definitive answers.

Used unthinkingly, algorithms can be counterserendipitous, but they do not have to be so. Their real problem is a familiar one, going back to the earliest market research. Established patterns, verified scientifically, can be upended creatively in ways that the data could never have predicted. Market research once declared that Americans liked weak coffee; then came Starbucks. It is also true, of course, that unaided intuition has often failed. But findings of behavioral economics should not depress or intimidate us. Data analysis and tacit knowledge complement rather than oppose each other.[28]

Algorithms themselves need and are getting new approaches. The programming technique called fuzzy logic accepts the need for initially suboptimal solutions in exploring the world. Catherine D'Ignazio, who studied serendipitous computing as a researcher in the MIT Media Lab and developed an innovative news program, has found that major search and media companies have been trying to build more serendipity and information diversity into their services and recommendations, but it has not been easy. If more sophisticated and discerning algorithms are possible, it's likely they will originate in academic projects and start-ups rather than in the major platform companies. These initiatives, and the insight of a new generation into the mutually beneficial coexistence of digital and analog thinking, give me hope that technology—after financial crises and alarms of stagnation—can once again renew itself.[29]

THE EFFICIENCY PARADOX

1

FROM MILL TO PLATFORM

HOW THE NINETEENTH CENTURY
REDEFINED EFFICIENCY AND
THE TWENTY-FIRST HAS TRANSFORMED IT

We are living in a second age of efficiency. Journalists and entrepreneurs do not use that word as often as they used to. We'll see synonyms later. But never far from our minds is consciousness of the value of getting the greatest possible output from available inputs, whether increasing production or profits, or reducing time.

My claim that preoccupation with efficiency in the short term may harm efficiency in the long run risks being considered a heresy by some and a truism by others. I hope to show that it is an obvious proposition when one reflects on it. It is also obvious, as I shall suggest in succeeding chapters and in the Conclusion, that combining efficient algorithms with holistic analog understanding can produce far better results than using either strategy alone. But it is not always simple to defend the obvious. It is helpful to see efficiency as a concept that has developed over the past two hundred years or so, and as a set of practices that are much older. The idea of efficiency, as we shall see, emerged in the age of the steam engine and was best expressed not by the eighteenth-century metaphor of a shop's division of labor (essential as that remained) but by the substitution of continuous production for the fabrication of one unit at a time. The greatest enterprises invested vast capital and employed up to a hundred thousand workers or more to keep it in operation. Both classical economic liberalism and rival doctrines like Marxism reflected this model; it should not be so surprising that even communist governments admired Western mass production.

The importance of technologies of uninterrupted ("continuous process") as opposed to batch production was first underscored by the Swiss architect and critic Siegfried Giedion and the American historian Daniel J. Boorstin in the mid-twentieth century. Rollers, belts, and other devices changed the nature of consumption as well as production. Cable television programs like *How It's Made* reveal how much of today's industrial processes are already automated, especially when compared to episodes of the *Industry on Parade* series broadcast on network television in the 1950s. Today's programs will probably look equally quaint in even less time. But further reducing labor costs on assembly lines is not the kind of efficiency that interests us here. It is a new kind of enterprise that has—unforeseen by even the boldest futurists—taken over what Vladimir Lenin called the commanding heights of the economy, dominating its agendas. "Silicon Valley" evokes the mixture of admiration, fear, and scorn once inspired by the grimy industrial metropolises of the Northeast and Midwest, but while an approach to Chicago or Detroit or Pittsburgh by automobile or train can still be a visually striking experience, nothing on the peninsula south of San Francisco is tall enough to inspire awe, stupendous as its wealth has become. The server complexes of its companies are scattered as inconspicuously as possible around the globe. Yet the giants of Silicon Valley have ideas about social organization as radical in their own way as Lenin's, and they share with classical communism a passionate faith in efficiency.[1]

This chapter will investigate the contrast between continuous process efficiency (which fascinated painters as well as photographers and filmmakers in its monumentality and awesome concreteness) and platform efficiency, which is far more profitable but concealed and evanescent and that takes a leap of artistic imagination to dramatize. It will suggest how matchmaking by electronic networks takes advantage not only of the steady if recently slowed improvement of the efficiency of integrated circuits, but also of the ability of ingenious computational techniques—algorithms—to multiply the speed of these circuits manyfold.

This efficiency raises a profound question, the chapter will argue. Why have these platforms apparently had such little effect on the self-perceived satisfaction of the United States and other nations in which they are most advanced? Why are citizens around the world so unhappy with their governments, so ready to look to extreme solutions? One reason may be that the platform revolution has been diverting talent and capital from other technological projects that could be more transformative. I cannot identify them, nor rule out that they are already well advanced and may flower soon. After all, the U.S. boom after the Second World War was in part based on innovations like broadcast television and dry photocopying that actually were under development during the darkest years of the Great Depression, along with Alan Turing's theoretical work that helped make the platform economy possible.

The question, which I don't pretend to resolve, is why the platform corporation, so profitable for its investors so far (especially the early ones), has been such an underachiever. Enthusiasts will insist that major innovations commonly have troughs of disappointment; the best is yet to come. This is especially the viewpoint of Facebook and its founder, Mark Zuckerberg, who in early 2017 published a manifesto acknowledging mistakes and vowing to build better communities and a better planet with the help of Facebook's users. To many adversaries such promises have long been "silicon snake oil" and "future hype"—to quote the titles of 1990s and early 2000s books by disillusioned technologists. To critics on the left in particular, the new bosses are not so different from the old bosses, just equipped with state-of-the-art surveillance and manipulation in place of the goon squads of yore. Some wary journalists see an existential threat to their own profession in declarations like those of Zuckerberg. I am not sure any organization really has such power. I will suggest at the end of this chapter that the most serious unintended consequence of platform efficiency may be its opportunity cost, its claim on resources that would in the long run do more to promote real efficiency.[2]

One paradox of the movement for efficiency is that innovations that have promoted efficiency and rationality have arisen in spite of discouraging data, driven by intuition and emotion. That does not mean that gut feelings alone are a more reliable guide than data-based analysis, but only that data, and tools for analyzing it, never can take the place of the imagination in foreseeing future patterns of human behavior. Most such intuitions fail. The exceptions fill inspirational and business books. Venture investment has a high failure rate built into it. Yet out of the inefficient maelstrom emerged some of the world's most efficient technology.

The history of efficiency should rightly start with nature itself. As biophysicists have discovered, DNA stores energy far more densely than the most advanced technological systems. The control of gene expression allows complex and robust organisms to develop with stunning speed. Tiny variations in the genomes of fruit flies can produce strikingly different behaviors. Evolution has been prodigiously successful in optimizing the flow of information. Leveraging limited resources is our biological heritage.[3]

The quest for efficiency seems to be built into human biology as well, as revealed by anthropological and archaeological evidence. There have been tens of thousands of years of innovations in tool making that sometimes reached dead ends but occasionally produced masterpieces of functionality. Think of the Australian Aborigines' boomerang, or the Central Asian steppe nomads' composite bow. Is any cutting tool more efficient than traditionally forged Japanese blades, or sharper than the obsidian knives flaked expertly by pre-Columbian Native Americans?

Turning to the West, many ancient Roman medical instruments were so well adapted to their purpose that similar ones are used today, and their quality was not surpassed until modern times. Roman troops were famous for their ability to assemble bridges and fortifications with a speed that dazzled their adversaries. There was even a kind of mass production of oil lamps, stamped and marketed with early trademarks.[4]

Recent archaeology has revealed more dynamism and technological innovation in the ancient world than historians of fifty years ago acknowledged. The slave economy, for example, did not rule out labor-saving machines like water wheels, just as steam engines were used on slavery-era sugar plantations in the early nineteenth century. There was a great deal of efficiency in practice. But the concept of efficiency as we know it had no clear place in ancient life. The ancient Greeks and Romans (and other Mediterranean and Near Eastern societies, including Egypt), had administrative and record-keeping systems that worked for centuries. But they had no doctrine of systematic improvement of output. The classical historian Peter Thonemann has underlined that Roman society in particular was based on principles of patronage, loyalty, and obligation. There was no theory of wages, interest, or productivity. Prestige was often more important than functionality. Books were written and read as rolls that were stored together in chests. Writing was *scriptura continua*, no space between words, which space would have increased papyrus and parchment use slightly but made reading and education far easier. The difficulties of reading—manipulating the scroll, looking ahead to determine word breaks—were part of the performance skills of an educated person. That kind of inefficiency was a feature, not a bug in today's terms.[5]

Europe of the Middle Ages and the early modern era was a time of growing practical efficiency—but also without an underlying theory. The black letter handwriting that seems so quaint and old-fashioned today was actually a relatively rapid and legible style of writing for those accustomed to it. The Romans had the optical knowledge and the glassblowing and metallurgical skills to make eyeglasses, but there was no market for them. Aging literate people had educated slaves to read to them. The Romans made excellent cloth presses (one of which survives at Herculaneum) and could cast bronze letters, but they felt no need for printing.[6]

By the eighteenth century, Denis Diderot's *Encyclopédie* and its Scots imitator, the *Encyclopaedia Britannica*, summarized the knowledge and improvement in dozens of trades. In *The Wealth of Nations*, Adam Smith showed how the separation of the making of pins into distinct operations by specialists could multiply the number of pins each worker could make per day. There was an even finer division of labor in the manufacture of needles in medieval Persia.[7]

Still, Smith was an exceptional pioneer. The nineteenth- and twentieth-century sense of efficiency was not quite present. A nineteenth-century political economist, whether laissez-faire or socialist, would be deeply interested in measuring just how much more productive a pin workshop would be than a traditional one. Many products were still made according to artisanal tradition and style rather than after systematic study of customer needs. The French technology theorist Jacques Ellul has pointed out that the armorers who made swords for late medieval mercenaries each followed a craft tradition and decorative style without studying the ergonomics of combat. Every soldier had to adapt his fighting style to the instrument.[8]

No eighteenth-century figure was more celebrated than Benjamin Franklin for his union of practical ingenuity with investigations of scientific theory, despite or because of the limits of his formal education. The designs of Franklin and his contemporaries—he never patented his inventions and encouraged further adaptation—for fireplace linings significantly improved the efficiency of wasteful conventional fireplaces. But late-eighteenth-century inventors still had no scientific way to quantify savings in heat produced per unit of wood. Only in the mid-nineteenth century did thinkers like the brewer and scientist James Joule develop consistent units to measure heat production: the British thermal unit and the SI (metric) Joule.

The two inventions that introduced modern efficiency were the work of other geniuses of the early nineteenth century, now known mainly to specialists: the millwright Oliver Evans and the paper manufacturer Henry Fourdrinier. If we look at plates of Diderot's encyclopedia as edited by Charles Gillispie, many of the workshops were not so different from those of the ages of Leonardo da Vinci or Galileo. Masters, assisted by journeymen and apprentices, made each product, though Smith's principle of the division of labor was beginning to spread. Goods were still fashioned individually or in small batches.[9]

Oliver Evans was the founder of continuous process efficiency. He is less well known than Franklin, Eli Whitney, Samuel Morse, or Thomas Edison, but for two centuries he was at least as influential as any of these. As Siegfried Giedion wrote in his classic *Mechanization Takes Command*, before there was any real American industry, "a solitary and prophetic mind set about devising a system wherein mechanical conveyance from one operation to another might eliminate the labor of human hands." Grain was raised to the top of the mill by a chain of buckets and conveyed by gravity through each of the stages of milling with belts, screws, and other continuous conveyances. Individually these were not entirely new; some had existed since antiquity. The idea of an integrated system that processed raw materials and semifinished products was still a breathtaking step in efficiency. Evans's system seemed shaky and he lacked Franklin's persuasive powers, but in "the power of his vision," Giedion rightly concluded, "Oliver Evans' invention opens a new chapter in the history of mankind."[10]

The second of the landmarks of classic modern efficiency was the Fourdrinier paper mill. Ever since its introduction in China, and to this day in the production of Japanese artisanal papers like washi, paper was made from fibers in individual sheets. Papermakers were highly skilled workers who formed powerful guilds; books and newspapers were still costly. A French printer named Nicolas-Louis Robert was the first to understand the potential of continuous paper production. As the historian Mark Kurlansky has pointed out, Robert's invention of a wire framework used the principle of today's conveyor belts, but actually preceded their invention. (The first use was by the Royal Navy for the manufacture of ship's biscuits in 1804.) In his machine, a moving screen received the wet fibers and agitated the pulp laterally to distribute it evenly, as sheet paper artisans did. After the water was removed, the semifinished paper was rolled on to a series of drums, the final ones heated, for drying. The paper manufacturers Henry and David Fourdrinier made technical improvements in the Robert process, but not enough to make it practical, and they were forced to declare bankruptcy. It was the engineer Bryan Donkin who finally made usable continuous papermaking machines on the basis of Robert's idea. This complex parentage reveals an important feature of continuous process efficiency: even more than other innovations, it is the drawn-out result of failure, collaboration, and competition.[11]

The efficiency of production of paper, flour, and biscuits heralded two centuries of efficiency in the continuous production of consumer goods. Circular motion became ubiquitous. In war, it created the revolver and the Maxim gun. In peacetime, the humble spool of cotton thread, introduced in Scotland during Britain's wars with Napoleon, made possible Isaac Singer's sewing machine and the mass production of garments. (Through the eighteenth century, thread was generally made of linen and sold only in skeins.) The nineteenth century's most celebrated innovation, Thomas Edison's electric light-bulb, had a limited initial market. Until the late 1890s, it took a team of two skilled glassblowers a full minute to produce two glass shells with methods that had not changed in two thousand years. Thanks to decades of improvements at the Corning Glass Works, a new genera-tion of automated bulb machine was able to produce 400,000 blanks (glass shells enclosing the incandescent filaments) in twenty-four hours by 1926; in the 1930s the number increased first to one million, then to three million. Just as Nicolas-Louis Robert and the Fourdri-niers proved as important as Gutenberg for mass reading and educa-tion, so the now obscure inventor William Woods used continuous process efficiency to realize the potential of the Edison bulb. Other mechanic-inventors made possible the fully automated production and filling of glass bottles and metal cans, and the mixing of rubber in giant rotary blenders still used in today's robotic tire factories. On the farm, the continuously operating harvester machine replaced the scythe and the hand sickle; the grain thus harvested would by the twentieth century be baked as it passed through ovens on continuous conveyor belts. Advanced dairies in Europe and the United States even milked cows in slowly rotating stalls. As Giedion observed, the continuous disassembly line of Chicago's meatpacking industry helped inspire the workflow of industrialists led by Henry Ford. And the very sheet steel that automobile makers were using by the early 1930s was made in a continuous roll process that was pioneered by a steel mill superintendent, John B. Tytus, inspired by the design of his grandfather's Fourdrinier paper mill.[12]

Some of America's greatest nineteenth- and twentieth-century infrastructure also exploited the efficiency of repeated rotary motion; the giant cables of suspension bridges from the Brooklyn Bridge to the Golden Gate Bridge were spun from wire on location by the machinery and workers of John Roebling's Sons. Even news and liter-ature were shaped by continuous rotary methods. Giant Fourdrinier machines turned out the rolls of newsprint supplying the high-speed web-fed presses of newspaper barons like Joseph Pulitzer and William Randolph Hearst.[13]

Shopping and recreation were transformed. Department store customers entered and exited through revolving doors and changed floors with ingenious endless belts of stairs. And the West's great railroads, with their continuous circulation of vast tonnages of freight and millions of passengers, were the ultimate expression—and management challenge—of the mature industrial age. The ocean liners of the North Atlantic circulated according to reliable, fixed schedules, keeping to a wide band in each direction. Elite passengers came to expect a punctuality unheard-of in the centuries of sail. If the captain of the *Titanic* had slowed to a safe speed for avoiding sea ice as many subsequent writers and film directors have believed he should, the ship would have been over a day late and he would probably be remembered (if at all) by marine historians for timidity, not prudence.[14]

While many of the inventors of the new processes rose from the shop floor, sometimes to great wealth, industrialists and the middle class alike were beginning to perceive that empirical skills were not enough. With continuous process efficiency arose a new set of values and a new lexicon that can be called the first efficiency movement. It motivated not only investors, bankers, and aspiring managers, but also members of the growing ranks of the professions. There was no single doctrine of industrial efficiency in the nineteenth and early twentieth centuries, but there was a firm set of assumptions.

The first was quantification. While it may not have mattered to Benjamin Franklin to measure the output of his stove versus that of conventional fireplaces, nineteenth-century elites shared a growing enthusiasm for measurement. New statistical techniques were making it possible to present and evaluate data for more precise decision making. The profession of accounting was essential to large enterprises, especially to public companies. The physicist and inventor William Thomson, Lord Kelvin, made the most famous declaration on this subject when he said in a popular lecture in 1883 that "when you can measure what you are speaking about, and express it in numbers, you know something about it; but when you cannot measure it, when you cannot express it in numbers, your knowledge is of a meagre and unsatisfactory kind."[15]

Classic efficiency also depended on scale. While the left of the progressive movement feared monopoly, and independent producers and merchants claimed unfairness, left and right often agreed on the advantages of the big corporation for both consumers and workers. From the time of Andrew Carnegie's Edgar Thomson works in Braddock, Pennsylvania, in 1875, it was scale that permitted the installation of the most efficient and expensive new machinery, driving down prices to put pressure on competition. It was scale that let John D. Rockefeller monopolize petroleum distribution and refining and control, much of it even after the antitrust breakup of Standard Oil. And it was scale that made possible the earliest industrial robots; as early as 1921, inspired by the Ford assembly line, the A. O. Smith Co. of Milwaukee was selling a robotic machine capable of riveting ten thousand automobile frames each day.[16]

With scale came bureaucracy and professionalization. Even entrepreneurs who had learned on the job, like the superstar telegraph operator Thomas Edison, realized they needed degreed engineers and scientists, and American universities obliged with new technical schools and courses. One empirical occupation after another was reorganized as a profession with schools, degrees, and journals endowed by dynasties like those of the Carnegies, Mellons, Rockefellers, Vanderbilts, and Guggenheims. An ideology of codes, examinations, and credentials spread to include not only medicine, law, and engineering, but new academic fields like librarianship, public accounting, journalism, and business administration. Even on the shop floor, new positions like tool room clerk were created to allow highly skilled workers to spend as much time as possible at their machines.[17]

With size, too, came the opportunity and responsibility for private planning. The efficient corporation was large enough not just to dominate its market but to shape future technology from within. General Electric, Du Pont, AT&T, IBM, and other giants were proud of their research laboratories. While Bell Labs is now famous mainly for its introduction of the transistor, no detail was too small for its research, down to linemen's leather belts and mechanics' oil cans. Even in the Great Depression, the Pennsylvania Railroad laboratories in Altoona tested supplies of everything from lightbulbs to dining-car grapefruit, according to an admiring two-part article in *Fortune* magazine in 1936, observing that it was "a nation bigger than Turkey or Uruguay. Corporately it behaves like a nation; it blankets the lives of a 100,000 citizens like a nation."[18]

The scale of great twentieth-century corporations also gave them advantages in the labor market, as described by the economist David Weil in his book *The Fissured Workplace*. The large national corporation was able not only to pay higher wages and offer better working conditions than most independent companies but it led the economy in health care plans, pensions, and other benefits. Low turnover of skilled employees further compounded efficiency.[19]

Classical corporate efficiency also depended on relations with government bureaucracies. Corporate executives fought government regulation and recommended their own style of management to improve the efficiency of government. But beginning with the First World War and accelerating with the Second and the Cold War, many relied closely on government contracts. Historians of technology have shown how national armories advanced mass production when the ideal of interchangeable parts was still technically challenging and costly. IBM was rescued from the Depression by the bookkeeping demands the new Social Security system made on employers. (IBM's founder and leader, the master salesman Thomas J. Watson, Sr., simply had a correct intuition that the world somehow would soon need the expensive equipment he was stockpiling, and the ideas his research laboratory was developing, during the early years of the Depression. His more rational competitors largely lost out.) After the Second World War, the initial market for Fairchild Semiconductor's integrated circuits was almost exclusively the military and the space program until the mid-1960s. The demanding specifications of critical defense contracts also pushed Fairchild and other mid-century companies to reliability levels that would have otherwise taken far longer to achieve.[20]

Corporate executives believed they had the right and duty to plan the technology of the future. Company-sponsored exhibitions in the World's Fairs of the 1930s attempted to buoy the public with the wonders their organizations had on their drawing boards, including radical infrastructure changes that would need political approval. By the years after World War II, management academics and gurus encouraged corporate leaders to regard themselves as private planners of the nation's future for the benefit of all stakeholders. It was implicit that corporations like the Bell System, General Motors, General Electric, Eastman Kodak, and IBM could manage innovation indefinitely in the public interest. And why should they not, since their well-funded laboratories had impressive records, and until the 1990s, newcomers like Polaroid, Microsoft, and Apple Computer generally complemented rather than threatened them? Even Xerox Corporation, perhaps the original disruptive company of the postwar era, did not compete with Kodak in photography or (despite a brilliant research staff) with IBM in computer hardware.

Finally, twentieth-century efficiency was elitist. As Samuel Haber, Thomas C. Leonard, and others have shown, the idea of a guiding minority directing less discerning masses was never far from reformers' minds, whether in industry, government, or education. Even one of the bitterest foes of the corporate elite, the rebel economist Thorstein Veblen, envisioned a new Soviet of Technicians who could increase the nation's output three- or even twelve-fold. Mainstream politicians—Theodore Roosevelt and Woodrow Wilson alike—endorsed the superiority and eugenic improvement of the white race and fretted about the reduced birthrate and "suicide" of its most intelligent men and women.[21]

The efficiency creed of the great corporations did not remain static. The authoritarian time and motion study introduced by Frederick Winslow Taylor, and anathema to labor unions, became kinder and gentler under the industrial engineers Frank and Lillian Gilbreth, who achieved national fame by running their household and raising their children according to the ideals of efficiency. Lillian Gilbreth sponsored some of the first research on the effect of seating on worker health as well as productivity; paternalist "welfare capitalist" companies like the Larkin Soap Company of Buffalo (pioneers of the direct selling to networks of friends and neighbors that was later perfected by corporations like Avon and Amway) and the National Cash Register Co. of Dayton made health and cultural opportunities part of employee life. (Frank Lloyd Wright's Larkin administration building in Buffalo, sadly demolished in the 1950s after the company's demise, was equipped with an atrium, an early air-conditioning system, and an Oliver Evans–style flow of correspondence from the top to the bottom floors.) For a few leading companies, efficiency became a way of life.[22]

The greatest change in corporate ideas of efficiency occurred in the Margaret Thatcher and Ronald Reagan years of the late 1970s and the 1980s, when energy shocks, inflation, and labor discord challenged received ideas in business. When the management guru Peter Drucker published *The Age of Discontinuity* in 1966, what was remarkable was how much of the efficiency synthesis he felt had to be preserved. The global business environment had become far more diverse and pluralistic: "We need government as the central institution in the society of organizations. We need an organ that expresses the common will and the common vision and enables each organization to make its own best contribution."[23]

On the moderate left, the Harvard economist John Kenneth Galbraith warned of underinvestment in public goods but also accepted big corporations (and labor unions) as technological and social necessities. Even Soviet communism had subscribed, in its own way, to many ideas of efficiency developed under capitalism. Stalin's USSR openly embraced Henry Ford's modernist vision, from the mechanization of agriculture to the vertical integration of the vast River Rouge complex, which turned raw materials into finished automobiles. Russia's Five Year Plans were based on the acknowledged efficiency of Ford production methods, and Stalin himself praised American efficiency as "that indomitable force which neither knows nor recognizes obstacles." Soviet filmmakers celebrating collective farms were not ashamed to make the Ford logo stamped on tractor radiators clearly visible. To Marxist-Leninists the contradictions of capitalism doomed it to periodic crisis and mass unemployment. Soviet planning would fulfill the promise of technological efficiency and surpass the West. A 1957 confidential report of the USSR Academy of Sciences, discovered by the historian of technology Slava Gerovitch, declared that "the use of computers for statistics and planning must have an absolutely exceptional significance in terms of its efficiency. In most cases, such use would make it possible to increase the speed of decision-making by hundreds of times and to avoid errors that are currently produced by the unwieldy bureaucratic apparatus involved in these activities." In the era of Leonid Brezhnev, Soviet planners and computer theorists believed that a centrally planned national network, which Gerovitch has dubbed the InterNyet, could at last accomplish the economic goal of the Soviet state, the rational and harmonious development of the entire economy.[24]

The world was riveted by the virtual end of European communism in 1991, the dissolution of the Soviet Union, and the independence of former satellites. Vast complexes like Magnitogorsk, inspired by the Gary, Indiana, works of U.S. Steel and once the pride of the Soviet system, were now revealed as the height of inefficiency in squandering energy and other natural resources. (When staying at the Moscow hotel of the USSR Academy of Sciences in 1988 I met a Finnish forestry consultant who had come to help with perestroika in his industry; he mentioned that Soviet yields per hectare were only a quarter of those of his own country.)[25]

But another kind of transformation was taking place in the West. A decade after the IBM PC and its clones had begun to transform office work, a new kind of capitalist efficiency was taking shape as century-old corporations faced crises and new empires arose. Not that continuous process efficiency was abandoned. It still existed and was making fortunes but it had lost its excitement in a West that had long anticipated a "post-industrial age." Contractors overseas could mobilize industrial armies of young people from the countryside.

The two decades from the late 1970s through the early 1990s were a transitional era. They brought in a new model of efficient organizations and new self-identified and pejorative names: "Reaganism," "Thatcherism," "third way," and (the current favorite of the left) "neoliberalism." The era from 1945 to 1975 now appeared as a golden age; the Arab oil boycott and the rise of Japanese competition tended to replace expansive optimism with fear.

The first great change was reduction of administrative levels. Few people today have a good word for hierarchical organizations. But we have to remind ourselves that in the late nineteenth and early twentieth centuries, the punctilious routine of European civil servants was the envy of American reformers bent on curbing patronage and corruption. By the late 1950s and 1960s this was all changing. Even as some business historians and theorists like Alfred D. Chandler, Jr., were celebrating the multidivisional corporation as the embodiment of technical rationality, academic and popular critics were ridiculing its conformity, the tedium of the assembly line, and the mind-numbing routine of middle-management bureaucracy. When Wall Street entrepreneurs began to challenge management with hostile takeovers and leveraged buyouts in the 1970s and 1980s, they signaled a new age in which share prices and immediate return on shareholder value outweighed old-style corporate statesmanship. The index of Drucker's *Age of Discontinuity* has sections on topics like "management," "unions," "government," and "knowledge workers," but no reference to shareholders or capital markets.

Closely related to administrative flattening was the rise of the doctrine of shareholder value. Thanks in part to the growth of private- and public-sector pension funds, managers were under increasing scrutiny from institutional investors seeking maximum returns for their customers. This seemed at first to be a progressive cause, questioning management insularity and complacency. Ironically, it was New Deal liberals who first promoted this idea. Adolf A. Berle, Jr., and Gardiner Means had warned in the early 1930s of the growing power of a professional managerial class controlling corporate decisions without owning much of their companies. It was time for investor-owners to assert themselves. In fact, Peter Drucker coined the phrase "pension fund socialism" in the 1970s and devoted a widely reviewed book, *The Unseen Revolution*, to it in 1976.[26]

In the "flatter" corporations, more executives reported directly to the chief executive officer, and incentives like stock options became an increasing part of executive compensation. The results proved disappointing to progressive critics of the corporation—pay became far more unequal—yet the new corporation seemed more efficient than ever.[27]

The troubles of the American automotive industry in the late 1960s and the 1970s helped catalyze a crisis of older ideas of efficiency. The River Rouge plant so admired by Soviet technocrats covered two thousand acres in Dearborn, Michigan, and employed 100,000 workers at its peak in the 1930s. The historian David L. Lewis has called it "easily the greatest industrial domain in the world," "without parallel in sheer mechanical efficiency." While Ford always bought parts from thousands of small suppliers, the ideal of the Rouge was to begin with iron ore, coal, rubber, and other raw materials in a single integrated process celebrated by photographers and artists of the time. Though General Motors, with its multiple brands "for every purse and purpose" and its friendliness to customization, seemed to be the antithesis of Ford, it still followed the pattern of multilevel bureaucracy—even more so than the autocratic, family-owned Ford of the 1930s. GM even acquired suppliers like ball bearing makers instead of dealing with them at arm's length. By the 1970s, outsourcing had replaced this insourcing. As the historian of management fads James Hoopes observed, Jack Welch at General Electric was able to sell many units (with the encouragement of his advisor Peter Drucker) because more efficient computer technology had reduced transaction costs.[28]

The radical new model of the 1970s and 1980s was not GE, though, but Apple Computer. Unlike its rival IBM and the prodigiously expanding Xerox, Apple maintained a relatively small core of designers, marketers, and planners and outsourced many of its other functions. Its researchers combined and modified others' ideas creatively, even radically, but it had almost no basic research to compare with IBM's Thomas J. Watson Research Center or Xerox's legendary Palo Alto Research Center (PARC). Apple's philosophy proved right in the 1980s when Xerox's personal computer program stalled and Apple applied its technology to the Macintosh at consumer-friendly prices.

Meanwhile, efficient manufacturing itself was reaching an impasse. A new generation of young workers who had never experienced the Depression were rebelling against management's search for ever faster production. "Alienation"—a luxury in years of breadlines—seeped from academia into popular culture. In many industries, what now appears a golden age of American manufacturing was tarnished by stress and fatigue. One reason for the later health care and pension crisis of the automotive industry is that so many workers of this era gave priority to early retirement benefits in their contracts.[29]

. . .

Along with a new style of executive compensation, a new model of the efficient organization emerged, the "workplace fissuring" described by Weil. The essential cores of organizations are surrounded by contingent workers, often outsourced and rarely unionized, with high turnover. In the new corporate environment of the 1980s and beyond, management's image of the ideal employee shifted. Under the aegis of Frederick Winslow Taylor and Henry Ford, it was the person who would follow a fixed program determined by professional experts and do so until promoted to supervision or retired. In the new flexible enterprise, it was the worker who would respond promptly and creatively to constantly changing policies. A former Larkin Co. executive, the writer and publisher Elbert Hubbard, created the first encomium of unquestioning corporate obedience in his 1899 tract, *A Message to Garcia*, reprinted in forty million copies for distribution to employees of organizations from the New York Central Railroad to the United States Army. The pamphlet's ubiquity reflected the doctrine of efficiency in organizations around 1900. Almost exactly a century later, in 1998, a physician named Spencer Johnson published a similarly praised and detested parable, *Who Moved My Cheese?*—this time about mice who adapt to a new strategy rather than continuing to pursue their former goals. Instead of demanding single-minded obedience to an order, the new flexible corporation was ready to reward those adaptable enough not only to respond to but to anticipate change. *Who Moved My Cheese?* sold 26 million copies in its first decade, according to sources cited by Wikipedia. Critics accused each book of glorifying obedience, but there was a difference. The flexible subordinate was now portrayed as obeying not a single individual— a superior who would reward faithful and enthusiastic service—but inescapable trends of technological and social change that superiors also were compelled to follow. Indeed, by the 1990s, the flexible "learning organization," sometimes explicitly inspired by the body's immune system, had largely replaced the old stable quasi-military structure in management theory.[30]

Just as flexibility replaced static hierarchy, privatism eroded whatever remained of noblesse oblige in relations with competitors and governments. Cold War corporations—not only aerospace companies but technology giants like AT&T and IBM—had close ties to the federal government. In some ways AT&T and IBM were monopolies, but they repaid their status with gestures toward the public good. As Jon Gertner pointed out in his book *The Idea Factory*, Bell Labs licensed the transistor to all manufacturers for the relatively modest fee of $25,000 instead of asking for substantial royalties. The technology of Larry Ellison's company Oracle, with a 2017 market capitalization of $177 billion, was based on papers outlining an innovative concept for managing large databases published by the IBM staff computer scientist Edgar F. Codd in 1970, and never patented. There was a high opportunity cost to being a national treasure. Oracle's rise must have been all the more painful to IBM executives because they had originally shunned Codd's breakthrough as a threat to their existing product.[31]

The dissolution of AT&T and the Bell System in 1984 signaled that no company was too large or too respected to be challenged by newcomers. One of the pillars of the new efficiency was set in place. The Gilded Age fortunes had been made by combining formerly independent oil producers, steel plants, and railroads into giant organizations, justified as lowering costs through scale; now efficiency could mean dismembering them while they were still apparently fully functional. New, leaner competitors with lower overheads (including investments in research as well as bureaucracy) could undercut prices of formerly premium services and hardware. The fact that a previously unknown microwave-radio entrepreneur in the Midwest, Bill McGowan, had been able to get the U.S. government to support his 1974 antitrust suit against AT&T, prevailing over the Bell System's overwhelming legal resources, showed that no organization was secure.[32]

A corollary of the new corporate model was globalization. Gilded Age trusts may have relied heavily on foreign capital and sold in international markets, but they were run almost entirely by nationals of their own countries and permanent immigrants. Today a typical giant U.S. corporation may earn 80 percent of its revenues overseas; taxation of this income remains a thorny issue. But as the business journalist Daniel Gross has pointed out, the headquarters of U.S. multinationals are also cosmopolitan by pre–World War II standards: "Forget about influencing policy; many of today's leading U.S. CEOs can't even vote here." Some critics on the left perceive a new world overclass more loyal to each other than to their fellow citizens. Resentment of this cosmopolitan elite played a major part in the victory of Donald J. Trump in the 2016 presidential election, but (in contrast to the River Rouge model) the interdependence of many key industries on international supply chains is likely to frustrate economic nationalism.[33]

By the 1990s, management theorists were revising long-standing assumptions about the nature of the corporation. In 1989 the Harvard Business School economist Michael C. Jensen foresaw "the demise of the public corporation." During the previous decade he and other academics had trained a generation of elite consultants and executives to regard return to shareholders as the sole purpose of business—a break from older views that balanced investor interests with those of employees, customers, and the public. The "agency" theory promoted by Jensen and his colleagues had already bestowed an Ivy League pedigree on the corporate raiders and dismantlers, who could portray themselves as efficient reallocators of assets and foes of transaction costs. The promise of compensating executives for their true contribution to shareholder income never realized its potential. There were too many ways for executives to manipulate results with creative accounting, often increasing their compensation even in bad years. As predicted by Campbell's Law, the criterion of measured profits can be manipulated to give a false idea of what they are supposed to measure: long-term benefits to shareholders. By 2014, hundreds of companies were using nonstandard accounting methods to justify executive bonuses. Agency theory, designed to reduce conflicts between executives' and shareholders' interests, may increase them in the long run.[34]

A second wave began with the Internet boom of the 1990s. Another Harvard Business School professor, Clayton Christensen, began a new phase of thinking about technological change when he coined the phrase "disruptive innovation" in a paper he coauthored with a senior Harvard colleague, Joseph L. Bower, in the *Harvard Business Review* in 1995. Christensen's own innovation was to question the conventional business wisdom of listening to customers and giving them what they ask for. New and revolutionary technology is often inferior to established methods. At first it appeals not to existing users but to buyers with different backgrounds and needs. Only with time and further refinement does it compete with and eventually dominate conventional products, Bower and Christensen cited the computer disk drive industry, in which established firms scorned new compact formats with initially reduced storage capacity—drives that ultimately made the mini- and microcomputer industries possible. That segment may not have been the best example. Few of the original manufacturers survived, but Seagate (which Bower and Christensen singled out) had emerged as one of the most dominant and best managed companies in the global drive industry by the early twenty-first century. Disruption, however, can be very real. Since the mid-1990s, the most striking example has been Eastman Kodak's failure to compete with its dominant film products by developing the digital technology of its own laboratories.[35]

Around the time Christensen's *The Innovator's Dilemma* appeared, a new business form was emerging, one that could challenge even earlier "disruptive" companies: the platform. Under continuous process efficiency, the point was production of material goods, their retail distribution, and speedy freight and personal transportation. Platform entrepreneurship, which began not with the personal computer but with the World Wide Web and its graphic browsers in the 1990s, is different. A platform is a web-based service that provides a framework for other services or transactions. Economists had long believed that the firm, with all its overhead and bureaucracy, was a necessary institution for reducing transaction costs. But what if technology could match exchanges of goods and services? That idea appears to date from an academic book that appeared in 1996, *Invisible Engines: How Software Platforms Drive Innovation and Transform Industries.* The platform company may combine the functions of commission sales, advertising, and information brokerage. It may be a de facto employment agency or taxicab company. Its attraction is that it centralizes information and services that otherwise would require searches and a multiplicity of sites. It can organize these as streams of feeds and suggestions and turn the user's behavior online into information that can be marketed to third parties. Best of all for investors, it can even induce users to do nearly all the work. A platform company may manufacture and distribute goods of its own. Microsoft, IBM, and especially Apple still sell billions in hardware. But the greatest room for growth appears elsewhere: getting paid by other businesses, and by individuals, to improve the efficiency of transactions.[36]

It was not only the well-known exponential growth of processor speed and storage that made software revolutionary. It was a small number of ingenious ideas that reduced the need for brute force, techniques like error-correcting codes (without which online commerce and communication would collapse), data compression (which multiplies storage capacity), and public key cryptography (which, built into web browsers and server software, makes secure Internet sessions possible). These ideas multiplied the efficiency of hardware; brilliant computational shortcuts could be the equivalent of massive hardware and its brute force. They are concepts for solving a problem in the speediest possible way, ideas that can be expressed in code. Take the numbering systems of product codes, the basis of electronic commerce and (as applied to books) one of the foundations of Amazon .com in the 1990s. It was worked out by a Dutch mathematician named Jacobus Verhoeff and is a formula for adding an additional digit to a number. This number, which you may have seen preceded by a dash in nonbook product codes as well, has no significance in itself. Called a check digit, it is there only to allow a computer program to verify the real number by processing it with a complex formula that results in a single-digit answer. If that number does not match the check digit (for example, because the customer mistakenly transposed two digits), an error notice appears. Few people entering numbers ever think about how they are generated and checked. That is the beauty of the algorithm, but also a pity, because it lets us take the economic power of mathematics for granted.[37]

We have all heard of Jeff Bezos, founder of Amazon.com. Only technical specialists and historians have heard of Jacobus Verhoeff. Yet when Bezos planned to transform online retailing, bookselling was a natural beginning because, thanks to Verhoeff's algorithm, more books had standardized product numbers than any other category of merchandise. Likewise, until recently, few laypeople knew the name of Karlheinz Brandenburg or the other German and American computer scientists who, in the late 1980s and 1990s, developed MP3 and other music compression algorithms that made possible the efficient use of digital storage in devices like Steve Jobs's iPod. The recorded music industry, complacently selling for $16.98 compact discs costing less than a dollar to manufacture, was memorably disrupted.[38]

When added to massive storage in remote computers over the Internet, efficient algorithms make possible a new style of quantitative analysis that has come to be known as big data. In the age of the slide rule and the punch card, people also felt overwhelmed by data, and early business education was based in part on techniques for analyzing it. But the ability to store and analyze unprecedented records was not just a more powerful version of the statistical thinking of the continuous process era. It has allowed far more precise identification of the productivity and profitability of employees and the value of customers. Michael Lewis's best-selling book *Moneyball* (2003) implied that any manager could emulate the Oakland A's general manager Billy Beane in identifying more sophisticated measurements of prospective employees' contributions. The problem of big data is that competitors usually have access to similar data sets and algorithms, so competitive advantages are similar to what accountants call wasting assets—tools, machinery, and other objects that lose their value over time—and techniques need constant refinement. Platform companies accumulate such enormous volumes of data that, unlike athletic teams, they become difficult to dislodge from first place. They also have the ability, as the political economist William Davies has observed, to follow and possibly manipulate trends in public sentiment without public scrutiny. Nineteenth-century statistics were to a great extent a public institution; twenty-first-century post-statistical big data are becoming a proprietary tool. As judges today privilege findings of secret algorithms, courts undermine the competitive advocacy testing of disputed evidence essential to criminal and civil justice.[39]

A foundation of much big data in turn is user-generated information. Gathering and entering data can be hard work, as in polling and focus groups. Platform efficiency is based in part on encouraging customers to create data without pay. Amazon's customer rating system was the best-known early version of the idea. An even deeper revolution was the Google PageRank algorithm, which (unlike earlier search software) relied on relationships between the links that countless website owners chose. Scientific bibliographers like the information scientist Eugene Garfield had pioneered using the citations in scientific papers to point to the works that had been most influential and thus presumably of highest quality and interest. The founders of Google, the computer science graduate students Larry Page and Sergey Brin, extended this idea beyond science to the entire World Wide Web. We will see more about it in Chapter Two. Despite acknowledged problems and the need to revise the algorithm constantly against manipulation, the relevance and quality of results soon exceeded those of all rivals.

A corollary has been user classification. Systematizing authorities of the nineteenth and early twentieth centuries were still trying to create a single hierarchic order of knowledge. Twenty-first-century readers and even some professional librarians now pay more attention to tags, keywords that may be proposed by lay readers, rather than classification specialists. The Princeton, New Jersey, Public Library, for example, still uses the Dewey Decimal System but shelves nonfiction books (like technology studies) in subject "neighborhoods" drawn from different Dewey ranges.

Despite the growing importance of feeds from social media and anxiety that Facebook and Twitter have become default information sources, search does not seem to have declined as an information habit in managing the explosion of data. While Google does not publish its annual number of searches, a search industry site interprets its statements to mean that searches increased by over 50 percent from 2012 to 2016 alone, now exceeding two trillion annually, 15 percent of which have been for keywords never previously searched. Social media might replace some web surfing, but they also seem to be generating even more searches. Since 2012, when he coauthored a paper, "Tracking the Flow of Information into the Home," the communication scholar W. Russell Neuman and his colleagues have been giving new life to an old distinction in their field. Information *push* in Neuman's terms is dissemination by influential media in the days of relative information scarcity; information *pull* is users' preference for getting media products on demand (whether through search or streaming services). Google and other modern search engines made it possible to use information more actively, to request it specifically rather than receive it from a limited number of outlets.[40]

Information pull in turn helps to create another defining feature of platform efficiency: personalization. Industrial-age mass media put a premium on typical consumers subdivided by broad demographic categories like age, gender, geography, and estimated income. There were also mailing lists of people with special interests—enthusiast buyers of books on cacti and succulents, for example—but these were expensive to rent and not always up-to-date. The big data of online retailers and search engine companies could identify tastes and predict behavior more accurately and at a lower cost. Platform colossi like Google and Facebook have thus become the most lucrative advertising agencies in history. Users of Google will note how often they are served advertising not only from the company they were originally looking for, but from its competitors, an opportunity no print or broadcast medium can offer. Thanks to such power, from the time of its initial public offering in 2005 to the calendar year 2016, Google's advertising revenue grew by over 1,000 percent from $6.07 billion to $79.38 billion.[41]

For some corporations, the platform idea offers another strategy opportunity: dematerialization. Technology companies originally built on distribution of physical products, especially IBM and Apple, have been shifting to web-based services. Amazon.com now makes more profit from its web services than from its retail operations.[42]

Personalization and cloud-based services have been made even more popular by the spectacular rise of mobile computing after many false starts in the decade after 1995. The adoption rate of smartphones after the introduction of the iPhone has been one of the most rapid in the history of information technology. It took over a quarter century from the introduction of the Apple I computer in 1976 for the household acquisition of personal computers to grow to about 60 percent in 2003. That level was reached in only eight years from the introduction of the iPhone in 2007 to 2015—mostly in the midst of a historic recession. (In fact, economic hardship may have helped promote the technology; smartphones and their apps have become the primary gateway to the web for almost 20 percent of Americans, especially low-income and young people.) Thus, both for better and for worse, many web resources are optimized for the personal, mobile, small screen rather than for the office or home monitor. Social scientists were quick to recognize the potential of this trend; even before the iPhone's introduction, the psychologist Sherry Turkle described the new mobile ethos as "always on, always on you." For platform companies and advertisers, the ability to reach consumers based on their real-time location has been a fantasy come true despite consumers' option of disabling disclosure of their coordinates.[43]

Platforms are one of history's most efficient types of business enterprise because they need so few employees and can be even flatter and leaner than other organizations thanks to artificial intelligence. Facebook, with $28 billion in revenue in 2015, had a staff of only about 17,048. With a net income of $10 billion in the same year, it was earning over $586,000 per employee. The classic twentieth-century technology corporation, IBM, still slightly surpassed it with consolidated net income from continuing operations of $11.9 billion. But with about 414,000 employees in 2017, that amounts to about $28,700 per employee. For all the prowess of IBM's supercomputer Watson there is far more profit in using algorithms to gather information from user-generated data and in analyzing it to target advertising to consumers than there is in selling advanced services to corporations.[44]

Ubiquitous computing has created new categories of place-based efficiency that take advantage of the Global Positioning System (GPS) built into smartphones. As platform companies, Uber, Lyft, and others do not own taxis or limousines or employ drivers. They sell their services as superefficient intermediaries matching customers and driver-owners with algorithms that track location and adjust prices to demand. In practice, Uber can assure customers in large cities that they can get a ride—at a price—within five minutes regardless of weather, traffic conditions, or special events.

Uber may thus be the most rapid success of a consumer platform-efficiency company. And while many objections have been made to it, especially in Europe, it is indeed efficient, according to economists who have studied its operations. For many city dwellers, even surge pricing is cheaper than paying for, maintaining, and insuring a car. Whatever else can be said about the company and about the ethics of its policies toward its own drivers and its competitors, it is highly efficient in matching riders and drivers. In early 2017, at least, its rates (below cost in many locations) were significantly less than what its customers would have been willing to pay, according to a study by the economist Steven Levitt (with the company's data and cooperation). Levitt determined that customers who spent $4 billion on Uber rides in 2015 would have been willing to pay $11 billion more, yielding $7 billion for society as consumer surplus, "an economist's dream," according to Levitt's coauthor, Stephen J. Dubner. Buoyed by such statistics, private investors have embraced the platform economy so fervently that, in February 2017, Uber's market capitalization of $62.5 billion exceeded the $49.9 billion valuation of Ford Motor Company, River Rouge plant and all. Despite allegations of misconduct by executives, the company's value had increased to almost $70 billion when a new CEO took office in late August 2017.[45]

Uber's business model, like that of many smaller platform companies, is based in part on the ambiguity of American labor and tax laws. When a person is an employee, following directions and thus subject to minimum wage laws and employer tax and insurance contributions, and when he or she is an independent contractor is often unclear. Software lets Uber take advantage of that ambiguity by combining elements of independence (freedom to set one's own hours and use competing dispatching services) with incentives that can amount to soft direction, a technique known as "choice architecture."[46]

The most common objections to services like Uber is that they have used lobbying power to gain unfair advantages over existing services by changing regulations, and that surge pricing is yet another way for the rich to jump to the head of the queue. But the real problem may be that it is not a radical innovation at all and thus does not do much to create a more efficient society—for example, by making trips unnecessary—rather than matching drivers and passengers more expeditiously. We will look at the effects of ridesharing programs in Chapter Four.

. . .

The first objection to platform efficiency is in fact that it is not deeply disruptive at all. And this criticism has been made most strongly not by Silicon Valley's progressive critics but by the academic most closely identified with the idea of disruption, Clayton Christensen himself.

Christensen and his colleagues Derek van Bever and Bryan Mezue have recently distinguished two kinds of disruption: efficiency innovation and market-creating innovation. One makes existing goods and services available to more people at lower prices. Uber's goal is different, to make transportation constantly available at a market-clearing price that may be lower or higher than conventional companies' charges, but it follows the efficiency pattern. Efficiency innovations often eliminate jobs; market-creating innovations introduce new categories of products and create jobs.[47]

To use the Christensen–van Bever–Mezue analysis, the bicycle design introduced in the 1890s and still prevailing today was not just a faster or less expensive machine than its mid-century predecessors. It redefined and stabilized a new technology in a way that extended its reach in society by orders of magnitude. The most popular earlier bicycles were the so-called penny farthings, with one enormous wheel directly below the rider and a smaller trailing wheel. While the big wheel's diameter minimized jolts on the still unpaved roads of the era, it also risked serious injury to riders who pitched forward when the wheel struck an obstacle. These spills, called headers, actually appealed to many of the youthful and affluent male risk takers who were the earliest cyclists. In the new "safety" bicycle, the combination of diamond frame, pneumatic tires, and ball bearings made riding not only safer, less costly, and more comfortable but actually faster than earlier models, winning over macho racers along with women, the middle-aged, the elderly, and better-paid industrial workers and craftspeople. In the late maturity of the continuous process era in 1960, another market-creating innovation was the Xerox 914 photocopier, which was not just a neater substitute for wet-processing photostats but a device that could sometimes make duplicates of higher quality than the originals. It also rendered Edison-era mimeographs and spirit duplicators obsolete and launched one of the companies

with the highest rate of return on capital in history. (A $10,000 invest-
ment in the company in 1960 would have grown to $1 million by
1972.) By contrast, an Uber or Lyft vehicle is, apart from the operator's smartphone, like that of a conventional black car service.[48]

Yet the primacy of immediate needs means that more challenging
technological innovations are underfunded, even though they might
make society as a whole more efficient: for example, improved storage
batteries that would simplify the use of renewable energy and extend
the range and efficiency of electric cars. The sense of military emergency that promoted government spending on basic research during
the Cold War has declined, and climate change has become a partisan
issue. Physico-chemical systems present more challenges and constraints than electronic networks and logic; making efficient devices
may take years of apparently wasteful experimentation. Examining the
development of U.S. jet engines after World War II, the historian of
technology Philip Scranton has concluded their success reflected not
scientific program management but "non-linear, irrational, uncertain,
multi-lateral, and profoundly passionate technological and business
practice, yielding success not through planning but through dogged
determination, a certain indifference to failure (which secrecy aided),
and massive expenditures of public funds." Yet the result has been not
only a leap in the speed of civil air transportation but enhanced reliability and reduction of costs per passenger mile compared to piston
engine craft. Before its explosive growth in the 1960s, the Xerox Corporation also had a prolonged and difficult childhood. Two decades of
research and development by a small photographic supply company
in Eastman Kodak's shadow, Haloid (it was later renamed after its
breakthrough, xerography), were needed before the inventor Chester
Carlson's dry photographic process patent of 1938 could be transformed into a commercially successful device. High-temperature
fusing of toner to paper made fires a recurrent threat; at one point
prototypes would catch fire if a copied document had too many
zeroes and letter o's. A small fire, fortunately unnoticed by customers,
broke out at a major trade show as late as 1960. Even now, lithium-
ion batteries, the most efficient type, can be a hazard. In autumn 2016
the Korean electronics giant Samsung recalled millions of its flagship
Note 7 smartphones after hundreds of incidents of fires caused by

faulty batteries from two different suppliers. Users of premium electronics demand both compactness and full-day power reserves, but
lithium-ion batteries, the only ones that can meet these requirements,
use flammable electrolytes. As *The Economist* put it, "catching fire if
something goes wrong . . . is their nature."[49]

The first problem of platform efficiency, then, is that it promises
faster returns than market-creating innovation can, in large part
because algorithms can be tested and applied to larger systems at a
pace exceeding those of physico-chemical innovations. Programs can
now learn rapidly from experience, defeating top professionals not
only in games like chess and Go but in contests like no-limit Texas
hold 'em poker, in which an AI program developed at Carnegie Mel-
lon University took $1.8 million against top-ranking players. Soft-
ware and hardware advances are, of course, not completely distinct;
modern lithium-ion batteries, for example, need sophisticated programmed controls for safe operation. But the relative difficulty of
market-creating innovation is not likely to go away. This disparity
helps explain why, in the midst of dazzling improvements in software,
the economy rebounded more slowly after the recession of 2008 than
after previous twentieth-century crises.[50]

There is a second problem of the new efficiency of financial
transactions. Far from reducing the social overhead represented by
finance, it has paradoxically increased it. Readers of 1990s Silicon
Valley manifestos like *The Road Ahead* (1995) by Bill Gates, Nathan
Myhrvold, and Peter Rinearson believed they were looking forward
to "friction-free commerce," in the authors' famous phrase. In fact,
for their users, Amazon.com and other advanced retail sites have
taken much of the work out of buying. Owners of Amazon's Echo
voice recognition microphone/speaker can use the company's Alexa
system to place orders without even having to tap on a screen; Microsoft, Google, and Apple have launched similar electronic assistants.
And the efficiency-minded who do want to touch something can opt
for one of Amazon's Wi-Fi-enabled buttons that can be attached to
appliances for placing instant orders for relevant branded supplies,
like detergent for a washing machine. Researchers at the micropro-

cessor colossus Intel predicted in 2009 that by the year 2020 consumers might place their orders just by thoughts picked up by sensors implanted in their brains. While the chip maker seems to have let that project drop quietly during the recession, it is unlikely to disappear.[51]

Friction nonetheless has a way of coming in the back door and reversing at least some part of efficiency. Amazon.com hosts two million third-party merchants whose offerings are presented along with Amazon's own. Some orders from them are fulfilled through Amazon's own warehouses; others are shipped directly from the vendors. Vendors may have different warranty policies for the same merchandise, and varying consumer ratings and delivery times. Furthermore, they use specially developed software to adjust their prices to those of other Amazon and non-Amazon vendors; under "dynamic pricing," quotations may change without notice. Amazon uses a complex and secret algorithm to select the default vendor in the "buy box," the link that adds the item to the consumer's shopping cart. The algorithm also lists other vendors below the winning one; still others are visible to customers who click yet another button. Amazon vendors use special software to calculate their prices; it might set a higher or lower price. So far, these variations have been minor annoyances compared to the generally rock-bottom prices, convenience of ordering—the Amazon interface is exceptionally well designed—and speed of delivery in the Prime program. Amazon's competitive power has helped reduce inflation; in fact, Amazon's margins on sales are so small that (as we have noted) its real profit comes from web services it provides to other companies and governments. The unanswered question is whether major acquisitions may turn Amazon into a different kind of company, anti- rather than pro-competitive.[52]

Thus the consumer is blessed with the full efficiency of Amazon if and only if he or she is willing to accept the choice that Amazon's algorithm, wrestling with the competing algorithms of various vendors with different satisfaction ratings, has decreed. A consumer looking for the lowest price may have to invest more time in considering the full list and weighing vendors' reputations. The memorably named website camelcamelcamel.com lets buyers review Amazon price histories spike by spike and dip by dip and set up an email for notification when a price drops to a pre-set level, but that requires additional time for decisions about trigger prices. It is useful mainly for expensive discretionary goods, especially consumer electronics, subject to brief seasonal manufacturers' price breaks. With or without such tools, what began as a simple and highly efficient system for shopping has become a complex one in which the best offers can appear and disappear suddenly depending on the dueling calculations of rival algorithms and platform vendors' surveillance of one's buying patterns. Likewise, online travel services originally appeared to simplify decisions by comparing the best hotel prices but have given rise to a new level of aggregators like kayak.com, which claims to find the best offers from other booking sites (though hotels have countered by offering their lowest prices for direct reservations). The complexity of booking travel has had an unexpected side effect: a revival of travel agencies, once mortally threatened by web booking.[53]

Evaluating customer ratings on web goods and service sites and on social media has also become more complex. According to *The New York Times*, marketing researchers who have compared Amazon customer reviews with both professional consumer organization reports and resale value have found that user comments are unreliable guides to quality. In practice it is almost impossible for comparison site owners to screen out shills. In 2012 an academic data-mining scholar estimated that fully a third of online reviews were faked. One publishing entrepreneur was briefly making $28,000 a month writing Amazon reviews for self-published authors. At the local level, looking for a computer repair shop, I noticed that one had exclusively five-star reviews with similar syntax, raising questions about the customers' identities. There were no signs of authenticity, such as an occasional mild criticism. None of the reviewers had commented on any other kind of establishment. Other review genres, especially of apartment complexes, conversely seem devoted to the airing of consumer grievances. To make matters even more complicated, some genuine online reviewers of books appear sincerely positive about almost everything. The central problem, though, is that reviews are subject to social influence bias: bandwagon effects and ratings bubbles. Fake reviews can be surprisingly influential in producing cascades of genuine positive ones.[54]

Favorable or not, reviews display the workings of Campbell's

Law. Their influence reflects reviewer behavior, making it necessary to discount reviewer bias. Social scientists and webmasters create algorithms to separate real from faked reviews, but these efforts encounter an age-old problem. As in document and fine art appraisal, the very tools developed to detect fraud can be used to commit it more ingeniously. In the end, it's not that customer reviews are useless, but they are much less time-efficient than they at first appeared. It often takes significant time to read through them and find the pros and cons of each product or service. Professional book and product reviewers did limit consumer information, but if you trusted their judgment it was more efficient to follow it than to try to divine the wisdom of the crowd.[55]

It is also not clear whether the platform economy of online retailing is more efficient than that of conventional stores. There has been a plausible argument that it reduces greenhouse emissions when compared to conventional bricks-and-mortar shopping by reducing automobile trips. In principle, parcels ordered on the web and delivered to the consumer's door result in lower carbon emissions than multiple shopping trips. Amazon, at least in 2012, claimed "a greener shopping experience" through "the efficiencies of online shopping" on its website. In reality, the results of algorithmic efficiency become almost impossible to measure once they begin interacting with human behavior. People diligent about reducing their carbon footprint can indeed save trips and time. But evidence from a study in Delaware suggests that others may compensate for their time and mileage savings with other types of trips, for example, for entertainment. The efficiency of rapid gratification—down to hours rather than merely overnight with some services—also means that more items are shipped and delivered in separate packaging to consumers, goods that when shipped to retailers may be bundled by the dozen on shrink-wrapped pallets instead of individually boxed. Just as electronic inventory control has made possible leaner manufacturing, some consumers are making last-minute purchases, enabled with smartphone apps, a way of life. "Planning Ahead Is Dead," announced an essay by a proudly unorganized writer. Amazon's heavily promoted Prime program offers, in exchange for an annual fee, free two-day delivery of many of its products, encouraging impulse orders. One form of efficiency—swift delivery—conflicts with another, the savings of combined shipments that were apparent to consumers in the era of the Sears Roebuck catalog. While the cardboard industry has been a leader in recycling, sales of boxes have been growing rapidly as a result of the convenience of online ordering, and recycling has its own environmental costs in shipping. What began in the 1990s as an environmentally efficient concept now is a tangle of unanswered questions, and brands like Amazon and Microsoft have been opening bricks-and-mortar outlets.[56]

Turning from retailing to banking and investments, we would expect two things. First, finance would be a lower proportion of the economy as measured by GDP. Surely credit cards, online banking, smartphone payments, and other innovations, especially the decline of the cost of processing transactions, plus bank mergers, would be expected to reduce finance's share just as changes in seed, fertilizer, and harvesting equipment have reduced that of farming. Second, with more efficient financial means of assessing new ventures, and with an apparently endless stream of innovations announced in scientific journals and magazines, the number of start-ups should be increasing during recovery from the 2008 financial crisis and recession. Unfortunately, the reverse is true in each case.

The first prediction, a declining cost of financial services to society, has not been realized. (I call it a prediction only retrospectively; the popular futurist books of the 1960s and 1970s, for all their enthusiasm about computing and automation, do not seem to say much about financial technology.) The economist Thomas Philippon has called attention to the growing share of financial sector costs in the GDP, observing that they are now significantly higher than in the days of J. P. Morgan. Around 1910 the financial sector consumed about 4 percent of GDP; in 2014 that proportion had more than doubled, to 9 percent. The rise has not been steady; there was an initial climb in the 1920s, and a drop in the Great Depression through the early postwar years, and then another steep rise from 1970. This tendency has contrasted with trends in other industries that adopted new information technology on a large scale, especially retailing, with its scanners and precise inventory control. Why has the financial system not been more like Walmart?, Philippon has wondered. The share of retail and wholesale distribution both dropped during adoption of new information technology.[57]

There are two explanations for the difference. The immediate one is that financial institutions have been using the efficiency of lower information and processing costs, and that of algorithms, to trade more often in the hope of higher profits. In 2011, Philippon reports, there were $700 trillion in derivatives—securities based on the value of underlying assets or other financial data—in force. Foreign exchange trading volume has increased two-hundred-fold since 1977. There is also no evidence that the increase of trading volume has enhanced the classic goals of financial intermediation: more accurate prices of investments and more efficient management of risk. Trading mechanisms may not have created the financial crisis and recession of 2008, but they did nothing to prevent it. Nor did the recession change the pattern of inefficiency through hyperefficiency. In 2016 *The New York Times* reported that a Royal Bank of Canada study had determined that a single security could have as many as eight hundred prices in twelve different markets. One electronic trader complained that "the level of complexity has grown to such an extent that it is unknown to most market participants. Instead of finding natural buyers and sellers, we're finding intermediaries who come in and are benefiting from the complexity." Others lamented that it is impossible to know the price at which an order will be executed, and that the software updates required by the financial system's complexity can lead to potentially ruinous breakdowns, as the trading company Knight Capital experienced in 2012. A market-making newcomer, IEX, has claimed to restore fairness to transactions with a minute delay that will neutralize the advantage of traders working with the fastest algorithms. But the other existing twelve exchanges have argued in opposing it that adding it as a thirteenth recognized exchange will only make the financial system more complex without the claimed benefit to the independent investor.[58]

Such reform proposals, whether or not effective, are symptoms of a trend that is still not completely understood. It is not clear *why* banks and other organizations and individuals have embraced the high-frequency trading as much as they have, or why buy-and-hold

policies fell out of favor. Technological innovations like trading algorithms alone rarely transform society; there must be a cultural change,
a latent demand for the innovation. Eastman Kodak and other major
corporations declined to finance Chester Carlson's xerography patent
because they saw the market as limited to the replacement of wet-
process document copying. They did not realize how many people
would want to copy documents if the price could be reduced to ten
cents or less. Resistance to the new technology was rational; identifying a disruptive technology in its early stages, when it is inferior
and more expensive than the conventional alternative, takes unusual
imagination. Similarly, there was a hidden demand for highly complex
automated trading strategies that reached its full extent only when the
tools were ready.

What drove this cultural change? One common explanation
might be called pathological. Progressive critics of Wall Street see
an epidemic of greed and materialism and the resurgence of the arrogance of billionaires in an alleged new Gilded Age. It is not hard
to find extreme avarice in American and world society, but that is
hardly an explanation. As Philippon observed, the capitalists of 1910,
while ruthless suppressors of workers' strikes, actually spent far less
on financial intermediation than their successors do now. On the
other side, many of the players in the derivatives market include
what remains of the "pension fund socialism" that Peter Drucker
predicted, acting not for moguls but for participants in public and
corporate retirement plans, seeking the highest possible returns while
controlling risk—and thereby sometimes increasing risk and jeopar-
dizing returns. Some of their clients may be billionaires, but they are
also trying to get the best deal for the pooled funds of the 99 percent. Most of us participate at least indirectly in the algorithm-driven
market.

(So far we have derived enormous benefits from another side
of electronic efficiency: index funds that maintain portfolios tracking common measures of securities markets like the Standard &
Poor's 500 and the Wilshire 5000 Total Market Index. Repeated studies show that no active human portfolio manager can equal returns on
indexes, partly because almost no managers are consistently right in the
long run, and partly because management expenses are far lower with-

out trading commissions or high-salaried analysts. The Pennsylvania-based Vanguard Group, whose founder John Bogle introduced index funding in 1976 with the encouragement of the Nobel Laureate economist Paul Samuelson, has been at the forefront of indexing. On Vanguard's blog, one of the company's analysts has described the concept as "a monster of efficiency," citing continuous reductions in management fees over the past forty years. Indexing may be, in his view, the best chance to reverse the growth in financial overheads highlighted by Philippon. But as indexing continues to grow in popularity, it also has become important enough, with over 30 percent of stocks and bonds under management, to feed back on the market itself. Companies included in indexes like the S&P 500 have higher valuations related to performance than others in the same industry that are not on the index. So if the proportion of assets managed by index funds and robotic trading rises, it is still possible that their scale may influence markets in unexpected ways. In fact, some critics have warned that by reducing the number of active analysts in the name of efficiency, indexed investments are endangering the quality of the information on companies' prospects that securities prices are supposed to provide.)[59]

A minority of economists and management scholars have been studying the values behind the algorithm-driven market. They see a deep shift in economic attitudes, one that can be elusive because it reflects quiet assumptions rather than ideologies. Paul H. Dembinski sees two twentieth-century trends behind the rise of what he calls financialization. This means not only the growth of the financial services sector, but the belief in financial measurements as the key to the success of a society. Two modern forces are behind financialization, he argues. One is the "efficiency ethos," the idea that productivity is the ultimate measure of good. The other is risk management, the system of protecting financial assets through instruments that limit possible losses at an acceptable cost. Efficiency and risk management are united by modern portfolio theory, for which the economist Harry Markowitz shared the Economics Nobel Prize in 1990. Well before that year, before the rise of modern networked computing, Dembinski argues, Markowitz and others helped create a new kind of economic actor, "Homo financiarius," concerned not with agriculture or manufacturing but with the optimal disposition of "temporarily idle liquid savings" under uncertainty using (as Markowitz put it in 1990) "sufficient computer and database resources" usually available only to institutions. The ethics of efficiency meant that fiduciaries controlling stock in public companies had a duty to support a change in management that raised shareholder assets no matter what the long-term effect on a company's employees, customers, or communities.[60]

Meanwhile, the economist Gerald F. Davis sees the rise of finance as nothing less than a transformation of American selfhood as well as of business institutions. While he does not use the word "financialization," he, like Dembinski, sees the hegemony of the financial sector as the driving force of the economy. The transformation goes beyond the growth of the service economy that flourished as industrial productivity drove down the cost of manufactured goods, increasing disposable income. The rise of finance is tied to a new way of looking at life as a portfolio—not just of conventional financial assets but of personhood and relationships: "human capital" for our education and abilities, and "social capital" for our network of family members and friends. In the "portfolio society" as Davis describes it, people may know little or nothing about the underlying assets held in trust for them by intermediaries like banks and mutual fund companies. Thanks to the efficiency of personal computers and the web, it is possible for an individual to survey all his or her assets and liabilities in a single view, from bank accounts and securities through credit card statements and mortgage balances. In fact, this information can be downloaded and displayed graphically wherever there is Wi-Fi or cellular telephone service. We might say, paraphrasing Descartes, "I monitor and transact, therefore I am."[61]

Publicity about tools for the managed life obscures an alarming underside of personal finances. Most Americans, according to a survey released in early 2017, live from paycheck to paycheck. Sixty-three percent of all households, and even a majority of Americans earning over $75,000 a year, lack cash reserves for a $500 emergency. While there are apps for encouraging savings, it may be that the net effect of our abundance of financial information gives us only an illusion of control.[62]

There is one final defense of financialization, arising from the

legendary fortunes of Silicon Valley. It may be harsh on underper-
forming corporations and their executives, but it mobilizes capital
for transformative new ventures, and it encourages the emergence
of innovators challenging established corporations. In fact, high-
technology entrepreneurship continued vigorously through and after
the 2008 recession. As the economics and technology writer James
Surowiecki has reported, the number of Silicon Valley companies
receiving initial support from investors doubled from 2007 to 2012,
and a total of $238 billion in venture capital was invested from 2010
to 2015, partly thanks to new technological tools. There are signs,
though, that the golden age of start-ups is over. Early in the web era, it
appeared that individuals and small partnerships could compete with
giant corporations—and indeed many could, if only because implementing new systems in large organizations took time. Twenty years
later, the advantage appears to have shifted back to big business. The
number of Americans working for big companies has been increasing, not declining. Concentration is especially apparent in platform
enterprises like social media. A recent study by economists at MIT
determined that while more technology companies than ever have
been launched recently, fewer of them are succeeding. In social media
even a previously strong competitor with an elite user base, LinkedIn,
was almost forced by declining share prices to be acquired by Microsoft in 2016. Twitter's stock price is weak, despite its own excellent
demographics and its possible role in helping decide the 2016 election. It may be that in the battle for attention online there is room for
only one profitable platform in each category. (One exception is the
search engine Bing, still overshadowed by Google but a profit center
for Microsoft.)[63]

In itself bigness is not opposed to efficiency. It may be bad for equality and bad for democracy, but in the continuous process era it often
created genuine economies of scale. Studies have shown that today's
large corporations are less likely to invest their research in radical
innovations and more likely to focus on improving existing technology. But by being so efficient and rational in their use of resources
they also may be neglecting the necessarily inefficient process of making technology even more efficient.

Sometimes intellectual property was virtually given away, as we have seen of Bell Labs' transistor and IBM's relational database concept. There was often a generous public spirit in these organizations. The Shell Oil Company granted to Princeton University Press the royalty-free use of the printing plates for one of its prized resources, a stratigraphic atlas of North and Central America, when it decided to have it published in the mid-1970s. It could have been a lucrative project, but Shell executives of the energy boom era valued academic goodwill (when the industry was competing for geoscience graduates) above additional profits. All Shell required—and it was readily granted—was a low-priced spiral-bound edition. In the rise of Silicon Valley, it was not necessarily the pioneers of theory and pure research but the agile so-called fast followers who dominated their industries. Xerox PARC developed the graphic personal computer interface and mouse but was unable to manufacture systems at an acceptable price; the Apple Macintosh transformed computing with Xerox's technology. It did not help that the top Xerox executives of the 1970s were veterans of Robert McNamara's cost-slashing ethos at Ford Motor Company, not visionary entrepreneurs like Joseph C. Wilson, who had retired in 1966 after transforming a previously quiet family business in Kodak's shadow.[64]

Some economists believe that even if ample funds were available for fundamental market-creating innovations, they are much rarer now, that over the past two hundred years from continuous process industrialization to the post-industrial age of the platform, we have invented all the basics and have reached a point of diminishing returns. As we have seen, the favorite metaphor of economists like Robert J. Gordon and Tyler Cowen is that we have harvested the low-hanging fruit. The historian of military technology David Edgerton has shown just how much of today's technology is a refinement of older ideas. Even the electric car is based on the twenty-five-year-old principle of the lithium-ion battery; most improvements have been in software control. The technology analyst G. Pascal Zachary has lamented that contrary to popular impression, "the specter of stagnation looms over the world's innovators. Low-hanging fruit is nowhere to be seen in fields as crucial as digital electronics, biomedical devices, or space technology." Against this viewpoint is the optimism of other economic historians, notably Joel Mokyr, who argue that while the fruit may be higher, improved instruments are letting us build taller ladders.[65]

Platforms like Google, Facebook, and Amazon do many things more rapidly and cheaply than previous technology, but their form of efficiency does not do much to make society as a whole more efficient in the way that, for example, a battery or microchip based on a new principle could. Yet the world's present financial institutions do not seem to be harvesting the fruit picked from Mokyr's long ladders.

The paradox of efficiency is that progress toward greater efficiency is wasteful. A succession of management doctrines has promised to slash costs and reduce overhead, thus increasing profits and shareholder value—in the short run. Yet in companies with an innovative culture this strategy can threaten long-term growth. One famous experiment was the implementation of a concept called Six Sigma at the 3M Corporation, known for blockbuster products from cellophane tape in the 1930s to sticky notes in the 1980s. Geoff Nicholson, creator of the Post-it note and later a 3M public relations "ambassador," believes that the search for predictably profitable innovations at 3M and elsewhere has been a failure. "The Six Sigma process killed innovation at 3M," he told the technology website ZDNet.com. "Initially what would happen in 3M with Six Sigma people, they would say they need a five-year business plan for [a new idea]. Come on, we don't know yet because we don't know how it works, we don't know how many customers [will take it up], we haven't taken it out to the customer yet."[66]

The frontier in the agenda of Silicon Valley is not in industrial processes or business decision making, but in the home where networked appliances would communicate in an Internet of Things. The best-known reservations about these plans come from security experts who correctly observe how easy it might be to hack domestic technology if even the sites of government agencies (including the CIA itself, from which secrets have been repeatedly disclosed to WikiLeaks) and major corporations have turned out to be disturbingly insecure. This means at best that much of whatever time is saved by electronic intercommunication will be consumed by monitoring and updating security software. Since the Internet of Things will also integrate products and software from many manufacturers, it will also be a challenge for households to resolve inevitable conflicts and mis-communication, which are likely to grow as the square of the number of products connected.

The irony of the efficiency movement is that in its latest and most domesticated form it is not about optimization of resources at all, except in conservation of energy by more sophisticated web-connected thermostats and in theoretical savings from app-based light switches. And even these are vulnerable. The *New York Times* correspondent Nick Bilton reported in January 2016 that a still undi-agnosed failure of the software of the advanced Nest thermostat caused rapid drainage of a battery that in turn allowed his home tem-perature to drop to 64 degrees Fahrenheit, a rude awakening for his infant. Such a failure, he continued, could lead not only to discomfort but to burst pipes and major damage. Silicon Valley's terms of use also make recovery of damages much more difficult than they are when old-style electromechanical equipment fails. In a system of interde-pendent, information-sharing appliances, one such glitch could easily cascade, sending the rest into their own failure modes à la Rube Gold-berg or Jacques Tati. It might be tragic rather than funny. Even the apparently innocent app-controlled LED lightbulb can, researchers have shown, allow hackers to seize control of a home's entire lighting and turn on strobe and other effects. Internet of Things enthusiasts may object that there are means to safeguard home networks against hacking, but it's hardly efficient to spend time configuring network settings in order to save the effort of getting up to adjust a lamp. In fact, it may be counterproductive, since frequent brief interruptions of sedentary work and leisure make us fitter and more alert. A number of desktop programs and mobile apps have been designed to encour-age standing up and moving.[67]

Many experts and journalists consider the Internet of Things to be the final payoff of the quest for efficiency in its latest, networked form. While it does offer the largely commoditized appliance indus-try a chance to join in electronic planned obsolescence and premium pricing, it also sadly illustrates how sophistication can mask a tech-nological dead end. Silicon Valley executives may well enjoy coming home to a world that is an extension of the network management issues they address at work, just as watch collectors enjoy expensive and observable complications like chronometers and moon phases that they are unlikely to use, yet the Nest episode shows why many other consumers may think twice.

What are needed are products and services that not just do existing things more smoothly but extend our capabilities as the Xerox photocopier did. To do this we must recognize that fundamental innovation is inefficient and that it takes a kind of intuition and commitment that Six Sigma programs and other systems are not able to model. The economist Albert O. Hirschman, reflecting on development projects, adapted Adam Smith's idea of the Invisible Hand of the marketplace to the Hiding Hand of new ventures. If humanity had consistently known the obstacles to its greatest projects in advance, it might not have attempted them. Hirschman cited Martin Luther's reflection that if God had revealed to him all he would have to go through to reform the Church, he never would have begun it, but instead God had given him blinkers like a horse. We spur ourselves on by exaggerating future benefits. Hirschman also quotes the Polish philosopher Leszek Kolakowski's metaphor of a caravan painfully making its way through the desert from one watering hole to the next, drawn on by mirages of gorgeous scenes ahead. No people has been more affected by this mentality for better or worse than Americans. In fact, self-delusion, underestimation of risk, and overestimation of profit—rather than strict rationality—were the true driving forces of the expansion of American society. Many of the voyages in the age of exploration— Spanish, Portuguese, and French as well as English—were carried out with maps and instruments woefully inadequate by today's standards, and often with little knowledge of the indigenous people. If the true risks had been known, there would still have been some bold adventurers but not necessarily equally optimistic investors.

We are familiar with the dismal rate of success of Gold Rush prospectors, but mining in general was blessed or cursed with the Hiding Hand. The historical anthropologist Anthony F. C. Wallace, analyzing the high disaster rates of a group of nineteenth-century Pennsylvania anthracite mines, found that the entrepreneurs systematically underestimated the frequency of fires, explosions, and floods. Sources suggest that the investors regarded themselves less as calculating profit seekers than as heroes of industry. And despite the appalling injury rate, the miners (independent workers hiring out their own labor) also were proud of courting danger. The great engineering projects of the nineteenth and early twentieth centuries presented one unforeseen obstacle after another, and there were spectacular failures, like the collapse of the original Panama Canal project of France's most celebrated engineer, Ferdinand de Lesseps. The American canal project that succeeded it surmounted almost incalculable obstacles of its own. We have already noted the extreme risks facing the development of jet engines before their triumph in safety and economy, and near-disasters during the twenty-year path from the original xerography patent to the introduction of a safe and economical office machine. Even the space program, from the original Apollo missions to the latest plans for manned flight to Mars, reveals the Hiding Hand. Consider the alarming 4 percent fatality rate of space missions, peril probably not fully foreseen; at least one former astronaut, Rick Hauck, has acknowledged that he never would have entered the program if he had known the risk. The doctrine of efficiency, in making our decisions more rational, may also be limiting our aspirations.[68]

Many of Silicon Valley's own favorite success stories are not about the rational calculation of risks and rewards using historical and market data and algorithms but about intuitive self-confidence. Bill Gates, Paul Allen, and Mark Zuckerberg all dropped out of college although data clearly show it generally pays to complete an undergraduate degree; each had a correct intuition, not supported by hard data, that he had an opportunity that would not wait. When Jeff Bezos, who did finish his engineering degree, was a young star of quantitative hedge fund management, he also knew that strictly rationally the odds were against his plan for Internet commerce. His reason for leaving a career that promised to be even more lucrative was that whatever happened, he did not want to be sorry at eighty that he had not tried to seize the opportunity—analysis he has called a "regret minimization framework." David Shaw, Bezos's employer and a former computer science professor, took a strictly data-based, rational approach and let his protégé depart.[69]

. . .

Neither the redistributionism of the left nor the market-driven doc-trines of Silicon Valley can take us beyond platform efficiency. It is indeed possible that, as Robert Gordon and others believe, we have exhausted technology's real bargains and that computer power will stagnate. But we cannot afford to assume that it will. Nor is it enough to say that we should return to the often irrational heroic risk taking of nineteenth-century business, if only because it took what we now consider unacceptable chances with human life as well as with capital. Rather, we need to acknowledge the Hiding Hand and find ways to reward the risks of the inefficient process of real innovation.

THE FAILED PROMISE OF
THE INFORMATION EXPLOSION

HOW THE QUEST TO MEASURE ELITE SCIENCE
EMPOWERED POPULIST CULTURE

The platform economy took shape in the 1990s and early 2000s so gradually that it became obvious only in hindsight. Amazon.com was still an online retailer; Web Services cloud platform was not launched until 2002. Napster, the first peer-to-peer music-sharing service, was established only in 1999. The famous (and sometimes notorious) *Encyclopaedia Britannica* salespeople were still going strong in the early 1990s, but their true competitor was not an online service but a Microsoft-produced version of the second- or third-tier *Funk & Wagnalls Encyclopedia*, rebranded as *Encarta*. The information economy was still one of discrete physical products. Even the technological avant-garde of multimedia educational CD-ROMs produced by the Voyager Company were not available online, and still are not, years after Voyager has ceased to exist. A pioneering analysis of network economics for a business audience in 1999, Carl Shapiro and Hal R. Varian's *Information Rules*, said almost nothing about either music file sharing, search, or social networks. Improvements in hardware, increasing speed of Internet connections, and Apple's iTunes platform for licensing digital music, together with the rise of mobile information devices after 2005, made a true platform information economy possible.[1]

Historians usually are skeptical of claims of unprecedented change. But the two decades beginning in the mid-1990s were just such a time. There was a deep discontinuity between the world of 1989, when the still flourishing print *Britannica* reached its peak of sales after a decade of PCs and five years of Macintosh computers, and that of 2012, when *Britannica* ceased print production. The efficiency of access to texts and images over the Internet seemed at that point—prematurely— to herald the disappearance of physical media entirely.

No surprise was more striking than the rise of search engines. In February 2002 I attended a scenario planning workshop at a California resort—a free-form exercise in imagining alternative futures—on the preservation of digital information, sponsored by the Library of Congress. One of the open questions was how Google, already essential for access to the online record, would ever become self-sustaining. I recall one participant raising the possibility that the federal government would need to take over Google as a national resource. None of us laughed or proposed instead that the still fledgling company was about to become the most successful advertising agency in history. Yet little more than two years later, the company's profits had soared to $286 million annually, and its 2004 initial public offering established its market capitalization at $23 billion.[2]

In 2010, W. Russell Neuman, whose work we encountered in Chapter One, and his students at the University of Michigan were able to quantify the changes in information supply and demand in ways that had eluded intellectual historians. Surveying the average newspapers, magazines, recent books, and television and radio channels available in U.S. households in 1960, they estimated that a typical family had access to a little less than a hundred hours of content (taking average reading speed into account for the print materials) for every hour they actually spent watching, listening, or reading. (Neuman was referring to the radio and television stations, magazines, newspapers, and recently published books available in the average home, not to public or academic library resources.) Considering similar families, their study examined all the digital as well as conventional sources available to them, and concluded that the ratio was by 2005 over 2,900, or about two weeks of unique content for every minute of every day spent consuming information. This seemed to be the information explosion so many futurists had perceived and predicted in earlier decades.[3]

Neuman and his collaborators did not accept the corollary drawn by many media prophets and critics that the public was smothered and even stupefied by overload. Neuman argued for a successful adaptation of human behavior in choosing information, a transition from push to pull. The classic information regime of the continuous process era made available a limited number of products to consumers: television and radio channels, recorded music and printed books in stores and libraries, at most a few local newspapers and a handful of national general-interest magazines. The positive side of these limits was a shared moderate outlook unfavorable to radical conservative or socialist ideas, a mind-set epitomized by a handful of trusted television network anchors and syndicated newspaper columnists.

Despite the radical change, few people in the platform era appear to feel overwhelmed, according to the study, because they have developed a new way to consume information. Instead of monitoring relatively few sources, they are more likely to seek out those that are linked to or recommended by other sources or by friends and colleagues.

As the Internet grew, a delicious libertarian spirit emerged. It not only was possible to make a fortune while remaining true to one's ideas; it was helpful to have a radical outlook. *Wired*, the flagship of Silicon Valley culture, was heavy with advertising. Its founding executive editor, Kevin Kelly, made his book *Out of Control* available free on the web; sales of the printed version continued to flourish. For a decade, many newspaper and magazine publishers seemed to have the best of both worlds: a new source of advertising revenue online that could more than offset the decline of print. National publications could offer advertisers what they appeared to want, an affluent and educated public. "Content is king" became a mantra. Since periodical readers were accustomed to advertising, so-called banner ads disturbed few, at least until more intrusive pop-up advertising appeared.

Still, the explosion of free websites, including those of small businesses and individuals, changed information habits. In the emerging era of information abundance documented by Neuman and his colleagues, selecting sites to visit—pulling information rather than having it pushed—was a challenge. Two complementary services appeared, the portal and the search engine. Portals—sites that organized and listed web resources—like Yahoo, America Online, and Excite employed people to select sites they believed would be of greatest interest to their subscribers. When search was expensive, trained professionals would translate queries into tight arguments for precise results. Some of them had degrees from schools of library and information science; others had equivalent experience. As misleading and even deceptive sites sprang up, these guides selected only the most genuine ones. But the concept of expert human guidance already seemed obsolescent in the mid-1990s. The initials in Yahoo's name wryly acknowledge the situation: Yet Another Hierarchical Officious Oracle.[4]

This strategy attracted millions of users in the late 1990s but had a fatal problem. New sites and pages were appearing faster than professional curators could evaluate them. Sites and pages within them also disappeared or were renamed. Controversies entangled portal managers' classification schemes. Should Messianic Judaism be classified as Jewish (by self-identification and the origin of many adherents) or as Christian (by its Evangelical theology)? The professionals could not avoid time-consuming religious, ethnic, and political controversies that could be challenging to resolve to all parties' satisfaction.

Classification was, in addition, only part of what users expected. They wanted to be able to search the web for specific information. The new platform companies had to be reference librarians as well as information selectors. This was even more difficult because of the limits of early search software. Most website owners allowed software programs called spiders to examine their pages and build indexes, enabling users to discover those pages that matched their searches. This could work well if a user was looking for something unusual like references to papers written about a rare species. It was not so easy to search for a common expression, like a celebrity's name. Search software had no efficient way to rank pages by quality. A search by relevance would list pages according to the frequency with which an expression appeared, but—true to Campbell's Law, the ubiquity of attempts to game measurement systems—site owners could stack the odds in their own favor by including hundreds of hidden copies of a word.

Inexperienced users of early search engines like AltaVista—which at one point indexed the highest number of pages—encountered the behavior immortalized in the early programmers' maxim: "A computer doesn't do what you want it to do. It does what you tell it to do." The search engines reported results dutifully and literally because they had no way of inferring what users really wanted. For example, they were not good at searching for synonyms. A search for "dieting" might not turn up a major article on weight loss if it did not use that exact word. This was an annoyance for lay surfers of the open web, but it was an economic risk for professionals using databases like Dialog that billed by time. For many early databases, skilled library specialists had to work with scholars and scientists to formulate a string of included and excluded words—sometimes further limited by their proximity to each other—to minimize time on the meter. Only later in the 1990s did it become common for libraries to license databases for free research by their registered users. Many of these databases had been professionally indexed by subjects and keywords. The open web was still hit-or-miss: highly inefficient.[5]

The philosopher and technology critic David Weinberger has identified the central problem that Yahoo and other portals faced. From the Middle Ages through most of the twentieth century, cultural authorities tried to establish classification systems to put human knowledge in orderly categories. Melvil Dewey, the founder of American professional librarianship and the entrepreneur who developed the modern file card, established a numerical order that, despite the 1876-vintage biases noted by Mr. Weinberger (including religious Eurocentrism and elevation of the paranormal), has remained remarkably serviceable even now. (Computer books fit neatly into the 004s at my local public library, for example.) But with the explosion of the number of titles and of interdisciplinary and hybrid subjects, top-down schemas became less and less useful. The web in particular was organized by chains of backward and forward links defying any single order. One book, article, or image may have dozens of possible keywords or user-supplied tags. Weinberger's title exaggerates but is still on target: *Everything Is Miscellaneous.*[6]

In the late 1990s nobody seemed to have predicted a solution to this bottleneck, the kind of problem that the historian of technology Thomas P. Hughes, adapting military jargon, called a reverse salient, a pocket of resistance in an advancing front of efficiency. Even optimistic futurists do not always expect them. The transistor, for example, overcame the problems of power consumption, heat, and failure of vacuum tube technology. Before its introduction, even the great science fiction writer Arthur C. Clarke was dissuaded from filing a patent for the communication satellite of the future he had described because vacuum tubes burned out so quickly and astronauts would be needed to replace them. The Google PageRank algorithm was a comparably radical innovation. Without needing any new kind of hardware, it began to solve the nagging problem of search, giving people more or less what they want rather than what they've asked for.[7]

PageRank is only one part of Google's ever-changing and largely secret algorithm today. Transparency has inherent limits. If the details were known and understood like those of Google's open-source Android software, they would be too easy to exploit. While the patent's equations are formidably technical, the principle was (like many other deep ideas) obvious in retrospect. Instead of relying mainly on professionals to select sites—they have a role at Google even now—Google's algorithm computes sites' connections to each other. It takes a populist approach rooted paradoxically in the organized elitism of scientific bibliography. In the mid-1950s Eugene Garfield, with degrees in chemistry and library science, launched a service that tracked the references of scientific, engineering, and medical (and later of some social science and humanities) journals. A subscriber to the printed Science Citation Index could look up how often each paper had been cited by other papers, and by whom. Instead of asking experts to rank peers according to their subjective judgment, academic deans and industrial employers could see whose papers were considered important enough to be cited by other papers—especially by authors who themselves had been cited most often. The research community was thus constantly and indirectly ranking each other. It was also writing its own history, recording the links among researchers, and helping them keep up with their fields as the number of journals continued to proliferate—for example, by identifying every paper that cited one's own work or a colleague's.[8]

As a bibliographic aid, citation indexes were applauded. As a measure of quality, they had critics from the outset, academics who considered them poor substitutes for traditional qualitative means like soliciting letters. I remember lunch in a Chinese restaurant in the 1980s with one of my former mathematics professors, and his indignation at the very concept. He declared he was going to write a letter of protest to Dr. Garfield, though I'm not sure he ever did. As a science book editor, I found such indexes almost useless in identifying prospective authors. I'll have more to say about citation indexing's other problems later. What is relevant here is how many people in the scientific world were using this form of measurement by the late 1990s, especially once the results could be found electronically rather than looked up year by year in big printed volumes or later CD-ROMs; the Institute for Scientific Information, which Garfield sold to the international media company Thomson-Reuters, went online as the Web of Science in 1997. By 2009 the Web of Knowledge, as it had been renamed after multiple expansions, included 23,000 journals and 700 million references going back to the early nineteenth century. In 2016 it was sold to private equity funds as part of a package of other Thomson-Reuters services. A *Nature* article reported that it was still highly profitable and likely to be resold.[9]

When two Stanford computer science graduate students, Larry Page and Sergey Brin, were developing their own search engine around the time the Web of Science went online, they were aware of Garfield's approach to indexing (as well as others) and cited his work in U.S. Patent 6,285,999, "Method for Node Ranking in a Linked Database," possibly the most profitable single patent of all time, though the algorithm of the present Google search engine has become far more complex. PageRank, like the Web of Science, showed how backward and forward links (in one case footnotes, in the other web page locations embedded as so-called hypertext usually visible to readers only as highlighting) could show how influential a source was: in the first case a journal, in the second a website. Just as *The New York Times*, *The Washington Post*, *The Wall Street Journal*, and their international peers are linked by countless online publications and blogs, so papers in *Nature*, *Science*, *The New England Journal of Medicine*, *The Lancet*, and the like are cited much more often than those in more specialized publications. Conversely, an article in one of those journals is more likely to be worth reading if it is cited often in one of the higher-ranking journals. For better and worse, citation analysis helped establish a quantitatively grounded pecking order among publications, affecting scientists' and managers' behavior, as my former teacher had feared.[10]

Of course, there was much more to Google's rise than the original concept. As a start-up Google originally indexed fewer pages than its competitors and returned fewer hits to queries. But early users found that its results were closer to what they wanted to find. Google didn't have all the answers but it often found good ones more efficiently. And its indexing software, the "spiders" that "crawled" the web, were reprogrammed to reduce their effects on the sites' performance. This efficiency had a cost; the vast server farms needed to store copies of crawled pages in response to user requests consumed corresponding energy and generated corresponding heat. The result seemed worth it. Google's algorithm and that of its main rival, Microsoft's Bing, know, for example, where a user is and the likely purpose of many requests. When Daniel M. Russell, a Google executive who held the enviable title of Über Tech Lead for Search Quality and User Happiness, spoke at Princeton in 2012, I asked in the question-and-answer session whether the company was working on improving the quality of the highest-ranking results. He replied that users' ideas of relevance and reliability varied by location and culture. In response to medical queries, for example, acupuncture and other alternative medicine ranked lower, he observed, on the East Coast of the United States than in East Asian cities.

The efficiency of search using PageRank and similar algorithms has not necessarily been synonymous with effectiveness—giving searchers the best possible result. While Google was still conducting

Yahoo's searches in 2002, for example, one study compared Google's own ranking of the relevance of search results with that of (elite) human judges: professors and graduate students at the University of Toronto. The judges agreed strongly with each other's ranking (a correlation of .475 out of 1.0) but not with the search engine's (a correlation of only .173). I have not found any similar studies published since then, but it is well known that Google and Bing employ human scorers to check on the quality of results. This might not be a serious problem if two reasonable conditions were met: first, people are willing to look beyond the first page of results, and second, that they usually have the background knowledge to evaluate them. Unfortunately, they are not, and don't. In fact, Daniel Russell's studies of Google users revealed some surprising gaps in basic computer skills. Only one in ten, for example, was aware of one of the most efficient shortcuts, Control-F (Command-F in the Mac operating system) for finding every occurrence of a keyword.[11]

It's an exaggeration to say that Google and the Internet make us stupid, as the technology critic Nicholas Carr argued in an article followed by a widely read book, *The Shallows*. Google and Bing do change intellectual habits and in principle can help free us from memorization to more creative thinking. But Carr and other critics like William Poundstone are right in noting that using the web creatively demands background knowledge to recognize which algorithm-served links are likely to be of highest quality. Professionals—at least we assume—have this knowledge. A physician, lawyer, or social scientist knows the reputation of publishers and journals and the biases of their policies and can easily reorder the algorithm's priorities. Users of academic databases like JSTOR do this routinely. Serious amateurs also can quickly see what is most relevant. Ideally our personal memory and our electronic resources share the work of knowledge. Each concentrates on what it does best—understanding fundamental principles and facts on one side, accessing massive data on the other— for both efficiency and effectiveness.[12]

The real problem is that search engines as they exist—even ones limited to supposedly more reliable information like Google Scholar—are inefficient ways to absorb an unfamiliar subject. The user needs the very knowledge that he or she is hoping to find—an idea going back to Plato's dialogue *Meno*, which raises the question of how a person can learn without already knowing. To make things worse, uninformed people don't always recognize their ignorance. Some of them, according to research by the social psychologists Justin Kruger and David Dunning, are sometimes firmest about topics they know least about. Another investigator, Brendan Nyhan, found that many people confronted with acknowledged facts challenging their views respond by reaffirming their positions. Search engines aid this tendency by making it easy to find information confirming just about any opinion. So despite Google's original declared mission statement of organizing the world's information and making it useful, it can be no better than the knowledge and attitudes of users. The outcome is that fewer than 9 percent of all Google searchers look beyond the first page of results, and about a third choose the top-rated link.[13]

Even in global politics and security, search engine optimization can have bizarre consequences, making the search for high-quality information inefficient. Governments around the world spend many billions of dollars on antiterrorism programs, yet searches for information on jihadism yield overwhelmingly pro-jihadi views. For instance, the Arabic word *khalifa* (pan-Islamic state or caliphate) returns links to nine extremist sites to one neutral one. In this case Google may begin to make an exception to the neutrality of its algorithm, or modify it to yield more acceptable results when the unfiltered ones might seem disparaging to a group. Search engine optimizers are not necessarily to blame; the algorithm may infer from the phrasing of the search, and from related searches by the same user, that he or she really is looking for extremist sites. This presents search engine developers with an embarrassing dilemma: appearing to tolerate or even abet violence on the one hand, or appearing to censor expression or police thought on the other. Social media programmers also may aspire to neutrality but cannot avoid personal bias in writing algorithms; some conservatives believe Facebook's culture skews its offerings toward liberal sources. Like search engines, social media sites confront a dilemma about controversial results. If their secret formulas are disclosed to demonstrate their fairness, well-funded special interests will exploit them to bend results. But as long as algorithms remain secret, conscious and unconscious manipulation can't be ruled out.[14]

. . .

Some of the most serious problems of efficiency, though, are free of extremism, commercial fraud, and personal gain. Professional researchers as well as students depend on the open-source reference site Wikipedia, created in 2001 after efforts failed to launch a free online encyclopedia written by the same kind of experts who contributed to conventional print reference books. Wikipedia was based on the idea that anybody, regardless of credentials or education level, would be free to create or modify an article—which, of course, could be modified in turn by other users. It was and remains nonprofit and advertising-free, relying on volunteers to present evidence on both sides of controversial questions. While Wikipedia's leaders claim that electronic and human oversight have been effective in detecting and eliminating vandalism, new cases still arise, including one long-lasting prank addition to the article on inflammation to the effect that volcanic rock produced by the human body causes inflammation pain. In principle Wikipedia is self-correcting because so many eyes are on each article. Its mechanism is admirably efficient at including new information, such as the deaths of famous people or revision of borders, that might have taken years in the days of exclusively printed reference books. Best of all, it remains free to anyone with an Internet connection—and also free to reprint and adapt.[15]

Despite its admirable openness, Wikipedia's efficiency has a self-sabotaging side. It meshes well with search engine algorithms; Wikipedia entries are often top ranked in Google's search results. But this can also be a threat. Google's own text boxes, compiled by algorithms using information from Wikipedia, compete with the encyclopedia project as a source of information and may have reduced traffic to Wikipedia's original entries. The need to protect the site and assure that articles meet high encyclopedia standards has also changed the organization. With multiple levels of privileges and robotic algorithms that can delete apparently noncompliant entries automatically, it has turned from a freewheeling collective to a more tightly run and hierarchical cadre that even admirers warn can be a barrier to keeping content fresh and diverse. (Women are notoriously underrepresented among contributors.) While the experience of consulting Wikipedia continues to be efficient, and content continues to expand, its operation is more cumbersome. The writer Tom Simonite suggested replacing the "anyone can edit" motto with "the encyclopedia that anyone who understands the norms, socializes him or herself, dodges the impersonal wall of semi-automated rejection and still wants to voluntarily contribute his or her time and energy can edit." The contributor of a commercial specialized encyclopedia article usually receives only a small honorarium, and may be praised or faulted by colleagues, but at least does not have to worry about the work being deleted or altered arbitrarily by anonymous strangers.[16]

Most journalism is still signed and is not open to alteration at will. But it has other technological challenges. The efficiency of mobile computing has had mixed effects on newspaper publishing. At a conference at which I spoke in 1995, run by the Annenberg Washington Program, progressive media critics worried about the growing influence of advertising as news moved to the incipient web. The technology boom in fact became a rich source of advertising for newspapers; the "Circuits" section of *The New York Times*, for example, was fat with advertisements from companies like J&R Music World (a former electronics superstore relatively inactive since 2014) and personal computer manufacturers. Many newspaper publishers and journalists were convinced that editorial quality would prevail in the digital future. Advertisers wanted affluent, educated consumers, who in turn would visit sites with authoritative, reliable information. Therefore, while print might be obsolescent, media would migrate successfully. Newsrooms continued to expand in the early web era. The news content of ten daily papers doubled from 1964 to 1999, according to a Columbia University School of Journalism report published in 2009. There were grounds for optimism in the new millennium, too. Newspaper advertising revenue continued to rise, to almost $50 billion in 2005. By 2013, that number had dropped by more than half, to $23.6 billion. So discouraging has been the situation that the major trade group, the Newspaper Association of America (now renamed the News Media Alliance), has not released industry-wide advertising statistics since then. Using the data of publicly owned companies that must include the information in shareholder reports, the Pew

Research Center has calculated a 6.4 percent drop in 2014 and a 7.8 percent drop in 2015. At the same time, there are fewer digital-only newspaper readers than many futurists once expected. More than half of all newspaper readers still limit themselves to print editions. Only 17 percent of all readers are digital-only news consumers, and only 5 percent are mobile-only. The rest are format omnivores. Statistics on magazines are harder to find. Aggregate circulation appears stronger than newspaper sales, but advertising is also declining.[17]

The problems of newspapers were visible at their peak. The *Washington Post* cultural reporter Paul Farhi, writing in *American Journalism Review* in 2005, pointed to the industry's conventional strengths (including local monopolies after consolidation, large reporting staffs, and elite readership). Their profit margins of 23 percent, according to one analyst, were one of the best of any industry. But Farhi also presciently identified what proved to be an Achilles' heel. The strong profits reflected living off capital, raising prices as readership declined while failing to invest in "plants and people." Meanwhile, web-based companies began competing for the boring but intensely profitable business of classified advertising, which accounted for fully 36 percent of newspaper profits. Craigslist was especially damaging in two critical areas. Even with charges for employment ads, it was able to undercut a major profit center of urban dailies, and it damaged alternative newspapers that did not have the retail and corporate display advertising that mainstream papers had been able to retain.[18]

In the decade after the high point of profitability, the efficiency of social media in holding readers' attention, plus platform companies' new advertising models, sent newspapers and some magazines into a tailspin. It was bad enough that younger people were abandoning not just print but digital newspaper reading in favor of new websites and videos, which became competitors for advertising. Google bought the advertising-supported video site YouTube for $1.65 billion in 2006. By 2016, a *New York Times* article estimated YouTube's annual revenue at between $4 billion and $8 billion. Still worse, the major platform companies have been wresting control of online advertising from newspapers and magazines themselves to arrangements that give decisions on acceptance and placement, as well as a substantial share of revenues, to the platforms. Advertising was long a notoriously inefficient business, like the entertainment industries with which it was intertwined. The late-nineteenth-century department store magnate John Wanamaker, who helped establish the close connection between great retailers and city newspapers, remains famous for his witticism that half the money he spent on advertising was wasted, but he didn't know which half. Since the early days of the web, entrepreneurs and Silicon Valley have sought to put marketing on a more rational basis by tying it to customer data. User information, including previous purchases and search and browsing patterns, could at least in principle help target advertising. With hypertext and links to other sites, it was also becoming possible to measure not just the number of readers who saw an announcement ("impressions") but the proportion who actually visited the advertiser's site. It was as though a traditional direct-mail company could tell whether an envelope had been opened or simply discarded.[19]

The most successful of the advertising servers has been Google's AdWords. These small notices are shown to readers not by an advertiser's decision that a publication would be a good showplace—which helped sustain Henry Luce's high-priced *Fortune* magazine during the 1930s—but by the calculations of an algorithm. In place of the old price-per-thousand-impressions model is an auction based on the reward an advertiser is willing to pay for each click-through. It can vary from a few cents to $50. Using modern auction theory (which has won the Nobel Prize in economics), Google charges the winner not the full bid but the amount the runner-up was willing to pay. The rise of Facebook, and its expansion from a site for contact among actual friends to a comprehensive portal, has created new dilemmas for newspapers. By May 2016, Facebook was claiming an average of fifty minutes of its users' time a day, almost as much as eating and drinking and almost three times as much as other reading. Early web media specialists liked to talk about retaining eyeballs. Facebook succeeded in commanding attention where so many others—including newspaper sites trying to be all-around urban portals—had failed. Experts have engineered it brilliantly for personalization, surpassing anything else on the web. The Facebook algorithm selects items on an individual's timeline based on a secret psychological format designed to encourage participants to return as often as possible and to spend as much time as possible. The timeline that a participant sees is not the sum of friends' posts but a selection from them, along with other links, made for maximum engagement. (Psychologists are still debating whether Internet and social media addiction is a widespread problem, and whether extended Facebook use damages health and life satisfaction.) Given this attention, licensing newspaper and magazine content was a natural step for Facebook, which like Google has become in effect a spectacularly profitable advertising agency. There was nothing shocking about the willingness of most website owners to allow the spiders of search engines to index and even store their content; it was all in the interest of getting noticed. Google, aware of growing criticism of its impact on publishers' revenue, has responded by making it easier for them to control the free content they can access through its search engine; they had previously been penalized in search results if they had been too strict about access for nonsubscribers.[20]

If social media had opened up new advertising markets for newspapers, they would be seen as a benign extension market, much as mass-market paperback reprints and book clubs in the 1920s and 1930s were a net bonus for the book publishing industry. In fact, search and social media advertising did not supplement newspapers' own advertising sales, both print and digital; on balance, they cannibalized them. Just five platform companies—Google, Facebook, Twitter, Yahoo, and Verizon—accounted for more than 65 percent of digital advertising. From 2014 to 2015, Facebook alone increased its share from 25 percent to 30 percent. By early 2016, 85 percent of new digital advertising revenue was going to Google and Facebook. Unfortunately, the long-term net record of the Internet as a source of media careers in the "information age" has been dismal. According to the U.S. Bureau of Labor Statistics, combined newspaper and magazine employment declined from 576,200 in March 1996 to 276,800 in March 2016, a net loss of over 50 percent. Internet publishing and broadcasting jobs meanwhile soared from 32,000 to nearly 200,000. But that was a net gain of only 168,000, little more than half the legacy jobs lost. And the troubles of so-called legacy media have spread to digital-only sites. The prominent Gigaom failed in 2015, and Mashable and Salon were laying off staff in summer 2016. By December

2016 there were also staff cuts at Fusion, *The Huffington Post*, and *International Business Times.*[21]

In some ways the new world of newspapers is far more efficient than it was in the centuries of print circulation. Especially in the United States, finding even high-circulation out-of-town newspapers used to be a challenge even in the largest cities, if only because of the poor railroad infrastructure. (Their British counterparts have such a strong national scope that in 2014 Amazon.co.uk contracted with the newspaper delivery agency Connect for fulfilling its own shipments.) While many major U.S. newspapers now limit free access to articles, digital subscriptions cost a fraction of mail delivery. Electronic publication has also globalized reading habits. According to Pew Research Center's *State of the News Media 2016*, the electronic editions of the London *Daily Mail* and *Guardian* would rank them among the five most read newspapers in the U.S., the *Telegraph* and *Independent* in the top 10, and others from Australia, Canada, India, Ireland, and New Zealand in the top 50. Conversely, *The New York Times* had thirty million unique international visitors a month in February 2016, about 5 percent of them "engaged" readers, however the *Times* measures engagement. This global reach in principle offers new opportunities for advertising revenue and paid subscriptions—and for expanded international reporting when many overseas bureaus are closing.[22]

The efficiency of electronic publication is not limited to international distribution. It has also transformed journalists' relationship with their audience and each other. In the 1970s the historian Robert Darnton, who had worked briefly as a reporter, cited the findings of the social scientists Ithiel de Sola Pool and Irwin Shulman about newspaper writers and their audience. Journalists, the researchers had found, had little direct information about their readers' response to their work. Each imagined the reader to be like a friend or acquaintance, "supportive" or "hostile." Reporters would slant their facts and interpretations toward these expected archetypes. Comments sections today allow much more concrete feedback, but so many are intemperate that moderating them becomes an additional expense. When Darnton was a reporter, the layout of the newspaper was a map not only of information but of the hierarchy of reporters and their assignments. On today's web pages, and especially on mobile devices, this organization is less clear. When we read *The New York Times* or *The Washington Post* on a smartphone and compare it with the layout of the print version, we gain the efficiency of compactness and scrolling. It is easier to save an article or post it to social media. But we also lose (for better or worse) our sense of what the paper's editors think about the importance of the day's stories and their relationship to each other. We're less likely to notice which reporters' bylines are above the fold if there's no fold. For young people whose main exposure to information is social media on smartphones, there may be less interest in the whole of a single publication. A growing proportion of news stories are read through referrals by search or social media, a grazing strategy. Yet if the base of subscribers—especially print subscribers—continues to erode, there may be less new and original content to refer.[23]

From the journalist's point of view, information on actual reader behavior is potentially a great step forward from writing for a hypothetical favorable or skeptical audience as described by Pool and Shulman. There can be valuable insights in measuring readers' time spent on an article and social media posts. There is encouraging anecdotal evidence that some newspapers have used such programs to improve content, especially paying attention to topics that don't interest most readers conventionally. One newspaper group in Alabama, for example, was able to pool the resources of three papers to launch a mainly online investigative report of abuses in the state's prisons, a topic readers are conventionally expected to ignore but which led to over a half million page views. Foundations are supporting such projects by newspapers and nonprofit journalism organizations. But there are three core problems in measurement. First, reader engagement metrics are proliferating, recalling the old joke about technical standards, that there are so many to choose from. Second, the proprietary metrics of Google, Facebook, and other advertising programs are both highly sophisticated and at least partly secret. So newspapers not only have to support their own engagement analyses but to anticipate the ever-changing analyses of platform companies and other advertising providers. At least one major daily has a full-time staff person to guess the algorithms used by search engines and social media sites to recommend articles, so that writers and editors can choose topics and tweak style to maximize clicks. This takes resources from the actual work of reporting and writing. And third, reader studies can be inconclusive; treatment that pleases one segment of readers may bore another. Excessive concern with short-term popularity discourages journalism that recognizes issues early and makes news production less efficient and effective in the long run.[24]

There are also dilemmas if reader analytics show demographic differences of engagement: by gender, age, ethnic background, education, and income. It has been shown that a slight change in a headline, for example, can increase by an order of magnitude how many people read it. But it is also possible that tweaking writing for greater impact would reinforce the herd mentality that journalism scholars recognized well before the web.

By 2016 journalists and readers alike believed that social media were endangering the credibility of all news, thanks to the efficiency of propagating stories. Fake information is hardly a new issue. It even predates American independence. Paul Revere's famous engraving of the Boston Massacre of 1770 was an inflammatory and inaccurate version of the actual events, today's scholars believe, despite its inclusion in countless U.S. history textbooks. And it was just this exaggeration of the bloodshed and one-sided portrayal of British guilt that helped make the print so popular. Another American icon, Horatio Alger, inadvertently advanced false facts by instructing his sister to burn his letters, fearing exposure of his homosexuality. (As a young man he had left the ministry and Massachusetts for New York following a child abuse scandal.) Alger's first biographer, Herbert R. Mayes, confessed late in life that he had fabricated the missing information in his 1928 study. Meanwhile, its "facts" had made their way even into the first edition of the august *Dictionary of American Biography*. In the second edition, Alger's definitive academic biographer, Gary Scharnhorst, notes ruefully that three later lives of Alger were based on Mayes's book, and that so are countless other reference sources. The Revere and Mayes works confirm for the print age what prevails on the web. People accepted what they wanted to believe, whether the bloodthirstiness of British troops or (at the peak of debunking) the personal failure of an apostle of success. What is different is the web's efficiency at accelerating the spread of fabrications. The computer scientist Emilio Ferrara has examined the prevalence of fictitious personas supported in turn by their own "fake followers," some of them created by governments and politicians.[25]

The July 2016 referendum on the United Kingdom's membership in the European Union showed how prominent automated social media posts had become and how potentially confusing they were for journalists trying to follow and measure public sentiment. Researchers have discovered a strong influence of automated programs (bots) retweeting both "Leave" and "Remain" messages in the June 2016 Brexit referendum on the U.K.'s future in the European Union. A third of all Twitter messages, half a million, came from only one percent of the accounts, many of them probably automated, with "Leave" messages retweeted three times as often as "Remain." Another study revealed that of the two hundred most active retweeters, 90 percent were bot accounts. The prevalence of bots is due to the efficiency of social media in opening new accounts and accepting and diffusing messages without charge. Bots don't appear to have changed the outcome of the referendum. If an "echo chamber" effect existed on Facebook concerning the issue, preventing members from seeing posts by the other side, it did not stop people from seeing the posts of pro-Brexit politicians. Britain's tabloid press, still strong in the nation's declining industrial areas, may have had more influence on the outcome of the referendum. Likewise, there is no clear evidence that fabricated stories influenced the outcome of the U.S. 2016 election decisively. One economics study suggests that while people follow the well-known principle of confirmation bias in choosing and evaluating news, fewer than 10 percent are ready to believe anything supporting their position.[26]

The real issue is not that sinister forces are distorting voters' choices, at least not through false stories propagated through social media; the economists who studied fake news found that a false story would have to be as powerful as thirty-six television commercials to have made a difference in the presidential campaigns. Instead, it is that made-up stories are like invasive species choking off native wildlife. In a healthier circulation and advertising environment, they would be mere nuisances, but under stressed conditions they can be a serious threat. Paul Horner, a professional fake news writer, claimed to *The Washington Post* in November 2016 that his inventions had put Donald Trump over the top. That assertion may be the biggest fake news of all, but consider the advertising budgets that shady sites absorb through the efficiency of ad-serving programs. Horner alone has boasted of making $10,000 a month and many other fake sites clear $5,000. Many Eastern European fake news purveyors also were attracted not necessarily by the personality or policies of Donald Trump but by his followers' appetite for partisan fantasies. It's likely that many enthusiasts on both sides of the election savored negative stories about the other as satire rather than as literal truth, more as *The Onion* than as a publication of record. (Indeed, some *Onion* satires have been taken literally by newcomers to the site.)[27]

The controversy over fake news is rooted in the growth of extreme partisanship in the United States since the 1990s, a trend clearly connected with the rise of talk radio and cable television but still not understood. That should not be surprising. Separating causes from effects in landmark elections, and distinguishing the relative weight of issues, can take decades of study at the intersection of political science, economics, sociology, and history. There is already evidence, however, that voters who retransmit stories about Barack Obama, Hillary Clinton, and Donald Trump may see them as provocation (trolling), as fictions that reveal a deeper truth about the opposition's character. For example, birtherism and rumors of Obama's secret Muslim faith may be rooted not at all in Obama's African ancestry or Arabic middle name, but in his upbringing in Indonesia, in the cool self-control he learned as a child in Java—a trait that served him well politically but that unsympathetic voters might consider alien. Fake news may belong more to the study of folklore and urban legends than to the dark arts of propaganda and disinformation.[28]

By early 2017, as *Wired* magazine concluded, Donald Trump and his spokespeople were charging Democrats with fake news of their own, while sometimes appearing to deny the existence of objective truth in favor of "alternative" facts. Yet in the spirit of polarization, Democrats also made questionable claims about the Trump campaign, for example, that it relied on large numbers of bots, many devised by allies of the Russian government or orchestrated by the British big data firm Cambridge Analytica, with ties to Donald Trump's hedge fund billionaire supporter and computer scientist, Robert Mercer. *The Washington Post* showed how exaggerated these fears have been; Donald Trump's Twitter account has fewer false followers than those of Barack Obama or indeed the *Post* itself. Cambridge Analytica's prowess also probably falls short of progressives' suspicions; it worked no wonders for its original Republican presidential campaign client, Senator Ted Cruz. Another skeptic, the Bloomberg News correspondent Leonid Bershidsky, noted that Cambridge Analytica's algorithm had flooded him with solicitations for donations although it is public knowledge that Bershidsky is a Russian citizen, disqualified from contributing.[29]

A more likely technological explanation of the presidential outcome in 2016 was the Achilles' heel of the big data used by Hillary Clinton's campaign. In September the online magazine *Politico* profiled Clinton's big data guru ("Director of Analytics") Elan Kriegel, whom colleagues credited with bringing new efficiency to identifying key voters and the channels for reaching them. The article mocked Donald Trump for slighting the value of data and quoted a Republican data analyst's worries about his party being left in the dust. In retrospect the confidence of Clinton campaign manager Robby Mook in Kriegel's model (along with personal conflicts in the staff) was a possibly fatal weak point. The software, Ada, could generate hundreds of thousands of simulations, but according to a computer scientist who studied the program, it was flawed by assumptions built into it by Kriegel and his staff, biases that kept it from countering a loss of support. The campaign's real problem may have been that the data weren't big enough, that the campaign was not getting up-to-date polling information that might have revealed loss of support in time for the outreach that Clinton supporters in Michigan had been urging on her data-driven Brooklyn headquarters.[30]

The crisis of truth, though, goes beyond politics and even the economic consequences of dilution of support for quality journalism of all persuasions. It is, as the political economist William Davies has argued, the analysis of enormous data sets itself that has challenged the classical nineteenth-century statistical analysis that has been a foundation of factuality. Many citizens no longer believe in the integrity or accuracy of government figures. There are important political and social trends behind this suspicion, and sometimes real flaws in formulating questions and gathering data. But the existence of vast, automatically generated and privately owned and analyzed records of human behavior and attitudes is playing a growing part. "Sentiment analysis"—deducing consumer and political attitudes from people's online language—is starting to take the place of the data that were generally accepted and fought over by progressives and conservatives alike. The success of newspapers will depend not on whether social media sites find a way to detect fraudulent articles—deception will probably only become more subtle, following Campbell's Law— but whether they can develop their own techniques for drawing conclusions.[31]

The greatest threat is not any single rumor or accusation promoted online but the spread of suspicion and cynicism. The cry of fake news has begun to contaminate all news, as journalists find it difficult to ignore the clamor of social media and thus to help spread ideas even while debunking them. There is no way for algorithms or indeed for most citizens or journalists to distinguish lies and half-truths from genuine news; we rely on experts who often depend on other experts. There are also signs that young people may be less able to distinguish the quality of sources online, treating fact-checked media and social media posts indiscriminately. Even more alarmingly, mass skepticism (with "fake news" on its banner) risks becoming information nihilism, for which all findings are partisan assertions to be accepted or rejected according to one's identity or politics. The historian of science Robert Proctor has coined the word "agnotology" to define the deliberate spread of ignorance by the tobacco industry and other special interests. If everything online is suspect as being riddled with falsehoods and disinformation, then all news is suspect as biased, even though a solid majority of Americans believes in the principle of fact-checking. It is not surprising that in one survey, only 27 percent of people who got their news from Facebook trusted it (as opposed to the 75 percent of readers of print newspapers who trusted them), while other studies showed that half to three-quarters of Americans who had seen false headlines on the web believed them. Skepticism and credulity, once considered opposites, now appear not only to coexist but perversely to reinforce each other as part of a post-truth syndrome.[32]

Because of the Thomas Theorem that we have noted—the tendency of perceptions to beget new realities—the fake news controversy has seriously damaged the efficiency of political debate. Mark Penn, Hillary Clinton's former marketing guru, objected in *The Wall Street Journal* that the proportion of fake news accounts maintained by Russian hackers was too small to have decided anything. Yet before publication of any study, a striking 82 percent of Democrats, and 54 percent of all persons polled by CNN, believed that hacking had swayed the election for Donald Trump. Trump's own digital director, Greg Parscale, has said that electronic targeting of specific voters (actually pioneered by Penn) did decide the contest, but it was his own and his firm's work that did so, without Russian assistance. Meanwhile, the British consultancy Cambridge Analytica would like to share in the credit, and has attracted some of the blame as well. The result of such claims and counterclaims is that politics is increasingly perceived as a form of manipulative electronic sport among technical wire-pullers, with voters as pawns rather than as rational actors. Perhaps distrust of all news, rather than the election of Donald Trump, was the real goal of foreign interference.[33]

It's possible that newspapers—chastised by critics for oligopoly, complacency, and superficiality even in their financial heyday—may yet be shocked into a new titanium if not a golden age. *The New York Times* has published its own road map for such a transformation. But nothing can replace the lost state and local reporting that, as the crusading reporter turned academic press critic Ben Bagdikian noted, are essential to accurate information on public officials in America. Especially because of losses at these levels—New York City employment has been stable and staffs in Washington, D.C., and Los Angeles have actually increased—from 2007 to 2015 alone, the number of full-time U.S. journalists at daily papers dropped over 40 percent, from 55,000 to 32,900. It is true that the growth of jobs in digital-only publications, from 3,410 in 2005 to 10,580 in 2015, has partly offset the decline. Yet this once promising sector has been stagnant since 2013.[34]

Magazines have faced a different challenge from the efficiency of web distribution and platform advertising. According to the 2016 Pew Media Report, circulation of publications it classifies as "news magazines" has been remarkably stable considering the competition from the explosion of online video and other new media. This repeats the experience of magazines during the rise of television from the 1950s through the 1970s. Television's share of advertising revenue grew rapidly; it was almost double that of magazines by 1960, nearly triple by 1970, and almost quadruple by 1982, yet magazine advertising continued to increase. Magazines survived the rise of television because of their ability to build both circulation and advertising on the specific backgrounds and interests of readers. *Time* magazine could point to its popularity among frequent fliers, for example. It even printed a special edition for them, as it did for the highest-income households and for women subscribers. Magazines have always been more efficient advertising buys in this sense than nonfinancial newspapers.[35]

Like newspapers, magazines adapted to the web by publishing online editions with their own advertising stream. As blogs flourished in the first decade of the twenty-first century, the genre faced technological and financial realities. Search engines and the linking structure of the web directed a large share of traffic to a relatively small number of blogs, some of which developed into profitable digital publications; others were bought by conventional media and platform companies. By 2009, the journalist Benjamin Carlson reported that fully 42 percent of all blog traffic was going to the top 50 blogs. Thus the fantasy of the lone web citizen swaying public decisions with incisive commentary all but vanished, but so had the nightmare that a flood of free amateur content would destroy professional writing. The Matthew effect, named fifty years ago by the sociologist Robert K. Merton after the Gospel declaration ("For unto every one that hath shall be given, and he shall have abundance: but from him that hath not shall be taken away even that which he hath"), continues to apply to the power of cumulative advantage expressed through structures of links. The reach of institutional blogs swamped remaining solo bloggers. In fact, bloggers—independent and staff—helped save magazines by attuning them to the Internet-age news cycle that had threatened to make monthly and even weekly publication obsolete.[36]

The most successful metamorphosis of an old-line publication was probably that of *The Atlantic Monthly*, which significantly dropped its second name, supplementing the print magazine with a roster of blogs ranging from politics and technology to sports. Having written both for the print *Atlantic* and for its digital-only blogging platform, I can confirm that readers who cite my *Atlantic* essays rarely make the distinction between the magazine (print or web) and blogs. They treat everything as part of the magazine, and indeed some blog posts are included by online databases, such as LexisNexis and Factiva, that license text from multiple publications. Some articles occupy a bibliographic no-man's-land; Benjamin Carlson's piece on blogs cited above appears on the *Atlantic* website as part of the September 2009 issue but is absent from that issue's table of contents online and from at least two major library databases, ProQuest and EBSCOhost. Nor did management care much about the distinction at the time; James Bennet, the former editor-in-chief and president, called himself "agnostic" on the future of the print edition.[37]

The *Atlantic* model has shown that the promise of serious magazines to advertisers—that they can bring their products and services to the attention of affluent and influential readers—is still alive. But the new digital-print magazine is still inefficient in the sense that it demands more resources than ever, not just the kind of established thinkers who created the classic print *Atlantic Monthly*, but a staff of young editor-writers posting frequently on their own while (at least when I wrote for the magazine) working with outside writers. It takes a ceaseless content-generation machine—and one of consistently high quality—to sustain the 27 million unique clicks a month reported by *The Atlantic* in spring 2016. Paradoxically, *The Atlantic* and a few other elite publications benefit by cutbacks elsewhere. Between 2009 and 2016, over a thousand magazines ceased publication. Although about as many new ones were founded, the churn and the continued production of journalism degrees helped create a buyer's market for editor-bloggers who can help draw younger readers through social media. Of course, it is true that high-quality opinion magazines have rarely been profitable and have been heavily subsidized by wealthy owners and think tanks. But the virtual collapse of *The New Republic* in 2016 after four years under the ownership of a Facebook founder showed that even some of the super-rich no longer believe the prestige of magazine ownership is worth the cost. (*The Atlantic*'s traditional rival, *Harper's*, is still owned by a family foundation and has chosen a strategy inverting the *Atlantic*'s: firmly committed to print and relying on paid subscriptions behind a paywall.)[38]

While some economists may consider *The Atlantic* a model of the new efficiency for magazines, despite the high costs of its approach, the point is rather that it is an almost unique survivor of the golden age of the upper-middle-class magazine. It has succeeded by becoming almost a platform in its own right, melding traditional magazine content with the blogging of sites like *The Huffington Post* and the comprehensiveness of 1990s portals like Yahoo and AOL.

The (relative) paradise of magazine publishing is still fashion, not just because glossy print is still the best showcase for luxury goods but also because the editorial side of fashion publishing has traditionally aligned itself with leading brands. As fashion marketers have shifted part of their budgets from print to promotion via social media, leading magazine chains have remained their partners. Thus Condé Nast has been able to offset print advertising losses by offering brands new ways to reach its 100 million online readers and 175 million social media followers. Across all publications, luxury print advertising has fallen by about 8 percent since 2013, to $2.6 billion, but the digital sector has grown by 63 percent to slightly over $1 billion. This success just underlines the hardships faced by other categories of magazines. The decades-old norm of a wall of separation between editorial and advertising departments—between church and state, as it is often called—has been crumbling. Over two-thirds of magazine publishers responding to a survey now use their own editorial staff to create special features ("native" advertising) for sponsors—even *The New York Times*. Thus, as an online trade publication put it, most journalists may now be part-time copywriters. But outside the luxury and fashion market, this expedient is bringing its own problems, especially reader confusion on the boundary between editorial and advertising material, possibly at the cost of readers' trust. The one bright spot in the periodical advertising scene is the rise of glossy magazine supplements to newspapers like *The Wall Street Journal* and *Financial Times*. In August 2017, despite an overall 7 percent decline in advertising of its parent News Corp, the *Wall Street Journal* magazine reported an increase of 5 percent in both pages and revenue, an all-time high.[39]

In autumn 2017 the resignations and retirements of several prominent magazine editors prompted a new wave of foreboding in the industry, and *New York Times* media correspondents contrasted their departures and the imperiled heritage of the genre with the announcement of Time Inc.'s new cute-animal video series. The sale of Time Inc. to Meredith Corp. in November 2017 confirmed many fears. A publishing optimist might look, however, at the same events and recall that nearly all magazine paradigms follow cycles. Henry Luce founded *LIFE* magazine in the Depression by buying the name of a tired monthly that had prospered in the Roaring Twenties. *Vanity Fair*, discontinued by Condé Nast as an independent publication in 1935, was revived in the 1980s by S. I. Newhouse, Jr. Evidence abroad suggests that there are still unfilled niches in the U.S. In the U.K., which has a higher percentage of homes with broadband Internet than the U.S. does, paper editions of both serious and satirical magazines continue to prosper; *Private Eye* circulation was almost at a new peak in summer 2017.[40]

Looking at newspapers and magazines together, the positive and negative effects of extreme efficiency are clear. It's more efficient to get and read news. I have over a dozen newspaper and magazine apps on my iPhone and also get feeds from publications via Twitter. Some critics have charged that the web has created "echo chambers" in which polarized publics see only the news that fits their political outlooks. But it's not clear that the real problem is the suppression of intellectual diversity. Even the arch-skeptic Evgeny Morozov has asserted in a review of Eli Pariser's *The Filter Bubble* that personalization can actually improve serendipity. This is a difficult proposition to prove or disprove, especially (as Morozov notes) given Louis Pasteur's dictum of chance favoring the prepared mind. Some people—regardless of formal education—are probably more open to serendipitous discovery than others. There is at least evidence that polarization is not mainly the result of ignorance of opposing views. A study of web use by young adults conducted by the National Opinion Research Center of the University of Chicago revealed that the great majority drew on news from a variety of sources regardless of their own preferences.[41]

Other critics of the web note the bias of algorithms—not only conservatives who suspect Facebook of slighting their viewpoints but also progressives who detect censorship by algorithm. It is true that the makers of the dominant mobile operating systems, Apple (iOS) and Google (Android), have suppressed apps without an effective right of appeal. Sometimes their targets are apps inimical to their interests; for example, attacks on working conditions in factories making a company's smartphones. The main problem, however, is that algorithms are written neither to advance a political outlook nor to establish the truth but to maximize traffic and advertising revenue for the platform company. The sociologist of computing Zeynep Tufekci has described them as "billions of semi-savant mini-Frankensteins . . . spitting out answers here and there to questions we can't judge just by numbers, all under the cloak of objectivity and science." This sounds terrible, but is it really any worse than often equally arbitrary decisions made by editors at the peak of the print era? In fact, following the rise of ultra-nationalism and racism in the 2016 election and thereafter, many believe that algorithms should be used to curb the spread of online hate speech. The underlying problem may be that radical positions right and left, by inciting user engagement pro and con, tend to suppress balanced ones. In building traffic, moderation may be no virtue and extremism no vice, as Barry Goldwater prophetically put it.[42]

The second problem is that instead of replacing the human editor, social media algorithms interpose another layer between the editor and the reader, an opaque process, a black box. Publishers also must face the expense of developing usable apps for two platforms, getting them approved by the platform companies, and revising them with new operating system releases—in addition to maintaining the desktop versions of their publications, which also must be usable by both desktop and mobile readers. Book publishers also need technically proficient staff members to format data for Amazon and the few remaining bookstore chains. In fact, as the writer Craig Lambert has argued, many of the gains of high technology have come through outsourcing services to the user that were once provided for no additional charge by the seller's own employees—"shadow work," to use a phrase coined by the philosopher Ivan Illich. What is convenient for users can be the opposite for firms that have no choice but to conform.[43]

What about information sources that are *not*, like most newspapers and general-interest magazines, dependent on advertisers? Their editors don't have the burden of working around the algorithms of the platform oligarchs. Yet even in these areas of cultural production, the search for efficiency leads to inefficient use of at least some kinds of important information. As noted earlier in this chapter, the Google PageRank algorithm was a populist adaptation of an elitist surveillance technique. Meanwhile, researchers in the humanities and social sciences as well as the natural sciences have acquired access to a stunning range of sources from the earliest days of print, thanks to commercial and not-for-profit scanning and digitization projects. Formerly in the 1990s there was often a gap between the latest electronic issues of a journal and print copies of back volumes that might have to be summoned from libraries' remote storage or—still worse—be available only in microfilm. The ability of end users to search through decades of writing promised to correct much of readers' myopia and their unfortunate tendency to repeat or rediscover older work. Despite the common view that science advances so rapidly that older literature becomes obsolete, researchers actually are keenly interested in it. Many nineteenth-century books, especially those by giants like Charles Darwin and James Clerk Maxwell, are still revered. Information scientists have even identified a category of older article called "sleeping beauties," initially obscure, that are rediscovered and frequently cited. Some were the work of people almost unknown to their contemporaries; Gregor Mendel's 1866 paper on the genetics of peas, in a provincial Moravian journal, may not have been quite as obscure on publication as historians once thought, but it had to wait decades for its real impact. Even the greatest minds are not immune. One of Albert Einstein's papers written after he had received the Nobel Prize, coauthored with Boris Podolsky and Nathan Rosen in 1935, took decades to be cited widely. The information scientist Alessandro Flammini and his colleagues have found numerous such examples in a study of more than 22 million individual papers.[44]

Medical knowledge is especially oblivion-prone. The physician and writer Oliver Sacks cited a number of cases from his own practice, including geometric patterns in the headaches of his patients when he was a young neurologist. While undocumented in 1960s textbooks, these illusions had been described by forgotten writers, a hundred years earlier, in forgotten books and journals. Neglected social science papers, too, may have great latent merit. One management theorist, Craig Pritchard, reviewed eight entirely uncited papers in the contemporary journal *Organization* and discovered that while there were sociological explanations for their neglect, at least some of them had potentially valuable insights on major topics like pay disparity between white and African American workers. There may actually be serendipitous value in some of the most neglected papers, it appears. Alongside conventional citation analysis we might investigate whether there are ways to identify papers that deserve another look. Nineteenth- and early-twentieth-century journals and books now in the public domain might have hidden gems of observations and theories; data mining software, already used in current science, might be applied to the older literature as well as to more recent studies. Computer scientists, recognizing that nearly a quarter of major scientific discoveries have relied on some form of apparently chance discovery, have been studying how to seek out and recommend work that might not be apparent in conventional literature searches. The Semantic Scholar program of the Allen Institute for Artificial Intelligence in Seattle, Washington, is the best-known initiative, though I have found its results inferior to those of Google Scholar, the search engine's academic interface.[45]

The new efficiency of search, and the extension of citation indexing to older papers, would have suggested more attention to older work. Easy discovery should broaden search horizons, but the opposite has been the case. After studying citation patterns in 35 million articles in a variety of scientific fields from 1945 to 2005, the sociologist James Evans found that researchers were actually paying more attention to fewer papers overall and, generally, to the more recent ones. This seems unlikely and was questioned by some other scholars of scientific influence, but Evans was unconvinced by their objections. And the social structure of scientific influence helps explains the paradox. When scientists had to pore over print journals, there was no convenient way to judge the relative importance of papers, so past literature was cited more broadly. Electronic publication did put older and newer research on a more equal footing, but it also made it easier for scientists to discover which papers were most popular with their colleagues and to align themselves with trends. That is not necessarily good for scientific creativity, Evans cautioned. Agreement may not be a measure of truth or importance; electronic journals accelerate consensus by amplifying tiny differences in quality. The result may be that promising results and concepts that are not taken up rapidly by the community will fade from its consciousness. Electronic links may promote the "winner take all" phenomenon that the economists Philip Cook and Robert H. Frank noticed in the broader society in the 1990s. Relatively primitive indexing by titles and authors, mainly in core journals, actually helped integrate knowledge, a positive unintended consequence of inefficiency. Print browsing may have been serendipitous, encouraging more attention to productive byways.[46]

Scientific fashions did not, of course, start with electronic publication. The rise of big science and competition for government and foundation grants in the postwar era put a premium on appearing to be on the cutting edge. The idea of the wisdom of crowds, behavioral economists remind us, refers to the value of combining independent judgments, for example, of the number of jelly beans in a jar. The effect disappears when people confer and groupthink sets in. There are powerful social forces that support joining a consensus, even though thanks to the proliferation of journals and self-publishing it is easier than ever to share a novel idea. In spite of or because of this ease of access, the rise of the web has highlighted the importance of reputation, and there is much less reputational risk in supporting a popular idea than an unpopular one. There is relatively little stigma if most others make the same mistake. Conversely, there are risks in attacking the work of influential figures supported by major grants and well-staffed laboratories. Following the herd is a short-term efficient strategy for building an individual reputation, but a behavior that makes science less efficient at discovery in the long run.[47]

Social scientists offer other insights on the effect of new publication patterns and measurement technologies on science itself. Sociologists of science have shown how misleading citation analysis can be if it is limited to conventional raw data. On the most elementary level, older papers obviously have had more time to gather citations, so comparisons should be made among publications from the same year. But journals also have different policies that in turn affect the citation rates of their papers without any necessary relationship to their quality. The greatest challenge may be that short-term citation rates—those with the greatest impact on young scientists' careers—may not necessarily reflect the long-term impact of work on the evolution of a discipline. One frontier of the quantitative analysis of scientific influence is the study of the full text of articles and books as well as references. Yet it is not clear that any of these methods can address the cumulative advantage promoted by measurement itself. The price of greater sophistication is the added time needed to master the latest measurement techniques—time that may present an opportunity cost to researcher-administrators in their actual work. Recent research has also confirmed that bad publicity can be good for citations; work possibly of low quality can be rated highly if it leads to rebuttals in comments rather than to indifference. Just as Daniel Boorstin defined a celebrity as someone well known for being well known, papers can also gain self-perpetuating fame without necessarily having exceptional merit. In the Royal Society journal *Impact*, the physicist and complex systems researcher Matjaž Perc has found that some papers are cited just because they have been cited elsewhere so often. In fact, even in searching for articles critical of cumulative advantage, it is almost impossible to avoid giving preference to those papers that Google or Google Scholar, or another resource using a search algorithm derived from Google's PageRank principle, puts at the top of the list.[48]

Citation patterns show the conflict of two kinds of efficiency. Scientific and technological studies—like those underlying electronic data storage and retrieval—make life more efficient. But real innovation often cannot happen efficiently. While the importance of failure captivates popular science and inspiration writing alike, real setbacks can be hard to overcome, as I suggested when discussing survivor bias in the Preface. Many wealthy Silicon Valley entrepreneurs have been associated with a failed business at one point, yet the founders of Microsoft, Amazon, Google, and Facebook all became wealthy as young men, and Steve Jobs's exile from Apple was relatively brief. But at least venture capitalists have open minds. The rules of peer review in science are failure-averse, if only because most research communities have grown more rapidly than grant support. Many elite scientists are dismayed. The Nobel Laureate biochemist Roger Kornberg has protested: "In the present climate especially, the funding decisions are ultraconservative. If the work that you propose to do isn't virtually certain of success, then it won't be funded. And, of course, the kind of work that we would most like to see take place, which is groundbreaking and innovative, lies at the other extreme." The physics Nobelist Peter Higgs has doubted he would be considered productive enough to get funding today. More frequent and shorter papers have become the norm. Technological efficiency does not determine the pattern recognized by James Evans but does help to amplify it.[49]

The efficiency of following links among scientific papers has also affected the behavior of journal publishers and academic administrators as well as of individual researchers. One of the innovations of Eugene Garfield's Institute for Scientific Information was the introduction of a measure of the average number of citations of articles published in each journal, the so-called impact factor. It's an apparently simple formula: a division of the number of citations by the number of qualifying papers published in a journal. Garfield never meant it to be the principal measure of a journal's quality. Citation practices vary across fields; mathematics papers are cited much less often than biology papers, for example. But once the metric was available, deans, department heads, senior administrators, and many government agencies began to interpret it as a journal's worth. Some governments pay many thousands of dollars in additional support when their scientists appear in publications like *Nature*, *Science*, and

Cell. Journal editors in turn adjusted their mix of papers to favor those by authors with strong records of citation by others. Just as electronic availability of journals tended to narrow research to the most popular lines, impact measurement also rewards the choice of already popular approaches. Information technology, far from equalizing opportunities as many enthusiasts of the 1990s predicted, has privileged the more established laboratories, universities, and publishers. Impact measurement also has risks for quality itself; higher-impact journals have higher rates of retraction, in some cases after discovery of fraud.[50]

There is also an unintended consequence of the impact factor. It magnifies the value of striking data. The more unexpected the results, the more likely a paper is to be published in a high-impact journal, enhancing a researcher's chances for promotion and further funding. In addition to the well-known cases of fraud, there have been a growing number of retractions when replication of results by other scientists has failed. (We will consider the effects of this trend in medicine in Chapter Five.) It is much more common for later experiments to support the original paper more weakly. This tendency is known as the "decline effect." There is usually no deliberate deception. There are legitimate reasons for discarding data from early runs and publishing when results are clear-cut. Prestigious journals, eager for citations to keep up their rank, also are looking for results that will be widely cited. They are less likely to publish replication studies. Most papers are never replicated at all. Campbell's Law thus brings scientists and journal editors into a feedback loop that rewards fast and striking results that may or may not hold up.[51]

Another problem of scientific efficiency emerges from Evans's work. Some critics questioned Evans's focus on nonconforming science; they ask whether most progress isn't the result of incremental knowledge rather than revolutionary ideas. Evans made a significant point in reply: electronic tools take researchers to the end results of others' work, but they do not readily access vital underlying data, such as the billion molecular interactions studied in twenty-five years of DNA research. Electronic search, he concluded, actually accelerates the forgetting of essential data. The situation is probably even more serious than Evans thought. A few years after his paper was published, a study of data of 516 ecology papers published between

1991 and 2011 revealed that 80 percent of data was unavailable after two decades. It is true that this was a period of unusually rapid change in hardware (Zip Drives), software (Lotus 1-2-3), and operating systems. But while formats may be more stable now, the efficiency of acquiring data in many fields has created new problems. The Large Hadron Collider at CERN produces 700 megabytes of data each second, according to an article by the philosopher and policy scholar Mark Sagoff. The challenge is most acute in genomics, in which new sequencing technology reduced the cost per megabyte from $1,000 in 2008 to only ten cents in 2012, one of the most striking accomplishments of technological efficiency in history. The data generated by the latest genetic paradigm, the study of the body's bacteria as part of an internal ecosystem, will be staggering. The catch is that the efficiency of storage takes over a year to double. "Cheap" big data need media that are becoming relatively costlier—not to mention the salaries of skilled technicians who ensure the data's integrity and eventually transfer it to new hardware. There are a number of proposals, and some journals have clear policies on availability of published authors' data, but there is no solution in sight. Encoding information in DNA strands has been one of the most intriguing alternatives, but at $3,500 per megabyte it is unlikely to be economically viable soon. Meanwhile, an IBM study has estimated that 90 percent of the world's electronic data has been added in the past two years. Thus inflation in the absolute storage cost is likely to outstrip near-term reductions in storage costs even if Moore's Law continues to apply.[52]

The data tsunami, as it is often called, reveals a paradox of efficiency in the age of big data. It is more efficient for scientists to gather massive data sets and interpret them later than to design experiments around a hoped-for outcome—"hypothesis-free science" or "discovery science," as it has been called. The concept is still debated. Some epidemiologists, for example, have tried to use the frequency of searches, and users' locations, to track infectious disease. In 2014, the economics columnist Tim Harford, reviewing the failure of Google Flu Trends to predict the spread of influenza more accurately than the Centers for Disease Control (which relied on reports from physicians on cases actually treated), predicted the program would "bounce back, recalibrated with fresh data." Yet as of June 2017, Flu

Trends was still inactive and Google was providing only historical data. Meanwhile, a paper published in June 2017 concluded that "Google Trends seems to be more influenced by the media clamor than by true epidemiological burden." For Google, the search data represented little or no additional data-gathering or storage expense. For academic and government researchers in the absence of powerful new hardware or ultra-efficient algorithms, access to massive data sets might become prohibitively expensive, or might produce misleading conclusions. The efficiency of data acquisition has brought a quiet crisis to biomedical research in particular.[53]

Science might, of course, be an exception. Scientists are part of a tightly knit and highly competitive community in which multiple laboratories are racing to solve the same problems, and rewards go disproportionately to priority—a tournament, as economists call it. So it is especially interesting that the inefficient effects of efficient networks also are visible in popular culture. An efficient recommendation system for music, for example, would be one in which the most popular artists were also the ones whom the public judged to show the highest quality—as though by a Darwinian selection of "the fittest." The popular music market lets us see the impact of technological efficiency without the complications of prestigious gatekeepers. Enthusiasts of digital culture, like the media studies professor Clay Shirky, compare web technology to Gutenberg's invention of movable type, unleashing some unfortunate excesses but in the long run empowering human collaboration and innovation. But while publishers from the fifteenth century to the twentieth often had to guess what the public would want to buy, online publication lets all of us contend for mass attention. Online collaboration by millions of producer-consumers of culture will, in this view, be more efficient at recognizing quality than the guesses of powerful intermediaries. The computer scientist Jaron Lanier has deplored the resulting culture of the mashup and the collective mind, in preference to rewards for individual talent, as "digital Maoism." Evgeny Morozov has questioned crowdsourcing enthusiasts' populist disdain for the insights of professional critics whose experience and discernment advance civilization, speculating half seriously that someday even the collective judgment of crowds will be replaced by algorithms writing reviews of works composed by other algorithms. But even these objections to digital efficiency may overlook a more fundamental defect of technology in aggregating popular taste. It may not be so efficient in reflecting what people really think.[54]

Cultural success and failure does have something in common with science, the "first mover advantage." Early publication in a field does not guarantee a prize, and it is possible for a very advanced paper to become a "sleeping beauty" until its insights are rediscovered. But in general, the physicist M. E. J. Newman has concluded after studying citation patterns, a relatively pedestrian paper on what will become the next year's hottest topic will get more attention than an excellent one on this year's. Once a scientist has early recognition, he or she will continue to accrue further preference and access to resources, which will multiply what might have started as at best a slight superiority—Robert K. Merton's Matthew effect, which we encountered in Chapter Two.[55]

Music, literature, and art would seem to have less risk of a Matthew effect. Equipping and funding a laboratory demands big investments, so people shut out of early opportunities often don't have second chances. The arts may yield few fortunes but at least have a low cost of entry. Success is up to a broad public, not a relatively small number of senior peers, administrators, and grant committee members, though such humanist authorities can certainly help make careers. Yet the Matthew effect still applies. There is a variety of the first-mover advantage when large numbers of people rate and recommend music and other cultural works on the web, according to a study by the sociologists Matthew J. Salganik, Peter Sheridan Dodds, and Duncan J. Watts, published early in the social media era, in 2006. The power of personal recommendation had been widely recognized for decades, ever since the first studies of word-of-mouth recommendations at the end of the Second World War. Even after saturation with television commercials, later studies confirmed, people were more influenced in many purchase decisions by friends, relatives, neighbors, and sometimes their doctors. Down to the end of the twentieth century, when web reviews began to appear, people discussed choices face-to-face. In the age of the LP and the CD, music store owners and clerks could also affect decisions, if only by their choice of artists and albums to stock. The music department manager of the Princeton University Store in the 1980s, for example, was a professional musician who made Baroque CD recordings a specialty. Salganik, Dodds, and Watts set out to see how influence was expressed anonymously and electronically in the web age, including over fourteen thousand subjects.[56]

The researchers' method was to compare how the chain of recommendations and popularity rankings over time compared with the inherent quality of the music—as judged by people in the same sample, not by musicians or critics. If user recommendations and ratings were efficient, popularity of the music should be strongly correlated with judgments of quality by people listening to it with no other information. In fact, there was a positive relationship between rank and quality—the "best" music was seldom at the bottom of the scale and the "worst" rarely at the top—but it was surprisingly mild. The implication for the authors was that the process of recommendation tends to magnify modest head starts (as we have seen of scientific research) and turn them into a massive cumulative advantage that the public may consider obvious in retrospect, hence the circular definition of celebrity. For most musical works, as for most products, success and failure may be a matter of random fluctuations—in other words, of luck—as Robert H. Frank has argued. This effect did not begin with Amazon ranking or music download sites like iTunes; as Frank notes, it was present even in the face-to-face years.[57]

Lists—from commercial and tax documents to religious principles like the Ten Commandments—are an ancient genre. One of the first written records of Mesopotamia over 4,500 years ago is a list of 120 officials of the city of Uruk. Rankings are much more recent; for example, the ancient Greeks did not even award second and third prizes at their Olympics. Some books were known as sensational sellers, but newspapers did not compare their sales records with others. The lists that they published, beginning in the late Victorian era, were compilations of "best" books as recommended by cultural authorities. Today's fascination with quantified popularity did not begin until the 1930s; before that sales comparisons had been the province of trade journals. For the first time, widely publicized lists claimed to tabulate popular preferences: the *New York Times* best-seller list (1931) and the *Billboard* hit parade (1936). Magazine editors, probably beginning with Clay Felker and *New York* in the 1970s, began to add subjective lists like "Ten Best Restaurants" to their cover stories. With increasing competition for shrinking newsstand space since the 1990s, and with readers feeling pressed for time, lists have become an indispensable promise of easy-to-digest information for short attention spans. "Listicles" are so ubiquitous, online as well as in print, that the phenomenon is seldom discussed anymore. The media psychologist Stuart Fischoff called them "predigested food for thought when we haven't had the time to keep up but are nonetheless hungry to keep pace."[58]

It's in the web version of publications, though, that ranked lists thrive most vigorously. *The Atlantic*'s senior editor Derek Thompson has reported that after viewing an article, a reader's most frequent second click is not one of the featured new stories but the cumulative list of most popular ones—despite the list's location at a bottom corner of the page. The cumulative advantage of even an obsolescent article may persist for years, Thompson acknowledges, but the practice is too beneficial for *The Atlantic*'s own ranking and advertising income to stop.[59]

The power of top 10 lists and ranking goes beyond newspapers and magazines to the entire web. It is true that Amazon, Apple iTunes, and other platform companies do a lot of profitable business with works selling relatively few copies—the "long tail" of distribution that Chris Anderson has made famous. Collectively, these sell more copies than all the books on best-seller lists, especially because many of them are steady sellers while some extremely popular books fade rapidly. Still, the attention given to the very top sellers magnifies the effects noted by Salganik, Dodds, and Watts, turning small initial advantages into bonanzas that then appear due entirely to the quality of the books themselves. The same is true of music and smartphone software. As the economist Matthew Jackson expressed it, "being 11th on a top 10 list on the app store is a lot different than being 10th on that list."[60]

When we survey the effect of algorithms on information, news, and culture, the positive side of efficiency can't be denied. Even after the spread of paywalls and the closing and retrenchment of valuable publications, readers around the world have access to an unprecedented range of sources without charge. Wikipedia may be imperfect and may fall far short of the ideal inclusive community of reader/editors, but it is vastly superior to conventional encyclopedias in its ability to link rapidly to new sources. Science citation indexing gives researchers an overview of their fields far superior to anything available in the age of printed references. Plagiarism may be more efficient, but so is its detection. Social media may be a waste of time, and shadow work for the corporations that profit from their users' data, but also a remarkably efficient way to share sources and ideas rapidly. Cultural authorities in the alleged golden ages of culture from the 1890s through the 1950s deplored the trends of their times as much as their successors do today. Nostalgia is misplaced.

If, however, we compare the present not with a sentimentalized past but with the promise and potential of information technology, the picture is darker. Search engine algorithms have evolved to use artificial intelligence techniques like machine learning, a challenge for corporations and celebrities paying for search engine optimization (SEO) consultants who can boost their rankings. Those who can't afford such services may be at a disadvantage. Personalization of content may not be the absolute "filter bubble" that some critics fear, but it can take special efforts to see the strongest arguments opposing a user's point of view. Advertising rewarded by user clicks seems to be more personalized but promotes teasing and sensationalism that would probably be rejected by the same publications' print advertising departments. Most seriously, the efficiency of social media algorithms has diverted vital advertising revenue from publications themselves to platform companies—an obvious effect in retrospect but one that few editors and publishers seem to have foreseen until well into the web era. Adapting to the new environment requires dedicated staff to monitor "reader engagement" and optimize content for search and social media. This additional overhead is the opposite of the "friction-free" world promised by *The Road Ahead* in 2005.[61]

Technology enthusiasts may protest that it is simply more efficient for journalistic talent to migrate to sites like BuzzFeed and Vox, which have in fact improved their content. But most of their writers still depend on other sources for their facts, just as Wikipedia editors do. Wikipedia even has a ban against editors including original research in their work on articles. The only truly efficient thing about the new mobile-oriented information machine is the ability of plat-form companies to claim an ever-higher share of revenue, and in the long term threatening the media they depend on.

In the centuries of continuous process technology, it was manufac-turers, refiners, and distributors who seemed to have excessive power over information. From the 1980s to the onset of the 2008 recession, progressive critics of media like Ben Bagdikian and Noam Chomsky saw corporate conglomerates and their allies, corporate advertisers, as a threat to democracy through their oligopoly and alleged censor-ship of news. Meanwhile, conservative critics like the publisher Wil-liam Rusher and the columnist Jonah Goldberg perceived a cadre of staunch liberals opposed to the values of owners and public alike. And the two apparently contradictory views were in a way compatible: when print advertising was by today's standards lavish, building read-ership and thus revenue was more important than advancing a politi-cal agenda. Neither Google nor the newly founded Facebook appears in the index of the second edition of Bagdikian's *Media Monopoly*, published in 2004. But the loss of advertising revenue—to platform companies that produce limited content themselves—makes the old debate moot. And as we have seen, digital start-up sites have been experiencing some of the same anxiety about advertising revenue as legacy publications.[62]

Newspapers, magazines, and web-only sites face different versions of the same challenge. The press as we know it was born in the 1880s and 1890s, when a handful of publishers like the newspaper barons Joseph Pulitzer, William Randolph Hearst, and Adolph S. Ochs and magazine innovators like S. S. McClure realized that mass circula-tion and advertising could reinforce each other; quality could actually improve as prices were lowered and sales and advertising revenues grew. This model survived the Great Depression (*Fortune* magazine, a corporate showcase, was profitable despite its then-astronomical newsstand price of $1.00), the Second World War, television, Sep-tember 11, and even the first decade of the web. Media are cobbling together a new future with digital-only publication (a short-term solution at best), reductions in staff and frequency of publication, and higher subscription prices (resulting in an older if richer readership). The more efficient journalism has become, the less viable it appears to be.[63]

There is one remaining question, an obvious one. Social media advertising and programs like Google's AdSense (unlike AdWords, it depends not on a user's search but on the content of a web page and data on the user, including his or her location) promise the utopia of advertisers, efficient targeting of the best prospects. People are understandably concerned about use of their private data by marketers and fear the omniscience of platforms like Facebook and Twitter. But does social media advertising work? Is it *effective* as well as *efficient*? This might be an unfair question; Michael Schudson showed in his classic 1980s study that it is usually impossible to document what advertising accomplishes. Data-driven, personalized web advertising promised to be different, and it does give advertisers much more accurate data about how many times their announcements have been seen. The role of advertising in actual decisions (apart from direct web sales) is harder to trace, at least according to a study published by Gallup in 2014. Only 5 percent of Americans said social media marketing has "a great deal" of influence on their buying decisions, 30 percent said "some" influence, and fully 62 percent said no influence. Among Millennials reports of moderate influence were higher—43 percent—but there was little difference in the number reporting high influence, only 7 percent. As with all self-reported behavior these numbers are open to question. People may be more—or less—influenced than they recall or are willing to acknowledge. Of course, the same may be true of print advertising and of website advertising sold directly by publications.[64]

AdSense serves AdWords advertising mainly to smaller sites. For larger online publishers, a Google subsidiary called Doubleclick and its program Doubleclick for Publishers matches (larger) online publications and advertisers. The details are too complex for those not directly concerned, just as television viewers who did not subscribe to advertising journals did not generally know how commercials were created and placed. The difference is the impressive precision and monitoring that Google can achieve and its dominant position as a platform-based matchmaker with proprietary algorithms and access to far more data than it reveals. One website owner, Josh Marshall of the news site Talking Points Memo (TPM), made his feelings clear in a September 2017 article, "A Serf on Google's Farm." Google's monopoly is "comically great," reinforced by its ownership of the Chrome browser. While (unlike Facebook) it has shared millions of dollars with TPM, it has also created a sense of dependency. Crucially, Google is not an especially efficient master. For example, Marshall reports, his site's accounts of the mass murderer Dylann Roof led to warnings about the possible classification of TPM as a hate site. There was no noticeable loss of income from this or other Google false alarms, but probably because of its monopoly standing, Google had little incentive to improve its screening software, with stress and loss of time for the publisher.[65]

It is thus possible that what appear to be permanent shifts, based on hard data, are neither more nor less than fashions based on intuition, and that "native" advertising may yet return to newspapers and magazines. By supporting high-quality publications (along with more questionable ones, it is true), advertising can show the positive side of inefficiency. It's possible that a new generation of advertising buyers will rediscover the kind of institutional advertising that has gone out of fashion, affirming rather than trying to defeat the underlying uncertainty of advertising. But I must admit the outlook for such support is dark now. At the end of 2016 *The Wall Street Journal* made major cuts to its print edition and editorial staff after declines in advertising revenue. While there is already evidence that the power of online advertising has been exaggerated—Procter & Gamble withdrew $100 million from its budget in summer 2017 and claimed the effect on sales was negligible—the company's example has so far not been followed.[66]

Regarding search, even one of the platform giants is rethinking speed. Jaime Teevan, a researcher at Microsoft, has written a paper with academic colleagues reconsidering users' apparent demand for almost instantaneous search results. The computing public has come to equate speed with efficiency. In fact, as Teevan et al. observe, the rapid answers we expect may not be the best that the search engine could provide if given more time. If search engines were allowed minutes rather than fractions of a second, they could get answers to more complex questions that today lead to dead ends. They could also see results presented in more useful ways. The Teevan paper makes the important point that we often mistake electronic speed for efficiency because we have not experienced higher-quality results from slower and deeper searches. Koreans are even willing to pay for a texting-based service that transmits queries to many other subscribers for answers. Tomorrow's search engine interfaces will offer the option of deeper and more complex searches that will be more truly efficient in yielding the most useful answers and might even have an element of serendipity built in.[67]

There are even services that attempt to offer algorithm-curated serendipity. They work by combining users' lists of their own interests, their likes and dislikes of pages they are shown, and the reactions of other users who share their interests and tastes. But these offerings can be only as absorbing as the publishers and websites who have agreed to share their content. StumbleUpon, for example, shows me mostly listicles rather than meatier articles from major science review journals. There are also many striking, no doubt Photoshop-enhanced, images. So far, at least, I can get more consistently serendipitous links by subscribing to individual publications and writers on Twitter. I find Flipboard the most promising, since in addition to its own algorithm's recommendations there's an opportunity to comment and to follow individuals. The mobile graphic user interface is even better than Facebook's and Twitter's. Flipboard in itself does not do much to solve the problem of paying for original writing, but it shows that algorithms can be used to broaden knowledge rather than to make it too narrowly personalized.[68]

Turning back to the citation-driven world of science, Flipboard illustrates how suggestions might work on a more advanced professional level, helping identify possibly neglected papers, keeping track of new techniques in mathematics and data analysis. Newspapers and magazines with longer back files could also offer exploration and suggestion tools to their paying subscribers, making it easier to study trends and themes over time and to rediscover older ideas that may be relevant again. We are still at an early stage in the development of discovery and suggestion software. It took over two decades for the elegance of Google's PageRank algorithm to supplement the basic search options of pre-web databases like LexisNexis.

Despite this promise, it would be a mistake to rely entirely on algorithms to remedy distortion by other algorithms. We must continue to make room for analog learning. Algorithms can sometimes find hidden possibilities—as in spotting undervalued athletes or exploring unfamiliar lines of chess openings—but they can also easily become self-reinforcing, closing off promising alternatives that human intuition can recognize as intriguing. And they may leave organizations surprisingly vulnerable. If a decade of experience shows that a certain background set of traits are ideally matched to a job, and algorithms consistently screen applicants accordingly, short-term results may be impressive. But the price of success may be an organizational culture that is ill-suited for new conditions and generations calling for different qualifications, or at least a different mix of backgrounds. Algorithms, while usually regarded as technologies of the future, can tell us only about the past—including trends that may be reversed.

There are many applications in which analog technologies are indeed dead. But there is a kind of serendipity that comes from engagement with analog media, just as vinyl recordings have recovered modestly despite electronic downloads and streaming. The reason may be partly the superior sound of analog, but that is not the whole story. If audiophile opinion ruled, there would be a strong market for vinyl records of classical music, but their resale value remains low. It is the pleasure of rummaging through used recordings for discoveries that helps sustain remaining shops like the Princeton Record Exchange, which reports six hundred visitors daily and double that on weekends. It is not that we are going back to LP records; it is that analog sound is a different way to listen to music, inefficient to produce, distribute, and listen to, but still a potentially illuminating experience.[69]

In the next chapter we will see that the principle of a serendipitous analog reserve applies not just to the adult information economy but to schools and higher education at all levels. By refusing to follow efficiency at all costs, we can become both more efficient and more effective.

THE MIRAGE OF THE TEACHING MACHINE

WHY LEARNING IS STILL A SLOG
AFTER FIFTY YEARS OF MOORE'S LAW

Hopes for efficiency through information technology have been greatest of all not in the news media, the scientific publications, or the everyday search queries we considered in the last chapter, but in education. More than forty years after the arrival of affordable home and educational computing, schools still are labor-intensive. In 2013 there were over five million teachers in America at all levels. Continuing a trend that had begun around 1900, the national pupil-teacher ratio continued to decline in the early computer years of the 1970s and 1980s; after a slight rise, it was still about 16:1 in 2012, less than half what it had been in the days of J. P. Morgan. Most laypeople as well as educators considered the lower ratio an improvement rather than a loss of productivity. By contrast, farmers were once almost 40 percent of the U.S. population and now are 2 percent. Teaching continues to be a relatively inefficient process despite efforts among some of the most brilliant thinkers in education, psychology, and computing as well as the rise of machine learning and self-driving automobiles. Nor has there been significant improvement in most test scores since the computer's advent. That does not mean that information technology is useless in education; quite the contrary. It can amplify the efficiency and effectiveness of well-trained teachers. But where teachers are underqualified and hardware and software resources are underfunded, there is evidence that a little computer power may be more of a distraction—a temptation to excessive video game playing—than an aid to learning.[1]

Far from an afterthought or a 1970s trend, a technological revolution in education has been a high priority for entrepreneurs since the early electric age. It was a favorite project of America's premier technologist of the late nineteenth and early twentieth centuries, Thomas Edison, who promoted mechanical instruction as an application of his motion picture patents. Edison claimed in 1922 that current textbooks functioned at only "two percent efficiency." "The education of the future, as I see it," he continued, "will be conducted through the medium of the motion picture, a visualized education, where it should be possible to obtain one hundred percent efficiency." (He never defined what 100 percent efficiency would mean in education. Presumably, he was convinced that with the best audiovisual materials the same knowledge could be acquired in one-fiftieth of the time.) And in 1925 he followed up by predicting that by 1935 "textbooks as the principal medium of teaching will be as obsolete as the horse and carriage are now. . . . There is no limitation to the camera."[2]

Edison believed so strongly in this future that he invested significant money in it, and lost, according to his biographer Paul Israel. Originally a self-taught telegrapher—a member of the original geek culture of electromechanical tinkerers—Edison valued university science and recruited trained graduates as his assistants. For all his futurist optimism, he maintained a Victorian middle-class Protestant passion for moral uplift amid the sensationalist and racy fare offered by so many nickelodeon exhibitors to their plebeian spectators. To bypass the exhibitors and appeal to domestic, church, and especially school audiences, Edison had even invented a new film projection system, the Home Projecting Kinetoscope, or Home P. K., introduced in 1912. Using new nonflammable film stock in a fireproof enclosure, the film and projector were ingeniously designed to show a standard thousand-foot reel on only seventy-seven feet of film using an aperture that shifted when one strip of the film reached its end and reversed. Edison planned to sell ten thousand of these machines through his corporation but believed in the new medium so strongly that he funded the educational content personally.[3]

As they would be for other educational efficiency experiments in the decades to come, early newspaper reports were enthusiastic, if only because of Edison's heroic stature in American industry and press releases giving memorable copy to harried journalists. (One article declared: "Thomas Edison has finished his job of illuminating the world. Now he is engaged on an invention to illuminate the mind.") For all the Wizard's charisma, though, teachers and administrators were cautious and rejected the idea that the new technology could displace their roles and methods. They made the valid point that the films, while illustrating scientific and engineering principles and created by Edison's expert laboratory staff, did not fit teachers' needs. Few of the sixteen thousand school superintendents ordered from the catalog Edison sent them, and Edison soon shut down the program. In hindsight the problem was apparent. Instead of working with teachers and addressing their classroom challenges, Edison evidently believed his prestige would lead educators to revise their curricula around his catalog.[4]

Edison had a deeper problem that would continue to haunt many other efficiency movements. In thinking about education, he refused to accept how much inefficiency and waste are often necessary to create something efficient. After all, Edison himself was already famous for remarks about genius, inspiration, and perspiration, and especially for his persistence in mastering the details that made electric lighting economically feasible. Edison had boasted: "I can teach more accurate geography in half an hour to a class of young pupils by moving pictures than a pedagogue can in a month. . . . The moving picture art will largely supplement the art of printing for the transmission and diffusion of knowledge."[5]

Yet while Edison had no geographic education of his own, he was not prepared to spend months or even years with geography teachers creating films that would teach the subject more efficiently than conventional lectures and books. He underrated the time and money needed to create a successful product, by orders of magnitude. And this was not just because he was unfamiliar with instruction; he was making similar mistakes in imposing efficiency as a film producer. When overseas revenue declined during the First World War, Edison retained an "efficiency expert" and decreed a shooting ratio of 4:3—use of three-quarters of all film shot—a policy that demanded mostly single takes. In the 1990s, late in the celluloid era, a low ratio in Hollywood was 15:1. Other producers learned that creativity often demands waste and made their peace with the star system and salaries Edison deemed extravagant.[6]

As educational films became more widely available with sound and 16mm projectors in the 1930s, studies showed that while films did have promise in motivating students as Edison had predicted, they were hardly an economy measure. To the contrary, they could do little on their own; teachers had to be specially prepared to use them. They could make education more effective, but they demanded equal or greater resources to do that, a lesson more recently repeated with each generation of computer technology.[7]

The real future of technological efficiency would have to wait until the end of the Second World War and the rise of the stored-program computer. Its underlying concepts were much older, even predating Edison's Home P. K. In an introduction to his field published in 1912, the pioneering psychologist Edward L. Thorndike proposed the concept of a book that would let the student move to a new page only after he or she had demonstrated understanding of the previous one—an idea finally realized, as the entrepreneur and educational computing historian Brian Dear has observed, by the World Wide Web and its ability to link pages. After Thorndike and Edison, academic computing branched in two directions. The great pioneer of teaching programming to undergraduates, Dartmouth's John Kemeny, was not efficiency-minded at all. He approached computing as an enhancement of education, not as a substitute for teaching. An American of cultivated Central European background, like MIT's Norbert Wiener, he saw computing as the latest and most promis-

ing academic resource. (Kemeny co-developed the BASIC programming language that helped launch personal computing.) But there
was a second and more pragmatic strain of reform that rekindled
Edison's dream: the psychologist B. F. Skinner's idea that learning
could be accelerated by carefully planned rewards and individual
feedback. Unlike the free spirits of educational technology, Seymour
Papert and Marvin Minsky, who experimented with new computer
languages to empower children's creativity, Skinner was an unrecon-
structed admirer of industrial ways. He deliberately chose the phrase
"teaching machines," with its blue-collar connotations, and did not
hesitate to make claims for productivity in terms Edison and Henry
Ford would have approved. His projects with would-be manufacturers failed. He thought electromechanically and was isolated from the
already-flourishing personal computing scene. Yet despite his disap-
pointments, he could not help returning to the idea. In 1984, the
same year in which Apple's Super Bowl commercial for the Macintosh
promised liberation of the individual from authoritarianism, Skinner published a broadside, "The Shame of American Education," in
American Psychologist. He made bold claims for educational efficiency:
twice the learning with half the effort. The method was programmed
learning built into consoles that presented information in small steps
followed by questions that in effect were instant quizzes. Students
could learn systematically at their own pace, being rewarded imme-
diately as they grasped each essential concept. The Smithsonian's
National Museum of American History has preserved one of Skinner's original teaching machines, a wooden box the size of a large
briefcase with slots displaying questions from rotating paper disks and
rolls of adding-machine-style tape on which students were to write
answers. After the student responded and advanced the tape, the correct answer would appear in the slot. Over decades, other educational
psychologists developed more sophisticated electromechanical and
electronic variants. Trying to teach an entire class at a time, even a
tracked class, was wasted effort, Skinner and his followers believed.
So was expecting children to discover the principles of mathematics
and other subjects on their own. The most efficient way to make new
discoveries was to reach competence as rapidly as possible through
individualized tutorials, ancestors of the "adaptive learning" now on
the frontier of educational technology research.[8]

Teaching machines, as a review (also in *American Psychologist*) four years later revealed, originated in the nineteenth century well before Skinner's birth. But the movement seemed to have reached a dead end by 1988. "The fear of an Orwellian generation of robot-like children sitting passively in wholly automated classrooms has not come to pass," wrote a fellow academic psychologist, Ludy Benjamin, Jr. "Today children spend much of their time staring at a screen, but it belongs to their televisions, not their computers." The rising cognitive psychology movement, Skinner's bête noire, shunned programmed learning as potentially harmful. The University of Illinois's PLATO tutoring system, using advanced plasma screens and a military-developed form of programmed learning distinct from Skinner's, grew from self-paced instruction in the 1960s to become the first global social network and the seedbed of the video game industry. One major computer manufacturer, Control Data Corporation, invested over $600 million in the project, which promised to reduce educational costs and improve quality. Yet independent evaluation found happy users but few benefits, and PLATO did not survive the transition to personal computers, Macs, and the web. During the 1980s, too, Apple Computer began a $25 million experimental project, Apple Classrooms of Tomorrow (ACOT), bringing the latest technology to selected schools across the United States. It did not aim to make teaching more efficient by substituting computers for teachers, or by reducing the time needed for learning. It was high-tech instructional support, bankrolled in part by the Microsoft co-founder Bill Gates, rather than disruptive innovation. The Edison Project of the Tennessee advertising entrepreneur Chris Whittle was really Edison's Home Projecting Kinetoscope as a daily cable television program with commercials. These and other projects share an initial wave of publicity, a quiet winding down, and a series of evaluations that let the sponsors claim victory while skeptics deny improvement over conventional instruction. Government, corporate, and foundation sponsorship comes and goes. Most entrepreneurs, as usual, fail, with even outstanding products like the Voyager CD-ROMs we encountered in the last chapter apparently unplayable on current computers. This cycle contrasts with the genuine disruption—for better or worse—of the dominant platform companies: Apple's iTunes, Amazon's Kindle reader, Google Book Search, Facebook, Twitter, and others. All these have scaled, grown steadily and globally by orders of magnitude, while the kind of adaptive learning Skinner envisioned, with constant tutorial feedback and personalized electronic coaching, has not been realized.[9]

Why did Control Data Corporation spin itself off bit by bit instead of becoming the Amazon.com of education? (It sold PLATO in 1989, and the program's ultimate incarnation, while profitable for the British publishing conglomerate Pearson as recently as 2008, did not survive the recession that struck soon thereafter.) Why are so many educational experiments half-forgotten footnotes while other high-technology dreams have become realities? One answer is that individualized tutorial education might still work, vindicating the pioneers. The original researchers are often so influential that they are paradoxically forgotten as others develop their ideas; Robert K. Merton saw a similar pattern in science citations as obliteration by incorporation (OBI). While Xerox Corporation has survived, its role in developing the graphic interface that inspired the Macintosh is also known mainly to industry veterans and enthusiasts. Before Brian Dear's history of PLATO, even fewer people were aware of the University of Illinois's electronic engineering genius Donald Bitzer, who developed the system and its striking original orange plasma terminal screens.[10]

Another possible answer is that we are too early; breakthroughs in the near future could finally bring technological efficiency to education. Tutoring systems might someday learn from student mistakes and adapt to clarifying subjects just as machine learning enabled the computer AlphaGo to defeat one of the strongest human players of the ancient Japanese game Go—one in which human masters once seemed able to retain their edge over brute computational force for many years after Deep Blue defeated Garry Kasparov at chess in 1997. It's possible that tomorrow's computers will be able to work with human learning styles better than the best teachers can. Of course, it is equally possible that this turns out to be one of those tasks so complex that no efficient algorithm exists for it.[11]

If there is a breakthrough, though, it will be expensive. CDC had real success in employee technical training in aviation and other industries and government agencies with ample budgets. Its courseware was disappointing in quality and ill matched to academic needs. William Norris, CDC's autocratic founder and CEO, failed to heed administrators' objections to his system's high costs because he believed CDC could ultimately take over the schools. Nevertheless, for all the hundreds of millions of dollars he had invested in PLATO, an investigation by the *Minneapolis Tribune* in 1982 revealed that students enjoyed it but did not learn more from it than from conventional instruction. When journalists talk about machines beating people, they are really describing the work of teams of skilled professionals, including human masters and grandmasters, defeating other human experts through the mediation of an algorithm and of stored databases like books of chess openings. Machine learning algorithms—which let computers recognize patterns and experiment with techniques, improving performance with time—need programming, too, even though new tools have brought them within the reach of nonexperts. And the challenge of the efficiency of educational technology has been all along not a theoretical impossibility but economic reality. In a report published by the Russell Sage Foundation in 1995, as ACOT was shutting down, the psychologist and computer scientist Earl Hunt explained why "teacher-centered" technology, enhancing traditional instruction but not necessarily making it more efficient in Edison's sense, was prevailing over intelligent computer-assisted instruction (ICAI), closer to the Skinner conception. The demands of ICAI for highly skilled development teams were no match for the constraints of school budgets. Hunt might have added the limited staying power and shifting focus of corporate and foundation support. "As the cost of computer power drops," he cautioned, "the computer programs become ever more sophisticated. . . . Expensive nonteaching personnel are always a target for the public budget cutter."[12]

Despite new initiatives by the Clinton administration and technology executives in the 1990s, skepticism remained. It did not help that students' expectations of production values had grown with the release of games like the *Grand Theft Auto* series. By 2011 a *New York Times* reporter, Matt Richtel, visited a school district that had approved a substantial tax increase for a technology-intensive program, only to find no measurable difference in standardized test scores, and lower budgets for other school programs. Yet the pro-technology educational reform movement has historically favored testing and objective metrics, so advocates can hardly claim that there are intangible benefits the tests do not measure, although good software may improve outcomes in long-term retention or in continuing interest in a subject.[13]

Beginning in the early 2010s, high-technology education reformers started shifting their attention from the long-sought utopian goal of the self-paced adaptive learning machine to the efficiency and effectiveness of conventional classroom instruction. Related to the electronic medical records movement that we will examine in Chapter Five have been efforts to put big data in the service of improving and individualizing instruction in conventional classroom settings.

The best known has been a project called inBloom, sponsored by the Bill and Melinda Gates Foundation, which received a total of $100 million, mostly from participating state school systems, according to the *Washington Post* education writer Valerie Strauss. InBloom was intended to compile massive databases of student performance that could be analyzed to improve individual instruction and give teachers a better sense of their effectiveness. The organization had the misfortune of launching at a time when privacy concerns, always a serious point in educational computing, were continuing to grow as the accounts of 77 million Sony PlayStation users were hacked. Impatience with centralized bureaucracies was already apparent across the political spectrum.[14]

The Gates Foundation made even more controversial grants in 2011 and 2012 for a pilot program using wrist-monitor bracelets to measure students' "galvanic skin response" to give teachers feedback on the level of engagement in their classes. Even the principal investigator, Shaundra Daily, an electrical engineer and computer scientist and entrepreneur specializing in instructional technology (rather than a primary or secondary school teacher), acknowledged that readings could not tell whether a student was engaged or just anxious, or discover whether a student was bored or just relaxed. As in the case of inBloom, the Gates Foundation should have foreseen opposition. It is one thing to gather statistics, another to record and store children's (inferred) emotional states. It has not helped the Gates Foundation's cause that the bracelets measured perspiration using a principle familiar from lie detectors. Teachers, too, were not reassured by Daily's acknowledgment that despite her intentions—and the foundation's clarification of its original wording of the grant announcement—the data could be used to judge their performance.[15]

Thus the movement for educational efficiency and individualized instruction through gathering and analyzing massive data sets reached an apparent impasse by the mid-2010s. Education researchers will probably revive the concept, but they are likely to face the same obstacles. Pre-college education, like politics, is local. Each school has its own environment and culture, and often more than one. Reformers tend to impose a uniform grid on diverse circumstances and parental and student cultures without recognizing that local conditions may demand different strategies in implementing changes. This neglect of how organizations really work led to the abandonment of Taylorism in its original form and remains a risk in twenty-first-century efficiency movements.[16]

Meanwhile, on the instructional side, new web-based initiatives continue to appear, especially video tutorials. But these face dilemmas of their own. What makes individualized efficient instruction especially difficult and potentially expensive is that few experts are able to see the world as novices do, an effect that economists and psychologists call the curse of knowledge. I discovered it when I taught a seminar course in the history of information as a visiting lecturer. My syllabus and reading list seemed good to the faculty committee, and a scholarly association even reprinted it. But while some students with strong backgrounds in history loved the course, others (including those from science and engineering whose participation I had welcomed) rightly found that I was assuming too much. Brain scans even suggest that the thinking processes of learners and professionals are physiologically different. Physics students and instructors may actually see different phenomena in the same computer simulation, and many students come to interpret their subjects as a set of rules to be memorized instead of a deep intuition. Overcoming this tendency—making education efficient in the sense of imparting better skills and more knowledge in less time—cannot itself be done efficiently. It takes many hours of experimentation to find what is effective. The first time an original course is taught is likely to be a beta version.[17]

These obstacles have not stopped educators and philanthropists from pursuing colorful web-based reincarnations of Edison's and Skinner's clunky devices and even PLATO's elegant plasma touch-screens of the 1970s and 1980s. One of these, a mathematics teaching program called DreamBox Learning, uses artificial intelligence to customize supplementary lessons with techniques inspired by video games, complete with individual avatars that can accumulate points with successful completion of units. Its patron, Reed Hastings, chief executive of the video platform Netflix, believes that the kind of individualized recommendation software that built his company can also transform learning. Skinner would surely be astounded that the program records fifty thousand data points for each student every hour, capturing not just answers, as Skinner's tape did, but each minute step taken in arriving at them. Thanks in part to Hastings's support, two million students were using DreamBox Learning in 2017, and parents and teachers say that many cannot get enough of it. As with PLATO, evaluators are not sure what DreamBox has added to conventional instruction. The head of DreamBox, Jessie Woolley-Wilson, found it especially encouraging that an independent study had at least shown that her program hadn't harmed student progress; most educational technology, she noted, has not even been demonstrably neutral. But critics who see an anti-teacher agenda counter that the improvement may have been due to instructors, perhaps motivated by the experiment, rather than to the technology.[18]

One no-frills online tutorial program, Khan Academy, shuns video game production values. Its original novelty was that the founder, a mathematically adept former investment banker, Salman Khan, is not a professional mathematician and may be closer to a beginner's point of view. His relatively crude production values fit the no-nonsense mood of the 2008 recession. Some students using his thousands of online videos to understand concepts—rewarded by "badges" for completion in a way that would have gratified Skinner—have surpassed their classmates rapidly, and Khan is a Silicon Valley hero. In the philanthropic sweepstakes, Khan has the backing of one of the biggest donors, Bill Gates. But Khan's engagingly offhand method, first developed for tutoring a cousin, has drawbacks. Teachers have found significant errors (such as misleading treatment of negative numbers) and have doubted whether his tutorials create deep understanding or are just old-fashioned drill dressed up for a new generation.[19]

The limits of Khan Academy suggest another possibility. What if the instructor offering free online materials is a professional expert, with a popular, acclaimed course? Isn't computer science itself, at least, suitable for a new and more efficient style of teaching that will contain ever-rising tuition and student debt? Would that not realize Edison's and Skinner's dreams for the future of education? The best-known MOOC (massive open online course) is the artificial intelligence course of Sebastian Thrun, now an adjunct professor of computer science at Stanford and an entrepreneur, previously on Stanford's tenured faculty and an executive and fellow of Google. By 2013, 7,500 people all over the world had successfully completed his MOOC, more than twelve years' enrollment of the most popular course in his Stanford department. It is hard to apply concepts of efficiency to this result, because 95 percent of people who had enrolled in the course had dropped out. This bothered Thrun but does not concern another prominent computer scientist, Robert Sedgewick of Princeton, who with his colleague Kevin Wayne taught a highly popular conventional course on algorithms for decades (with a text used worldwide) before launching a MOOC. Remaining an enthusiast, Sedgewick finds that many supposed dropouts were in fact interested in only part of a course. (The Online Course Report website ranks Thrun's course as 40 out of 50 with 160,000 total enrollments, and Sedgewick and Wayne's Algorithms 1 as number 7, with over 751,000.)[20]

Whatever the reasons for attrition, the MOOC dropout rate suggests that we are far from the Skinnerian ideal of an online tutor that could teach anything to anybody at their own pace. And there is an even more serious challenge to online teaching in achieving efficiency. From a public lecture that Sedgewick gave at Princeton and a telephone follow-up, I discovered that if you have to ask the cost of preparing a really good MOOC you probably can't afford it. Sedgewick had extensive experience and student feedback, yet to give his online lectures pedagogically useful dynamic examples, he had to spend fifty to a hundred hours for every instructional hour online—as opposed to Khan's improvisation of his early tutorials with little or no research. Edison had dreamed of replacing the "two-percent-efficient" textbook with "one-hundred-percent-efficient" film, but courses like Sedgewick's are difficult to follow and review without a text as reference. Sedgewick and Wayne's 992-page algorithms textbook had already sold 600,000 copies in four editions by 2013, and Sedgewick believes the MOOC has helped double the book's royalties. While MOOCs do make lectures by elite professors freely available, and some offer certification that can be an alternative to thousands of dollars in tuition, they really depend on wealthy institutions even if most professors develop MOOCs on their own time. They are like "freemium" software that adds to demand for the full-price product.[21]

There is an ironic twist to the now century-old quest for educational efficiency through information technology. For all the practical problems in realizing it, Skinner's confidence in technological tutoring has never been refuted. Devices and the web are helpful, but only to a point. A recent study by the Organisation for Economic Co-operation and Development (OECD) has suggested that while moderate exposure is helpful, overinvestment in educational technology can actually harm outcomes. Students who spend the most time on electronic devices have lower mathematics scores, for example. The psychologist K. Anders Ericsson has described striking improvements in elite athletics and musicianship over the past century—gains achieved mainly through better coaching and "mindful practice" rather than through electronic devices. Because of findings like the OECD report, even many parents in information technology industries now believe that intensive screen time should be postponed in favor of more humanistic methods in early years. One of their favorite movements, the Waldorf schools, was founded almost a hundred years ago by Thomas Edison's contemporary, the Austrian mystical philosopher Rudolf Steiner, who left a technical career to develop a pedagogical system based on the ideas of Goethe and Hindu spirituality. The religious basis of the school is no secret, nor is controversy over Steiner's ambiguous views on race, yet the parents do not appear to be converts to the tenets of Steiner's system of Anthroposophy nor are most of its doctrines taught explicitly. (The official website of the

Waldorf movement defines Anthroposophy as a "spiritual philoso-phy" that "strives to bridge the clefts that have developed since the Middle Ages between the sciences, the arts and the religious striv-ings of man.") Rather, the parents seem to be pragmatists who believe in indirection. If real efficiency is the ability not just to plug vari-ables into equations but to solve unfamiliar problems creatively, then apparently inefficient methods may actually be most effective. And studies over decades suggest that test results of Waldorf students are at least as good as those of conventional schools. The point is not that Waldorf is superior but that teacher concern with students as individ-uals is more important than technologies and spiritual beliefs alike.[22]

While the Waldorf schools share a unique quasi-religious phi-losophy that makes them unsuitable for public education, the Finnish school system has shown that human-based individualized instruction does not need intensive technology. It relies on making teaching an elite profession, well trained and well paid, and encouraging teach-ers to work with students individually on their goals, giving teach-ers freedom to experiment and avoiding high-pressure testing. The paradoxical result of not obsessing over tests is that Finland's interna-tional educational assessment scores are some of the world's highest. Thanks to their nation's judicious use of computers in the class-room, adult Finns surpass Americans and Canadians significantly not only in literacy and numeracy, but in tests of "solving problems in technology-rich contexts."[23]

The United States, without the social solidarity of relatively homo-geneous nations like Finland and with a tradition of local support and control, faces a special problem created by technology: an increas-ing gap between richer and poorer schools. Just as the results of the Finnish schools are due more to teacher preparation and morale than to equipment, the extension of broadband computing to American schools has had little impact on the most serious inequality, the poor preparation of many teachers for using information technology effec-tively, and the lack of resources for continuing education of teachers in low-income school districts as wealthy ones forge ahead. The tech-nology that promised to equalize students' opportunities appears to be increasing inequality.[24]

Whether schools are Waldorf or Jesuit, whether Japanese or

Finnish, technology is still secondary to the selection, motivation, and training of teachers. This can't be cheap, because the people with the human and academic skills to be excellent elementary and secondary teachers are not common, and their teaching skills need time and expert supervision to develop. The most efficient course is to accept the inherent inefficiency of the process.

Turning from the organization of instruction to students' personal technology, the decade from 2006 to 2016 saw a revolution in mobile computing that has changed the experience of school: the almost universal smartphone. By 2015, according to a Pew Foundation study, nearly three-quarters of American teenagers had smartphones, as did half of elementary school students by 2016. Other research found teenagers spending nine hours a day on media using all devices. New York City schools attempted to ban smartphones—students bringing them to school had to pay entrepreneurs to check them in trucks— but found the rule unenforceable. In the 1990s Seymour Papert announced a goal of "one laptop per child." Now most children, even many from low-income families, have smartphones significantly more powerful than the laptops of the late twentieth century, and schools don't know what to do about them.[25]

While information hardware has advanced more rapidly than even most technology prophets had expected, the all-digital lifestyle has not, especially in the schools. If you doubt this, consider pencil manufacturing. The graphite-clay pencil as we know it has changed little over two hundred years. In May 2016, *Stationery News* reported continued if slow (3 percent) growth in the sale of pencils, pens, and other writing materials, many of which are bought as school supplies. It is possible to enter mathematical equations and chemical formulas and diagrams with special software, but in working out any problem or exercise, it is simply more efficient to sketch it with a pencil before calculating the results. Calculations are now always made with pocket calculators or software, yet paper laboratory notebooks remain the norm for schools despite the growing popularity of software records among professional scientists.[26]

An idea from studies of culture is equally applicable to technological styles in education: omnivorousness. People's musical and artistic tastes, mixed in the mid-nineteenth century when competing Shakespearean actors could inspire riots among fans, had become stratified into "highbrow" and "lowbrow" by late in the century, when a new decorum prevailed in elegant theaters and opera houses. In the 1990s, though, sociologists investigating Americans' tastes discovered that elites no longer identified exclusively with high culture. They also had interests in popular culture and, far from being embarrassed by them, believed in inclusiveness. The technology that transformed personal computing, the Macintosh, was itself a hybrid, omnivorous product influenced by Steve Jobs's extended study of calligraphy after dropping out of the degree program at Reed College.[27]

Electronic devices have not killed notebooks, pens, and pencils in the schools or elsewhere, for good reason. The inefficiency of paper can help people study and live more efficiently. Smartphones in particular are not just tools but portals to a full range of media products and social connections. And they don't tempt only young slackers. In early 2016, for example, the Bronx High School of Science, home to some of New York City's highest-achieving students, began to shut off Wi-Fi access to students because their nonacademic media streaming was slowing down the school's many bandwidth-intensive educational programs. In fact, digital distraction by smartphones and other devices is on the rise both in high schools and in colleges. One study at the University of Nebraska–Lincoln found that on average, students spent 30 percent of their classroom time in noneducational electronic activity, from emails and social media to games. While all these activities can be pursued efficiently, many instructors believe distractions have made their teaching significantly less efficient. The problem is especially acute for students suffering from "FOMO"—fear of missing out—a syndrome that leads people to check compulsively for messages.[28]

(The distraction if not the passivity issue extends to the workplace. One nonprofit consortium, the Information Overload Research Group, has calculated that American white-collar workers waste fully a quarter of their time on messages and notifications processed by multitasking, at a cost of nearly a trillion dollars a year. Whether it's possible to justify this or any other number—sometimes an interruption can offer an opportunity, prevent a major loss, or make a new connection—there is no doubt that many people feel overwhelmed by data pushed on them through electronic devices.)[29]

Banning smartphone use in classrooms is likely to have unintended negative consequences. Studies in Singapore and the United Kingdom suggest that many students with FOMO will learn less if entirely deprived. It is pointless to try to reverse the march of mobile communication. Even scholars concerned about their effect on relationships, conversation, and the capacity for solitude, like Sherry Turkle, don't propose restricting their use by the young—which would only increase their appeal as forbidden fruit.[30]

Paper may not address the social issues created by mobile technology, but it does add a creative and productive form of inefficiency that can promote greater efficiency in later life. In education, the choice between paper and digital media has become one of technology's wars of religion. Even in the late nineteenth and early twentieth centuries, handwriting instruction was not monolithic. There have always been competing national traditions and methods. There were right- and left-wing schools of handwriting instruction, calling for disciplined uniformity on one side and expressive individualism on the other. In twenty-first-century America, partisans of italic and cursive handwriting, as I discovered when I blogged on the subject, sometimes are fiercer toward each other than toward keyboard-only enthusiasts. Italic advocates especially object to equating all handwriting instruction with cursive. When most people think of connected school handwriting, though, they visualize some version of the late-nineteenth- and early-twentieth-century Palmer Method. Its goal was to train students in a uniform, rapid, legible script that would make them an efficient and regimented workforce in keeping with the teachings of gurus like Frederick Winslow Taylor. (More recent research has shown that it is no more time-efficient than italic or even writing individual letters.) Palmer Method cursive handwriting was a form of continuous production of writing. While cursive instruction survived in the schools, the strict Palmer Method was in sharp decline by the 1920s, made obsolescent by higher-quality and lower-priced typewriters.[31]

The main advantage of the typewriter over handwriting was not

so much speed as uniformity and legibility, especially in large organizations exchanging documents among hundreds or thousands of
employees. Since the 1920s, handwriting has ceased to be a commercial skill. And even its advantages in education have been used against
it. Young people who do not learn to write rapidly and legibly, and
their parents, protest with some justification that their examination
scores are marked down unfairly. But what about typical children
whose writing is neither illegible nor artistic? There is evidence from
both neuroscience and psychology that handwriting, though slower
than keyboarding, benefits learning. Karin Harman James of Indiana
University used a pretend "spaceship" to scan the brains of children
who had learned to make letterforms and those who had not using
functional magnetic resonance imaging (fMRI); the former showed
more adult thinking patterns than those who had learned only passive recognition of the alphabet. Laura Dinehart, an educational psychologist at Florida International University, studied children from
low-income families and found that those who became proficient at
writing at an early age made better progress than those who had not.
Forming letters and words, neuroscientists and psychologists believe,
is more than a motor skill; it also involves thinking, language, and
motor memory. In effect, it is a form of all-around mental exercise
with benefits exceeding those of keyboarding alone. Skipping deliberate practice of writing and proceeding directly to keyboarding may
save time and often frustration, but efficient short-term effort may
make learning less efficient.[32]

The benefits of handwriting turn out to extend to older students
and adults. It is reasonable to expect that undergraduates would be
able to take better notes with a faster keyboard than with old-style
notebooks. Experimental results a few years ago were thus surprising. Just as the apparently more cumbersome printed book was more
efficient to comprehend than its electronic counterpart, students taking relatively inefficient handwritten notes score higher in examinations than those who use laptop computers—even when potentially
distracting web surfing has been disabled. Psychologists recognize
this paradox as efficiency with a phrase coined by the psychologists
Elizabeth L. Bjork and Robert A. Bjork, "desirable difficulty." Too
much efficiency can impair our ability to form memories that will

help us use information more efficiently later. Efficient isn't necessarily bad. It is often better to know how to retrieve information with a search engine than to spend time memorizing it. But if we want to learn something, research has shown, we have to make the effort hard enough if we want to retain it. It is almost as though there is, for the brain as well as muscles, an optimal level of resistance just as there is in physical exercise. Students taking notes with laptops often copy the instructor's words as literally as possible, almost stenographically, as one reviewer put it. Because the handwritten note taker cannot keep up with the flow of words, he or she is constrained to identify and paraphrase the main ideas, and thus has a better chance of retaining them and mastering the course.[33]

The psychologists Pam Mueller and Daniel Oppenheimer performed a series of experiments with undergraduates, to show how desirable difficulty affects classroom note taking. All volunteers viewed TED talks, video lectures of about twenty minutes, and were asked about them after completing a series of distracting tasks. (Other computer functions, including the web, were disabled during the videos, so distraction was not an issue.) As expected, students with laptops took significantly more detailed notes. But these did not seem to improve their test scores when examined either with or without a chance to review what they had written. One group of laptop subjects even was coached in note-taking technique and advised not to attempt a verbatim record. They had the opportunity to make the same kinds of notes as the longhand group, but more rapidly and in greater detail. This appears to have helped their recall of facts but not their understanding of concepts. It is possible that the inefficiency of taking notes in longhand stimulates us to make every word count, to restate key ideas more concisely. Only by restating ideas in new ways can we be sure that we have understood them. Something about the inefficiency of handwriting constitutes "desirable difficulty."[34]

A similar effect extends to the written word as well as to audiovisual presentation. Early-twentieth-century modernist graphic designers and typographers shunned Victorian ornamentation and aspired to present ideas functionally. Already in 1928 the German master designer-typographer Jan Tschichold cited the need of "modern man . . . to absorb every day a mass of printed matter which, whether

he has asked for it or not, arrives every day through his letter-box."
(Information overload is hardly a new concept.) Typography had to
obey, as streamlined vehicle designs did, "laws of economy, precision, minimum friction." In other words, efficiency. In bold type—
sans serif, of course—Tschichold declared: "The essence of the New
Typography [the title of his book] is clarity." (He later retreated from
this work's radical viewpoint, and from the Berthold foundry's spare
1898 font Akzidenz-Grotesk he had used, and designed a more traditional and still-popular font, Sabon.) In the twenty-first century clarity is prized aesthetically, but its value in promoting efficient reading
is much less clear. Comparing the performance of undergraduates
whose classes had been randomly assigned texts in a variety of fonts,
Mueller and Oppenheimer found that those with fonts considered
least legible showed greatest comprehension. One was the despised
Comic Sans; a second was a display font, Haettenschweiler, notoriously illegible as a text font; they were compared with the sans serif
type Arial. With both Princeton University volunteer subjects and
Ohio high school students, comprehension was greatest using the disfluent fonts. Inefficient reading somehow led to more effective learning. We should not make too much of this paper, widely noted in
the popular press, because there is such a range of disfluency and its
effects depend on culture. Modern Germans, educated with Roman
typefaces, find the nineteenth-century Fraktur (sometimes called
Gothic in the English-speaking world) difficult to read, but it was
perfectly natural to their ancestors who had absorbed it in their first
school lessons. One of the "disfluent" fonts in the study, Corsiva, is
based on the beautiful Chancery hand of the Renaissance first developed by papal secretaries, the opposite of Comic Sans.[35]

Disfluency still has limits. Even if students will understand a professor's ideas best if these are formatted in a nonstandard font like
Trebuchet, it does not follow that a student's paper will be best appreciated in it. Georgia seems to be the safest choice because it was commissioned by Microsoft from the illustrious typographer Matthew
Carter to be equally legible on screen and in laser and inkjet printing.
A professor reading it on screen will see nearly the same thing as one
who reads it on paper. And some professions are so used to older
fonts that any substitution would induce rejection, not closer reading.

Ever since the days of the IBM Selectric, the public domain font IBM commissioned for its standard golf ball head, 12-point Courier, is still de rigueur for Hollywood and television scripts, partly because of the happy accident that one page of it equals about a minute of production time. Innovation in screenwriting fonts is almost entirely limited to tweaks in Courier, and even some of these may not be acceptable. So it seems to be a rule that while acquiring new information is done most efficiently with a bit of optimal difficulty, the designer's old adage applies. The best font is the one that is unnoticed, as indeed Times Roman was known only to newspaper people and typographic professionals before Macintosh and PostScript introduced the masses to font literacy.[36]

The greatest experiment in educational efficiency is neither font design nor the technology of lecture notes. It is the attempt to substitute screens for print. In the 1980s and 1990s I was one of many commentators mocking the idea of the paperless office, and pointing out that the new efficiency of laser printing was enabling people to generate more print documents than ever—even though a dwindling *proportion* of all information was being distributed on paper. Yet contrary to my prediction of continued growth, the world appears to have reached a peak of paper consumption in 2013. For years, efficiency seemed to be on the side of screens over paper. In 2009 Jacob Weisberg, editor of the online magazine *Slate*, who had a few years before called for "an iPod of reading," declared that Amazon's newly released Kindle 2 "reader signals that after a happy, 550-year union, reading and printing are getting separated. It tells us that printed books, the most important artifacts of human civilization, are going to join newspapers and magazines on the road to obsolescence." A few years later, in 2012, Secretary of Education Arne Duncan joined in, declaring in a speech to the National Press Club that "over the next few years, textbooks should be obsolete," replaced by tablets and educational websites. But the question remained: Would a new generation turn from print books as they had from musical recordings on physical media? E-books seemed to have almost every advantage (except for being licenses rather than physical media that can be resold freely) over paper books. Manufacturing paper in rolls rather than as individual sheets was, as we have seen in Chapter One, a foundation of the age of continuous process technology. The e-book, which may reside temporarily in a device's memory but which in principle can never be lost or destroyed as long as there is a master on a server, appears a miracle of efficiency. It spares the environmental damage of papermaking (leaving open the effects of rare earth mining and electronic waste disposal), avoids the cost of transportation and warehousing, and is not subject to the inventory taxes that had been blamed for so many books going out of print in the 1980s. It can be searched even without a conventional index, highlighted and annotated temporarily without damaging the base image, and stored so compactly that a small library can be carried in a briefcase or purse. Even the relatively low-fidelity computer displays of the late 1980s and early 1990s, decades before Amazon Kindle, seemed to threaten print culture. The digital future feared by critics like Theodore Roszak in *The Cult of Information* and Sven Birkerts in *The Gutenberg Elegies* seemed to be coming true.[37]

The reality since Weisberg's original column has been coexistence of general-interest books, not the rapid triumph of readers and tablets that enthusiasts expected. The question for both digital advocates and traditionalists, however, was less about the habits of current readers than those of the rising generation, who have indeed deserted some print media like newspapers. But the reasons for their choices have not always been clear. Was it the act of reading documents in a broadsheet or tabloid format? Was it the increasing prices of newspapers after platform competition and electronic classifieds began to siphon off advertising revenue? Was it the style and mix of reporting? College students' textbook preferences are a clearer gauge of youth's information habits. And to the surprise of the digital prophets, young people are media omnivores, pragmatists who see value in both paper and screens. They were not alone; sales of physical books increased from slightly under 520 million copies in 2012, when Duncan made his prediction, to 571 million books by the beginning of the Christmas season in 2015. Even when a free digital download of a textbook is available, one study showed, a quarter of students buy a physical copy. Further academic research revealed why people aged eighteen to thirty still love print. Inspired inefficiency is a familiar concept to them. Naomi Baron, a linguistics professor specializing in reading habits, has found that students often cite better comprehension in slower, paper-based reading. Independent bookstores report a student preference for print, and Baron's research suggests that if digital editions were not cheaper, paper would be the strong student favorite.[38]

Just as Pam Mueller and Daniel Oppenheimer helped explain why more detailed electronic notes are less efficient for mastering lectures than handwritten notes, other psychologists have probed the kind of advantages that Baron's students have found in digital and print formats, which turn out to be complementary. A study by the reading specialists Anne Mangen and Jean-Luc Velay compared comprehension of a fictional work on Amazon's Kindle reader and in a paperback; in all but one category, print readers scored higher than screen readers. The human factors researchers Geoff Kaufman and Mary Flanagan found that readers acquired information differently when reading the same (fictional) material on screens and as hard copy. Reading on electronic devices improves recall of details in quizzes; reading printed text is less efficient for learning specifics but more so for understanding a work more broadly. Subjects who saw information on electronic devices were better at low-level recall, but those who saw the same data in print were better able to execute the higher-level *why*, as opposed to the lower-level *how* of a task. Even in games simulating real-life professional decisions, Kaufman and Flanagan discovered in a separate study, participants perceived the analog version as simpler and were more responsive to the game's goal of changing attitudes.[39]

This response to simulations suggests that the printed book—or newspaper, or magazine—is not just a material object for transmitting text and illustrations. It is also a three-dimensional space that we explore as we read. That does not necessarily mean that, for example, to understand Charles Dickens we should wait eagerly for each installment as the first nineteenth-century readers of his novels did, or that we should read Jane Austen in her original three-volume format that inflated the text for the lending library market. That is strictly for bibliophiles and library scholars. But all formats of print shape our experience of the text. They leave bookmarks as signposts.

A book is not just an object but a terrain. When we read a printed book, we remember a text more meaningfully because we are visiting a place. Chances are you remember actually handling books by Dr. Seuss, Maurice Sendak, and other great children's authors when you were growing up. Reading researchers have found that young children prefer to read print rather than electronic versions with their parents, and the topographic experience is probably a major reason.[40]

Because of this and other effects, studies by psychologists and comments by students on print and electronic media seem to converge on one metaphor used by Kaufman and Flanagan: the forest and the trees. Not only for mature adults who turned to electronic media after the age of thirty, but even for younger people who grew up with screen information, there is a consistent pattern. Electronic formats are more efficient for studying and grasping details, and incomparably more efficient when searching for information one already knows for review or further study. Print formats, partly because they seem to demand more careful reading, are better suited to grasping larger ideas. There is no point to arguing the merits of the two formats. Book sales patterns show that some kind of balance is likely to persist.

Baron's research may also have revealed what happened to the electronic tutoring projects of the later twentieth century. The goal of individualized instruction has not gone away, especially in science and mathematics. It survives in the online resources included with many textbook packages, accessible to buyers of print and electronic editions alike, but better integrated with the latter. Edison had dreamed of replacing inefficient paper texts with audiovisual materials; Skinner had imagined programmed "machines." The personal computer and the web have enabled the textbook industry to take the place of dedicated terminals like PLATO's, but there has been a catch. Although Edison and Skinner conceived of technological instruction as a more economically efficient alternative to traditional methods, the cost of the resources is now charged to student buyers of textbooks. An economics professor at North Carolina State University recently published an essay in *The Wall Street Journal*, claiming that the $250 Amazon price ($360 list!) of one leading economics textbook he was considering reflected a rate of inflation six times higher than that of the Consumer Price Index. His own excellent introductory text in the early 1980s had cost less than a tenth of that amount. The price, he argued, showed the inefficiency of the market in texts; the professors who decide on text adoption don't pay for the books, while the students may accept the prices because they are small compared to their tuition bills. Other professors dispute charges of excessive pricing. The sociologist Joshua Kim, for example, believes that texts costing hundreds of dollars can be fair value because of their included audio-visual aids for lecturers and personalized exercises for students. Whoever is right, the point is the same. Whether educational efficiency means more rapid learning or less expense for students, more efficient technology has not only failed to replace textbooks as Thomas Edison had hoped. New electronic technologies have helped increase rather than reduce the cost of instructional materials.[41]

Beyond lectures, notes, and textbooks, there is another side of education that receives less attention because it is harder to measure and often reveals its benefits slowly: the ability to ask questions beyond the assignments, to search for and recognize the best information, to make original observations, to debate and collaborate, and to produce new ideas. Silicon Valley's cult of the dropout is based on the accusation that colleges fail to teach just such things. And where information technology's detractors see personal computers and the web leading down the garden path to endless distraction, its champions see them empowering creativity.

The problem of the rise of the smartphone for education is that it is highly efficient for consuming media but less than ideal for creativity and experimentation. According to child development researchers, the effects can be positively harmful to small children who are still building the neural networks of their brains. We have evolved to need a variety of stimuli from infancy to the age of three. The delight of very young children with the stimulation of smartphones appears to many parents a sign of engagement and rapid mental growth. The small screen is superefficient in responding to the child's curiosity. Yet the psychologist Aric Sigman has called excessive screen time "the very thing *impeding* the development of the abilities that parents are so eager to foster through the tablets," harming "the ability to focus, to concentrate, to lend attention, to sense other people's attitudes and communicate with them, to build a large vocabulary." Frank R. Wilson, a neurologist, has gone further, deploring the decline of physical play as contrary to the crucial role of the hand in developing the human brain.[42]

For influential enthusiasts of mobile computing, like the *Wired* magazine editorial director Robert Capps, smartphones are unleashing a new age of networked creativity, thanks to our ability to upload photographs, videos, and posts to Facebook and other sharing sites. The smartphone's integration with the self, Capps declares, makes it our partner "in how we express ourselves, in what we hold out as beautiful and compelling, in how we try to emotionally connect, in ways abstract and literal, with our friends and muses." And while it is easy to cite antisocial examples in all these genres, it's hard to deny that some viral creations indeed deserve their renown. It is no longer unusual for prestigious art galleries to sponsor exhibitions of cell phone photography. Still, even large-format smartphones are small canvases, hardly ideal for composing music, making a drawing suitable for publication, or even editing photographs beyond the admittedly copious filters available in apps. The economics of Apple, which made its reputation in part by specializing in computers for graphic designers and musicians, invert its former priorities. Only 10 percent of the company's revenue comes from desktop and laptop machines; three-quarters comes from iPhones and iPads. Some of Apple's decisions have disappointed advanced professionals in the arts and graphics. *Wired*'s reviewer found that Microsoft's all-in-one Surface Studio, with a twenty-eight-inch ultra-high-density monitor, seemed irresistible to the magazine's designers. In December 2017, Apple responded by launching its most powerful desktop computer, the iMac Pro, and promised a new version of its flagship Mac Pro in 2018. It's hard to imagine composing a short story, much less a novel, on a smartphone or tablet without a separate keyboard. So no matter what mobile computing can do for creativity in education, it enforces a bias toward the small canvas.[43]

Equally challenging to creativity in education is the smartphone's promise of unending novelty. Part of learning, in fact of adult life, has always been productive boredom. Smartphones in themselves don't necessarily dictate overstimulation; there are even free apps for meditation. But they do offer instant relief from tedium, and that is not necessarily a good thing. The artist-philosopher Saul Steinberg once remarked that "the life of the creative man is led, directed and controlled by boredom. Avoiding boredom is one of our most important purposes." Relieving boredom with free thought can be a far more efficient way of using time than playing a game or watching a video. There is no doubt that students are much more likely to use smartphones to avoid boredom; according to a 2015 report by the Pew Research Center, fully 93 percent of smartphone owners aged eighteen to twenty-nine did so, as opposed to 55 percent of those over fifty. Those younger smartphone owners are also more likely to report themselves "distracted" or "angry" as well as "grateful." (The survey apparently did not ask about the objects of those emotions.)[44]

Sometimes relieving boredom does promote efficiency. Time spent waiting in line at supermarkets and airports need not be lost. But smartphones are still most efficient when receiving information rather than generating longer original work. Their small screens are actually more efficient than large monitors for reading most social media feeds—scrolling with finger swipes is more natural than working with keys and a mouse. Longtime readers of online publications have also discovered that many sites are now optimized, as I suggested in Chapter One, for mobile rather than desktop or laptop devices, which in turn helps drive users to the former. The ubiquity of cell phones also reflects the high cost of home broadband service for many low-income families. The Pew report notes the disturbing trend that a significant number of young people have Internet access only through their smartphones; this puts them at a significant educational disadvantage, especially in reading and creating longer documents.

Another kind of paradoxical efficiency also has been magnified by the smartphone: the challenge to "declarative memory," the information that we can summon instantly. Defenders of information technology have for decades cited Plato's concern that writing was endangering memory, and there has recently been a revival of memory-training techniques and even memorization as a competitive sport. The psychologist Anders Ericsson's pathbreaking work on expertise was his discovery that, with conscious practice, average people could memorize strings of letters far longer than what his fellow psychologists had assumed were natural limits of nine or ten characters. (U.S. telephone numbers and area codes were based in part on Bell Laboratories' research on memory capacity, which established a seven-digit optimum for local numbers.)[45]

It is obvious that information technology users in general, and smartphone users in particular, keep large amounts of significant data either in local device memory or in cloud storage like Gmail accounts. Even relatively primitive hardware, like inexpensive desk telephones, has to be able to store dozens of names and numbers in memory. It is not surprising that psychologists have found that people who know they will be able to retrieve information easily will be less likely to remember it. The mind prioritizes, and it's a good thing, too. Passwords, security experts keep reminding us, should be as randomized and hard to remember as possible, but we should also not leave them on a sticky note attached to the monitor or carry a list around. Even when using a mnemonic system to create relatively secure passwords, most people need too many of them to remember which belongs to which site—and the same security professionals also advise us not to use the same login for two accounts, and to change all passwords regularly. It does not seem a loss to outsource such data, even friends' telephone numbers that were once memorized. (Recently the developer of the most influential password guidelines, Bill Burr, has recanted his original advice, recommending long passphrases of actual words instead. But many or most sites will not yet accept them.)[46]

Technologically extended memory still can create inefficiency through efficiency. Because information of all kinds is so easy to retrieve, we are losing not just routine lists but essential facts that we need to evaluate and assimilate new information. Summarizing academic research on the technological augmentation of memory, the writer Sophie McBain found that a bias for reliance on electronic memory risks promoting "intellectual complacency, making people less curious about new information because they feel they already know it, and less likely to pay attention to detail because our computers are remembering it." Without a framework for assessing new information, we are less able to deal with it efficiently.[47]

Young people may be no more ignorant than their parents and grandparents, but the mobile web and social media give them a false sense of knowledge less common in earlier generations, when looking up a fact beyond the scope of an almanac or entry-level home encyclopedia meant a trip to the local public library. As we have already seen, strongly polarized identity has weakened the power of facts. People confronted with facts that tend to undermine their point of view don't modify their outlook; they strengthen it. (A classic case, studied by the psychologist Leon Festinger, was the Chicago religious movement of the 1950s, whose leader predicted the end of the world on a certain date. When the prophecy failed, followers did not quit in disillusionment but agreed with their leader that God had spared the world in recognition of their faith.)[48]

The web is not completely neutral in this post-fact tendency, which affects both students and adults. It is not just a stream of messages like traditional media but a cultural and political arsenal with resources to support almost any point of view. In fact, the algorithms of search engines are efficient at detecting the kind of sites that users are looking for. If students and others were more aware of the limits of their knowledge, they might search more carefully and deliberately. They might look for the strongest evidence and arguments challenging their viewpoints, if only to rebut them more decisively. But this would require them to have much of the very knowledge that they are seeking—a new version of Meno's Paradox.

Wikipedia is a partial solution to search results distorted either by widespread misinformation, like most conspiracy theories, or by systematic manipulation of search algorithms. The best articles have links to high-quality sources. But many others do not. And Wikipedia articles, precisely because they are written collectively, are much better as reference sources than as learning tools. Entries on technical topics present comprehensive up-to-date details, such as specifications of audio and video standards and formats, that no printed work could keep current. The openness of Wikipedia to public editing allows for instantaneous correction. It's a lifesaver for scientific and technical professionals and advanced students, and for others with readily answered questions like technical standards and specifications.

The strengths of Wikipedia's system nonetheless become weaknesses when novices try to study with it. Writing a clear explanation of a scientific concept for newcomers is an art because of the curse of knowledge, as we have discussed. At its best, the conventional print encyclopedia reflected a respected point of view and teaching style. Editors were experienced in helping contributors clarify wording for beginners. The disadvantage was that the revision cycle, especially in the late twentieth century, could barely keep up with new knowledge on many topics, and annual yearbooks were no substitute.

The co-founder of Wikipedia, Larry Sanger (an academic, unlike his more colorful globe-trotting ex-colleague Jimmy Wales), became unhappy with the inconsistent quality of the project, and the sometimes raucous culture of anonymous editors, and launched an alternative called Citizendium, in which contributors published their real names and accepted guidance from experts and editors. Citizendium was an experiment to determine whether volunteer free-culture spirit could coexist with traditional ideas of quality control. By 2017, after ten years, the venture appeared troubled. While Citizendium maintained its website and announced forthcoming articles, its official statistics page stopped at 2014 and even for that year showed under ten active contributors each day. It was even difficult to find a list of approved articles online. The lesson of both Wikipedia and Citizendium seems to be that experts and lay volunteers don't mix. If the latter dominate, most of the former will leave. But if the latter must submit to the former, both groups become unhappy, and the project falters. Professionalism and populism rarely coexist.[49]

There is thus no viable free alternative to Wikipedia. There is a partial solution to the limits of general search engines and the Wikipedia articles that are at or near the top of their responses. So-called federated search engines, available in libraries, index many of the dozens of databases and hundreds or thousands of electronic journals to which a library may subscribe, including the vast back issue files of the JSTOR academic journal database. These may include good explanatory articles from online specialized encyclopedias. Students often prefer them. But their search results omit important resources that may be included in those of Google.[50]

Students also are overconfident in their online skills. The ease of using Google, Bing, and other major search engines hides the implicit choices that search engine algorithms are making. Few students use the advanced search options of Google, even though Google itself offers web pages for searcher education. Librarians find that the structure of student searches also reflects a misunderstanding of how ranking works, sometimes almost magical thinking. (To find a good book on a topic, they will enter "good book on . . ." without understanding that authoritative recommendations probably don't contain the phrase "good book.") Students are thus subject to a form of the Dunning-Kruger effect, believing they fit the positive media stereotype of the "digital native" intuitively fluent in all forms of information technology. Media studies researchers say they have a lot to learn. Siva Vaidhyanathan, author of *The Googlization of Everything*, told *The Chronicle of Higher Education* that the digital native idea is a "myth . . . in the direct interest of education-technology companies and Silicon Valley itself." The notion of the technological "savant-like talent" of the young, he said, encourages "policies and buying decisions and pedagogical decisions that pander to Silicon Valley." And the technology writer and computer manual author David Pogue has observed that while many people have come to believe that all software questions can be readily answered by search, the decline of printed technical guides has left users unaware of many features, buried within desktop software programs, that could save them time and frustration.[51]

Silicon Valley's mistake is not in developing efficient algorithms, from which we all benefit, but in encouraging the illusion that algorithms can and should function in the absence of human skills. This is useful for the business model of most platform companies, to profit from user data, and most of us are willing to give up much of our privacy for a service that sometimes seems—to use Arthur C. Clarke's famous characterization of the most sophisticated technology—"indistinguishable from magic." Speed helps sell advertising based on our data, but it may not always be desirable. We saw in the last chapter that some computer scientists are advocating "slow search": higher quality through more complex processing. That idea should be taken to the next step, skilled search. We need to introduce desirable difficulty into search, to recognize that (as in music and sports) we can achieve surprisingly good results through deliberate practice.

When electronic information was sold à la carte, and by seconds of computer time, as it often was in the 1980s, there was no question that search was a skill, as we saw in the last chapter. A search was a privilege. Even in the mid-1990s, when I tried to use a dedicated LexisNexis computer in the library at the University of the District of Columbia near my apartment building, librarians seemed to panic that unauthorized access might void their subscription. Now in many college libraries, an academic version of the same database is available to all. But it is not always easy to make a research request that will retrieve the desired information.

Librarians and experienced researchers are able to set limits and use proximity conditions (like "within three words of") to make searches more precise. But search—whether of Google, a single database, or a federated database—is still largely a craft learned by trial and error. Reference librarians can show the way, but they don't have time to help with every query of every student. Some college libraries offer training in search. Yet the faculty are often unable to teach search in their fields, if only because they know too much. Thus search—as I discovered when I investigated Princeton students' information skills for an essay I wrote over ten years ago—is still a stepchild of the college curriculum.[52]

If students don't learn search naturally, it is challenge to teach it. The algorithms of search have become ever more complex, and must change constantly in response to attempts to manipulate them. And even after a carefully defined search, it takes experience to recognize what are likely to be the most promising results. Meno's Paradox strikes again: in order to expand our knowledge efficiently, we need to already know what we have been looking for.

Skilled search thus starts with recognizing our ignorance and branching out step by step. I call this method cognitive bootstrapping, finding resources that will expand the searcher's range of concepts and authors, leading to one level after another. One example of a technique is to find a single author and use his or her name as a condition of the search. In technological risk, this might be, for example, Henry Petroski, who has written widely on failure from an engineer's point of view. Or it could be sociologists like Charles Perrow and Diane Vaughan. Or it could be a military analyst like Scott

Snook. This method will yield not only peer-refereed articles citing these scholars, but reviews and essays in high-quality journals, newspapers, magazines, and online foundation and government reports that are not peer-reviewed. These names are also associated with concepts. Diane Vaughan's analysis of the *Challenger* disaster introduced "normalization of deviance." Scott Snook's work on friendly fire gave us a related and equally valuable concept, "practical drift." Perrow's examination of the linkages of technology is famous for a distinction between "loose" and riskier "tight coupling," as occurs in the design of most conventional nuclear power plants. Contrasting with Perrow's framework is another concept, the "high-reliability organization," which suggests that it is possible to train people in rigorous safety procedures even if the technology is inherently hazardous. While few people will need to follow through on an entire reading list, a skilled search can map a subject and its major points of view in a reasonable time and find brief summaries. People can understand the territory.[53]

Earlier I advanced the idea that a book is a place, a multidimensional map. That theme can be extended for search. Search is not just a way to get a serviceable answer to an immediate question but a means of discovery (a favorite term of today's librarians). It is a way to explore and find order in the apparently chaotic space of online knowledge. Because nearly every student will need to be able to explore and map new knowledge in a future career, search is one of the most useful skills of all, yet most educational systems around the world believe it develops naturally with experience. In one sense this is true. People do teach themselves many things without formal lessons or textbooks, and some are prodigies. But for most of us, music lessons and sports coaching help avoid common mistakes and develop good habits, even if practice can be frustrating at times.

Search education should begin no later than the first year of high school. Young people are used to casual searching but don't necessarily know how to refine a search that yields too few or too many results. To its credit, Google has pages of search tips and multiple programs for schools. Taught well, search can become an absorbing challenge, like working a crossword puzzle. As in many word puzzles, search depends on the multiplicity of synonyms for similar ideas. For example, not all articles on the death penalty will include the phrase "capital punishment," and vice versa, and some may be restricted to issues surrounding lethal injection. Website owners can deal with this issue by creating searchable keywords that do not necessarily occur in the text—one kind of metadata—but many important documents include no keywords. The synonym problem is a challenge to many kinds of electronic search, including the analysis of terabytes of e-mails and other documents in litigation. But the synonym problem is itself an example of the challenge of online resources: as of September 2017 there was still no English-language Wikipedia article devoted to it, though a substantial article, "Controlled Vocabulary," concerns the efforts of librarians and information scientists to standardize terms for subject indexes. Most people intuitively know what a controlled vocabulary is, but probably few are aware of the term. One advantage of Wikipedia over conventional resources, though, is that users (including undergraduates and even high school students) are able to fill in its gaps. Schools should teach skilled search by encouraging Wikipedia editing.[54]

There are two paradoxes in educational technology. One is that while a major goal of education is efficiency in learning, it can't—contrary to the hopes of Edison or Skinner—be achieved efficiently in the sense of cheaply. It takes well-trained and well-paid teachers and librarians to make information technology work in the schools. Critical information skills fall between faculty and librarians, although there are a growing number of training specialists who are meeting the need. The inflation of textbook prices reflects in large part the fact that a textbook today is really a framework that many instructors need for organizing courses. One or more professors may still be enough to write the main text, but even their work has to be peer-reviewed by colleagues, and it takes other skills to produce tutorial resources. The question should be whether these high-priced materials really help students better understand the subject. If they do, the cost should be considered part of tuition and included proportionately in scholarships. An open educational resources (OER) movement has been challenging conventional publishers by offering free texts and other materials, but its faculty advocates have discovered that creating and adopting high-quality alternative books requires far more time and effort than they had realized. Meanwhile, commercial textbook publishers have argued that textbook costs to students have actually dropped since 2007, thanks in part to expanded programs for textbook rental and resale. This is a doubtful claim, since students then cannot retain the book for reference under such arrangements. In at least some fields, especially when linked to MOOCs and other online programs, moderately priced textbooks—like that of Robert Sedgewick and Kevin Wayne—can be profitable for publishers and authors alike by reducing student resales and encouraging retail purchases.[55]

The second paradox is the value of the inefficient medium, paper, for more efficient thinking. As we have seen, searchable texts displayed on screens are a superior way to understand and verify details. In the humanities, historic runs of newspapers and magazines, available in college libraries, can at last give humanities education something like a laboratory experience. All this is wonderful. But so is the analog realm of paper. We have seen that it has an advantage in promoting the learning of concepts and relationships, which can then be explored further with electronic resources.

The relative inefficiency of using print resources can promote a more efficient use of our talents, according to Julio Alves, director of the Smith College program in writing, teaching, and learning. Noting the declining circulation of printed books in his college library, and what he perceives as the declining originality of student essays since the 1990s, Alves distinguishes between the immediate needs of research and the long-term growth of understanding. Database searches are efficient in answering questions directly and identifying resources that are most relevant to a query. But the relatively inefficient print library fosters another kind of learning, incidental, that can be deeper and more lasting: "The library stacks are a mine of incidental knowledge" that may no longer be our primary intellectual resource but that should remain a vital complementary one. In fact, the very word "serendipity" was rediscovered through a print reference book, *The Oxford English Dictionary*, by the sociologist Robert K.

Merton when he was a graduate student at Harvard. It is possible to browse an electronic edition of the *OED*, yet there is something about the printed page that registers in our peripheral vision and provokes more original investigation. There is still an experience in browsing, for example, the Eleventh Edition of the *Encyclopaedia Britannica* in one of the many surviving print copies that is absent in reading the free version on the web.[56]

In the first decade of the twenty-first century, in the aftermath of the 1990s web boom, some academic mandarins embraced the Silicon Valley dogma, celebrating the "bookless future" that their technologically conservative peers had feared when the web was still young. A few libraries attracted media attention by not including any printed books at all. Yet the users of at least one of these libraries were unhappy with the policy and librarians finally accepted the need for print, just as members of the Millennial Generation rejected the preconceptions of their elders about their choice of textbook formats. Fortunately, either-or thinking is less common now, tacit recognition that efficient means can sometimes be inefficient and vice versa.[57]

The goal of efficient learning through technology, which has captivated moguls and academics alike for a century, from Thomas Edison through B. F. Skinner to Reed Hastings, seems to have reached an impasse—perhaps because so many of its leaders (excepting Skinner) have been entrepreneurs, foundation executives, professional administrators, and politicians rather than classroom teachers. Information technology augments and enriches nearly everything in education, yet it has neither reduced the time needed for a degree, nor improved citizens' background knowledge or critical judgment. There are multiple reasons: the high labor costs of developing effective online learning (including open access textbooks), the illusions of mastery that technology can bestow on the unwary, the dilemmas of crowd-sourcing programs attempting to meld lay volunteerism and professional expertise. As I have acknowledged, given progress in machine learning, it is possible in theory that algorithms may yet learn effective tutoring techniques, for example, by analyzing large numbers of sessions of the most successful human tutors or even by experimenting on large numbers of learners to develop new strategies. But no matter how efficient technology might become in teaching concepts, it likely to remain inefficient at teaching critical judgment or creativity. The efficiency movement of the decades before World War I, an efficiency of obedience and uniformity, is no longer enough. Society can never be efficient without independent thought.

MOVING TARGETS

WHAT GEOGRAPHIC INFORMATION CAN'T DO

In the previous chapters we have seen how apparently inefficient, analog thinking can be more efficient for important purposes than newer information technology. In finance, commerce, media, and education, the technological and social worlds of a hundred years ago were no more humane than our own. But critics of information technology movements make a tactical mistake when they focus on the culture that we have lost and are losing. Technology advocates may disdain that culture and proclaim themselves transhumanists who are building a new and better culture by blurring the line between humanity and technology. It also doesn't help to predict out-of-control conscious robots, because after a hundred years of doomsaying there is more excitement about robotics than ever, while efforts to deal with the much more imminent threats of climate change have been so ineffective. Because technology advocates believe in efficiency above all, it is really the inefficient side of efficiency, and long-term gains in efficiency through apparently less efficient means, that are the point.

The fat mail-order catalog, the metropolitan department store, printed books in bookstores and libraries, and students' bound notebooks and printed textbooks all share an important feature. They are more than concrete physical manifestations of strings of characters and graphic files. They are all, even the ordinary newspaper, terrain—places that we learn to navigate, arrangements of information that help anchor and organize our memory even if we don't consciously recall the layout of the original page that we read. Electronic information is supremely flexible and searchable, adaptable to everything from a smartphone to a 4K monitor. We can choose formats and often typefaces. But when skilled editors and designers make these choices, we get something extra from our experience. Conversely, the smallest and most efficient information devices, smartphones, do not make us stupid but do—according to at least some studies—keep us from being as efficient as possible. The young, once considered a "born-digital" vanguard, are recognizing the value of the analog mode even if print newspapers don't seem good value to them at $2.00 to $3.00.

The advantages of the apparently less efficient medium should not be surprising. We are most efficient when we have vital facts in working memory, and thinking of real and imaginary places and structures is an ancient way of organizing our memory. The master rhetoricians of ancient Greece and Rome taught what has ever since been called the method of loci, or places. The orator or student imagines a house with a number of rooms, or in some variants a walled city. Some systems even use the human hand. Each room would be furnished with objects representing the ideas or facts to be remembered or narrated. The idea of the memory palace has gone in and out of fashion and is now a favorite technique of the revived sport of memory competition. Memorizers are usually advised to choose a familiar building, but the technique also seems to work with virtual ones. A pure textual outline is a less efficient way of memorizing facts than a set of connected images.[1]

If our minds grasp knowledge in such a spatial way, what does electronic efficiency imply for our ability to navigate our world? A growing number of researchers—geographers, neuroscientists, psychologists, anthropologists, and others—have misgivings about the effects of electronic aids on spatial literacy.

There is no disputing the benefits of geographic efficiency. During the last decades of the twentieth century, a network of satellites synchronized with the earth's rotation provided precise information to the U.S. military, but signals were degraded for most civilian use. With the U.S. Defense Department's release of accurate military Global Positioning System (GPS) location services to the public, following authorization by President Bill Clinton in May 2000, and the rise of smartphones a few years thereafter, the sense of location of a large part of humanity has changed radically. Today it is easy to pinpoint our locations by coordinates within a few meters and to construct itineraries for travel from virtually any location on a continent to any other. Visitors to a city can see annotated maps of their real-time surroundings with restaurants, museums, and other attractions, and upload their own photos. Motorists fifty years ago might visit an auto club office and get a set of strip maps customized with their route and notices of construction and other delays; today such routings are available instantly. Travelers can also see nearby hotels, restaurants, theaters, and other businesses displayed on their maps, and even preview actual buildings photographed by roving camera cars. One of my favorite advertising-supported apps displays a map of service stations with up-to-date prices reported by subscribers. And prospective home buyers can preview a neighborhood, with assessment and sales information and high-resolution street views, without stepping outside. Even Google text search does not afford the kind of apparent omniscience that Google Earth does. Travel appears to be reaching a level of efficiency few imagined even in the 1990s when quasi-secrecy still prevailed, despite remaining censorship and the European privacy movement.[2]

Before we consider what efficient travel means, and what we may be losing as well as gaining, it is worth looking at the most efficient travelers of all, if efficiency (as I suggested in the Preface) is the ratio of resources used to the results: the hunter-gatherers, seafarers, nomads, and traders of past eras.

Human beings are only the latest species with innate directional abilities. In fact, almost all animals have brains mainly to know where they are going. The neurobiologist Rodolfo Llinás points to the exception, the sea squirt, which uses a three-hundred-neuron brain to find a place for permanent attachment and then absorbs most of that brain. (In a conference I attended, but not in his book, he quipped, "That's called tenure.") Migrating birds and mammals may not have mental maps in the human sense, but use a synergistic combination of signals without the need for artificial satellites: the sun, the stars, earth's magnetism, photochemistry, scent, polarized light, and probably others. One prominent researcher on animal navigation, the geophysicist Joe Kirschvink, believes—leaning toward a hypothesis that he once opposed—that humans not only have vestiges of magnetoreceptors but may actually be able to use them to assess direction.[3]

Underlying locational skills is the capacity of the mammalian brain to construct mental maps of its surroundings. In 2014, Edvard Moser, May-Britt Moser, and John O'Keefe shared the Nobel Prize for Physiology or Medicine for their discoveries of the mammalian brain's navigational cells; O'Keefe had discovered place cells in the rat hippocampus in 1971, and the Mosers more recently had found grid cells that the brain uses to navigate latitude and longitude. Nature, the Mosers established, had been efficient in developing two sets of such cells. The grid cells of rats in their experiments, located in a region called the medial entorhinal cortex, remain constant as rats moved from one room to another. The place cells, located in the hippocampus, created a distinctive map for each room. Rats' memories, and ours, encode experiences with the place at which they occurred, just as many digital cameras and smartphones can record the coordinates of an image. This helps explain, for example, why we remember just where we were when we heard historic news, such as the assassination of John F. Kennedy or the attacks of September 11, and personal tragedies and joys as well. The Mosers believe that it is this dual system that makes the method of loci so effective.[4]

While human beings have an inherited locational sense, they have added a precious capability, cumulative development of skills—including perceptual techniques—over generations, by teaching and learning. Other species make tools; some may even use tools to make other tools. Primates and some parrots can solve complex puzzles. What is unique to people is the ability to develop, transmit, and refine our skills, including geographic knowledge. Pedagogy lets us ratchet our scope and abilities cumulatively from one generation to the next,

as the anthropologists David and Ann James Premack have suggested.
And people also have a capacity for planned exploration that at least
so far is not known in other species.[5]

The most impressive wayfinding was developed centuries before
European contact by those outstanding explorers, the peoples of the
Pacific Islands, at a time when mariners of the ancient Mediterranean remained within sight of the shore whenever possible. Most of
the Polynesians' voyages were also short, but they developed canoes
capable of traveling hundreds of miles. Each people had its own combination of methods. Together these comprised not just dead reck-
oning (calculation of a position from an initial reference point) but
observations of the sun, stars, currents, waves, atmospheric cycles,
movements of birds and fish, winds, and even odors. Polynesians'
knowledge of wind patterns enabled something like the slingshot
technique of NASA satellites, which use the orbits of the moon and
one planet after another to propel themselves farther into space. The
Polynesians' was the most energetically efficient travel mode imagin-
able, powered only by wind and currents with the occasional human
assistance. But it was not efficient in the same way that a dedicated
GPS device would be today. Teaching and learning navigation was
a time-consuming education relying on arrangements of sticks and
objects and lines in the sand rather than prepared maps and charts.
Aspiring navigators had to memorize hundreds of stars, distinguishing the useful ones from the rest. In a hierarchical, male-dominated
society, navigation was an elite craft. So it is no surprise that with
European conquest, skills and knowledge were lost among many
peoples, but not entirely. Polynesian and Micronesian men remained
some of the world's most enthusiastic and adept sailors as late as the
nineteenth century, traveling up to a thousand miles and for a year
or two in the spirit of exploration, and openly disdaining European
sailors intruding in their cumbersome vessels. In the twentieth century a New Zealand physician, Peter Lewis, learned some of the techniques and led a movement of indigenous navigators who revived
their study and instruction. By 1976 an American anthropologist, Ben
Finney, could find a Polynesian navigator who sailed a replica of an
eighteenth-century double-hulled canoe 2,700 miles from Hawaii to
Tahiti entirely with ancient techniques.[6]

The point is not some exceptional faculty of the South Pacific peoples, remarkable though their methods are, but the human ability to cultivate our capacity to memorize and guide ourselves by landmarks and environmental signs. The peoples of Europe, the Middle East, and Asia also developed ingenious forms of orientation. The Phoenicians' astronomy let them cross the Mediterranean regularly without keeping the coast in sight and even, according to Herodotus, may have enabled them to navigate from the Gulf of Arabia around Africa and through the Pillars of Hercules on behalf of Pharaoh Necho II of Egypt. (The founder of history and geography was not entirely convinced, but he found the claim at least plausible.) Vikings tracked the sun and may have exploited the polarization of sunlight in the frequent cloudy weather to explore the North Atlantic. The Inuit have established a network of trails using visual clues to connect their scattered settlements with each other and with hunting and fishing grounds in the Arctic. The writer Bruce Chatwin made the songlines of Australian Aborigines world famous. Peoples as different and distant as Lapps, Bedouins, and Navajo mastered the landmarks of their surroundings. Generally having no need for written maps of their own, indigenous peoples drew the very first maps for conquering Europeans, who sadly showed little gratitude. Only in the twentieth century did anthropologists begin to understand the sophistication of pre-contact wayfinding.[7]

Traditional wayfinding skills are obviously no substitute for contemporary maps, but they are also more than quaint survivals, and urban people can learn from them to value and develop their own wayfinding abilities. The anthropologist Claudio Aporta and the environmental scientist Eric S. Higgs have studied the geographical techniques of Inuit hunters, which traditionally have included "wind behavior, snowdrift patterns, animal behavior, tidal cycles, currents, and astronomical phenomena"—a deep understanding of their surroundings that may be efficient in needing no costly instruments but has a price in the years of training it takes to master using all of them together. Unsurprisingly, younger Inuit have been turning increasingly to global positioning, but the cautious reception by their elders is illuminating. The Inuit are pragmatic about new technology and have embraced the snowmobile despite the dependence this technology demands on outside sources of fuel and parts. They also see the value of GPS; using it, Aporta and a local young man were able to locate a lost snowmobile whose last location had been correctly logged. The snowmobile, while more efficient in time per mile and in human effort if not more environmentally sustainable than the dogsled, does have consequences for learning about the environment. Its speed makes it more difficult for experienced travelers to explain natural features to the young.[8]

After accurate signals became available to the public in 2000, the Inuit among whom Aporta did his fieldwork were able to buy moderately priced receivers, and Canadian organizations taught their use. GPS lived up to its promise to make traditional life more efficient, especially in the snowmobile era. On a walrus hunt, for example, it was possible to use visual techniques including animal tracks to return to a settlement even during bad weather, but using a snowmobile, errors and circling could waste precious gasoline. Even under normal conditions, GPS makes it possible to travel between two points in as straight a line as possible. Yet the same elders who had welcomed snowmobiles had reservations on the new navigational technology— doubts that are relevant even to motorists in temperate landscapes.

Experienced Inuit hunters saw the value of GPS, especially in a fog when they might otherwise have to wait until normal visibility returned. GPS was even more effective when combined with their local knowledge of ice patterns and shorelines; experienced hunters could sometimes save time if they did not attempt to follow the GPS reading precisely, knowing that ice might be obstructing the most direct path. One elder remembered a search for an overdue traveler. The GPS, he recalled, indicated a certain place, but the direct route it provided covered potentially hazardous and disorienting territory in which the search party might have been delayed. Without traditional knowledge, the traveler might have been at risk. And there is the additional hazard that batteries may be exhausted, receivers may malfunction, or there may be interference with signals. Ancient way-finding remains technological insurance, yet there is no compelling reason for the young to learn it.

·   ·   ·

Deskilling and loss of environmental perception are concerns not only for indigenous societies renegotiating their relationship with national and global economies. They concern almost all of us.

The best-known problems of highway GPS are far more glaring than the inability of the Inuit GPS to correct for terrain. In principle it would be possible to use geographic databases that worked around possibly hazardous features like pressure ridges; the market is obviously too small. For the motorist in more densely populated territory, the risk is different. It is that the efficiency of the GPS can induce uncritical obedience to its directions. To begin with, place names have evolved with little consideration for possible confusion. The U.S. has both Washington State and Washington, D.C.; New Mexico has not been part of Mexico for ages, yet some mail is still misdirected to near-namesakes. London has at least two Abbey Roads, ten miles apart. Even a community as small as my local Princeton, New Jersey, has both an Olden Street (on which most of Princeton University's engineering buildings are located) and an Olden Lane (which terminates in the campus of the Institute for Advanced Study three miles away on the other side of town). Mergers of municipalities as large as London's and as small as Princeton's—there was until recently a separate inner Borough and outer Township—have created the confusion. But it's also possible to mix up far-off destinations. Sometimes this happens to the culturally disoriented, like the Syrian truck driver who went 1,600 miles out of his way to a place called Gibraltar, England, rather than to the more familiar rock at the gateway to the Mediterranean. And confusions are also possible even for elite local residents. A taxi driver took a teenage daughter of Lord Spencer over two hundred miles in the wrong direction by choosing a Yorkshire town rather than a London soccer stadium when entering his destination.[9]

This episode, reported globally to the Spencer family's chagrin, was doubly revealing. It was not only that a dispatcher failed to notice the error. It's not unusual for double-checks to fail; serious errors usually result from independent problems with multiple safeguards. What makes this incident so telling is that a professional driver evidently overlooked the wrong direction for more than a hundred miles, despite the absence of road signs with his destination. An

Inuit hunter has to be conscious of as many topographic details as possible, whether or not using GPS. But young Westerners may be losing their awareness of landscape. A journey can easily become a voyage through a tunnel, especially when a passenger today has the option of paying attention to a mobile device rather than to his or her surroundings. For drivers and passengers alike, the consequences of attention to GPS rather than actual road conditions can be hazardous. In 2008, a British insurance company estimated that GPS errors had caused 300,000 car crashes, and 1.5 million readers of one tabloid reported experiencing a dangerous traffic situation as a result of faulty GPS guidance. This does not mean that GPS has been a net loss; it is hard to say how many serious navigational errors and even accidents have been prevented by GPS. But it does point to an issue described by the writer Ari N. Schulman from his own experiences in Boston and Washington, D.C. Especially in cities with non-grid street layouts, the turn-by-turn instructions of GPS compete for the driver's attention with signs (especially temporary ones not incorporated in the base map information), attention to pedestrians and cyclists, road surface conditions, and the many other variables with which a city confronts unfamiliar and even longtime drivers. As Schulman says, it is a challenging form of multitasking. And in cities the slight time lag of two seconds imposes an additional stress on the wayfinding brain.[10]

Fortunately, industrial and post-industrial society have had a laboratory of extreme geographic knowledge for over 150 years: the London taxi driver examination, which requires being able to describe a trip turn by turn between any two points in a network of 25,000 streets. Dating to the days of horse-drawn cabs, it reflects not just the duplication and similarity of names like Abbey Road, but also the complex topography resulting from centuries of patchworks of private landownership that resisted plans for radical redevelopment like the demolitions wrought by Baron Haussmann in Paris to create the city's boulevards in the 1850s. London has also grown by absorbing many of its suburbs. More recent designation of one-way streets complicates routes still further. "Doing the Knowledge"—as preparing for the examination is called—means spending about three years developing the kind of familiarity with urban terrain that hunter-gatherers learn in their own environments. The foundation is, significantly, not the study of maps alone but thousands of miles of runs on motor scooters, internalizing street names, landmarks, and road conditions within a six-mile radius of Charing Cross. Cabbies, like hunter-gatherers, need to draw on all their senses. Just as the navigators of the South Pacific learn the winds and currents, taxi drivers must have a mental model of traffic patterns to find alternative routes if necessary. Months of exercises using laminated maps in specialized schools follow; training takes two years or more. The metropolis with all its points of interest becomes a memory palace in its own right for the trained driver, but a dynamic one.[11]

Brain scanning has revealed that the memory palace actually has an anatomical counterpart. The neuroscientist Eleanor Maguire has shown that taxi drivers who passed their examinations shared an enlargement of a part of the brain, the posterior hippocampus, associated with memory in some nonhuman animals, for example, in squirrels that cache food for the winter. There may be a price for this adaptation; the other, anterior, part of the hippocampus was somewhat smaller in these drivers, and the difference may affect performance in other memory tasks. Their baked-in mental maps may also make it more difficult for them to learn changes in London's road system. But the main lesson of the Knowledge may be that without extensive formal education, at least many people have the capacity to deepen their sense of their environment, to know the way without consciously thinking about it or knowing how they know it. They are like outstanding physical athletes, whose exceptional skills have encouraged others.[12]

According to Silicon Valley values, the Knowledge, the drivers who spend years mastering it, the examination system, and London's traditional black cabs (which have helped keep the oldest Knowledge school from a threatened closing) are archaic, monopolistic vestiges preserved by outmoded laws. With GPS, ride-sharing apps, and autonomous vehicles—which we will consider later—there is no more need for an elite certification system. The Knowledge examiners represent everything that the technology industry aspires to disrupt in the name of greater efficiency. But there are also implications for those who do not seek an encyclopedic visual memory of their cities or regions. Memory is not just a passive databank that can be outsourced but a means of interacting with the world.

The commonsense, moderate position on technological assists—"they're only tools"—does not tell the whole story. There have always been people who deny that even typewriters are mere tools, who believe that they lead to less precise thinking, and that computers are even worse. One of the world's most distinguished mathematical physicists, Clifford Truesdell, whose work deeply influenced engineering, abjured even fountain pens, writing with quills instead, though he had no objection to such domestic amenities as air-conditioning. But while typewriters and computers have done no noticeable damage to physics or the humanities, GPS in excess may be harmful to our mental health. It's often too easy for the user to become the tool. Since GPS can be easily disabled with devices readily available on the web, and environmental and technical risks also exist, governments have been concerned about the ability of navigators to work with older means. The U.K.'s Royal Academy of Engineering conducted a test that concluded:

> People are conditioned to expect excellent GPS performance. As a result, when ships' crews or shore staff fail to recognise that the GPS service is being interfered with and/or there is a loss of familiarity with alternative methods of navigation or situational awareness, GPS service denial may make a significant impact on safety and security.

Significantly, confusion and repeated false alarms occurred even when the crew of the test ship had been informed in advance that failure would be simulated.[13]

A Canadian neuroscientist, Veronique Bohbot, has been studying the impact of GPS dependence on land-based wayfinding. While there is no evidence that heavy use of GPS depresses general intelligence, users' powers of orientation clearly suffer. The journalist Leon Neyfakh, who interviewed her, recalled his own experience after moving to Boston. With its agglomeration of communities mostly dating to the colonial era, the area is more similar to London than to any other U.S. city, though without anything like London's elite black taxi corps. Relying on the voice-synthesized turn-by-turn directions on his smartphone, Neyfakh was able to commute error-free to his office, but he soon realized that he had not learned anything about Boston's topography. Bohbot's work showed that following such directions, whether or not from electronic prompts, does not help us develop a clear mental representation of our surroundings. This was confirmed from a different perspective by the English engineering professor Gary Burnett, who found that subjects who had only followed directional cues tested significantly worse in their memories of their paths than those who had used conventional paper maps. The GPS-style method was originally more efficient. Subjects who used it made fewer mistakes. But in the long run, learning from their inefficiency made them more efficient in navigating their surroundings.[14]

The consequences of widespread GPS use have alarmed even some experts in the technology. Roger McKinlay, a consultant in communication and navigation satellites and a former president of the Royal Institute of Navigation, warned in *Nature* in 2016 that flaws in GPS systems were leading to serious errors and that major upgrades to those systems were needed—dramatized by a red lorry that got stuck in a narrow alley between two houses after following GPS directions. McKinlay emphasized that even with improvements there was no substitute for human wayfinding and the need to exercise it regularly.[15]

It would be plausible to assume that young adults are eschewing printed maps, despite these advantages, for the convenience of GPS. Evidence is mixed. American Millennials actually appear to be competent map readers, according to at least one test. Attitudes seem different in the United Kingdom. One British survey found that 80 percent of people between the ages of eighteen and thirty admitted they could not navigate without GPS. Another, focusing on young people, found that while they recognize the periodic unreliability of satellite navigation and agree with critics that reliance on it degrades wayfinding skills, they do not regard GPS data as maps at all and have little interest in learning to use paper maps. There is a certain logic behind this attitude. A textbook needs to be understood as a whole to master a course and pass an examination; a map does not, except for taxi-driver candidates in some jurisdictions. As I've traveled with both paper maps from many publishers and GPS, I've been struck by how each genre and each map publisher has its own strengths and weaknesses. On a business trip to western Virginia I used a smartphone app, a road atlas, and AAA city maps. I found them complementary. The "Western Washington, D.C." city map showed me the location of a suburban restaurant I was looking for but would have been almost useless in finding my way through a maze of interstates, arterial roads, and local streets at night. The app took me exactly where I wanted to go and helped me find a service station in the suburban thicket, but was not helpful in understanding just where I was on my journey. And the road atlas let me plan the whole trip and check my progress and get a sense of the landscape. The beauty of maps is that each technology and each design has its own trade-offs.[16]

There are stunning benefits in the accuracy of GPS, not least in public health. Many people who make emergency calls are not able to give a location—especially if there is no street address or landmark in sight—and are sometimes too seriously injured to speak. One of the original reasons for making correct signals available to the public was aiding police, fire, and rescue services. And it has made these more efficient. At the same time, it has created new problems for them. They arise not in everyday highway and urban situations but off the road in recreation, and the problems remind us of the Inuit elders' caveats. Some hikers and climbers may use smartphones or other dedicated devices, but neither can take the place of map-reading literacy in an emergency, according to climbing experts. Gavin Raubenheimer, a globally experienced South African mountaineering guide and rescue organizer, has observed that more people than ever are getting lost because even with maps they are not able to use GPS to orient themselves in the terrain. They know where they are, but they have not acquired the skill of converting the contour lines and trails on printed maps into actual routes back to safety. Raubenheimer once experimented with a mountain bicycle ride by two groups, one with GPS and the other (his) with map and compass. The GPS cyclists had difficulty understanding the approaching terrain with their devices; the map readers could discern the trails and roads ahead, just as Inuit hunters could do using only their traditional skills. The GPS cyclists finally decided to follow the map-and-compass group. The big picture turned out to be more efficient.[17]

Cell phones, GPS, and beacons have saved lives, but the sense of security they bring in the absence of training and navigation skills has been an issue for rescue services. Greg Milner, in his excellent book *Pinpoint*, has noted that Death Valley National Park rangers have a phrase for technology-driven misadventures, "death by GPS." Unlike printed maps, even dedicated units do not give warnings about rising elevations, slowly deteriorating road conditions, and other hazards, making the shortest distance between two points often the riskiest. In Idaho in 2011, the Canadian couple Albert and Rita Chretien, feeling confident in their new GPS on their way to Las Vegas, decided to try what they thought would be a more direct shortcut through Nevada. The route chosen by the GPS was an initially well-kept side road that unfortunately slowly rose to over a mile above sea level. Unable to turn around, their van—not designed for off-road driving—was immobilized in a muddy gully. Albert died trying to use the GPS on foot to get help; the battery probably had run out. Rita miraculously survived on a small food supply and creek water for almost two months. (Three outdoor enthusiasts in all-terrain vehicles discovered her, severely weakened, by chance while looking for elk antlers.)[18]

About the time of the Chretien tragedy, smartphones were already starting to take the place of dedicated GPS for many consumers, especially those whose vehicles do not have factory-installed systems. Inherently, cell phone navigation can be a lifeline, but it is too often a first rather than a last resort. Instead of keeping the phone in a backpack for emergencies as public safety officials advise, hikers are taking additional risks by keeping them on, even climbing to higher elevations under stress to get a signal rather than sitting still to await rescue after calling 911, as emergency services urge. A major in the New Hampshire Fish and Game Department told a *Boston Globe* reporter that he seldom saw hikers using map and compass anymore. Inexperienced hikers often do not realize that not just GPS but text and voice transmission can be weak in mountains. In extreme cases a search for higher ground to send a signal can contribute to fatalities. Only a few years after the Chretiens' misadventure, a disoriented retired nurse from Tennessee, Geraldine Largay, became lost after briefly leaving a remote Maine section of the Appalachian Trail, a heavily forested region that the navy uses for survival training. Her text messages were never received. She had a compass but did not know how to use it, according to the Maine Warden Service. The area was so remote that the woman's body was not found for two years, along with her diary of a month of attempts to get rescuers' attention. Largay's death may have been brought about in part by her belief in the availability of text messaging; she thought she had contacted her husband, who was resupplying her from towns along the trail. Learning orientation skills may have seemed unnecessary.[19]

The issues of GPS for safety and efficiency extend beyond casual hikers and climbers to professionals. For them the risk is not failure to learn skills—they are examined on them regularly—but the ability to respond rapidly when automated systems fail or malfunction. While civil aviation in general is safer than it has ever been thanks to sophisticated autopilot systems that can even alter course for weather or other unusual conditions, the rare crashes are all the more disturbing because most are preventable. Many aviation safety experts believe that despite rigorous original training, pilots do not get enough practice in sudden shifts from automatic to manual control. The basis of elite performance, whether in military operations or in athletics, has always been repeating actions so often that the correct response becomes automatic. The better and more reliable autopilot has become, the fewer the opportunities for such practice in actual flying. This has been a recurring issue ever since the loss of Air France 447 in the South Atlantic on June 1, 2009, when pilots were unable to recover control after icing of a crucial airspeed detection component transferred management of the highly automated Airbus A330 to the crew. The underlying issue—icing that disabled airspeed monitoring instruments called pitot tubes—was not inherently grave. And the technical failure had nothing to do with the plane's navigation systems as such. But the crash illustrates the psychology that makes all electronic control potentially hazardous. Often the most sophisticated and reliable systems pose the greatest danger because—like geolocation units—they are so complex that they give ambiguous clues about how to proceed when they malfunction. One leading analyst of engineering systems, John Doyle, has called such technology "robust-but-fragile." Its very success makes it possible for a small failure to cascade when it does occur. The Air France 447 pilots might have been able to fly by instruments alone if properly trained, but they were distracted by a series of confusing alarms and did not notice that their climb was putting the plane into a fatal stall.[20]

The greatest challenge of all to efficient navigation may be at sea. The reasons are apparent. First, apart from coastal trades and short ferry rides, the greater part of most ocean voyages and many on large freshwater seas like the Great Lakes occur out of sight of the shoreline and in the absence of buoys and lighthouses. Second, compared to highway and rail transportation and aviation, government supervision of oceangoing ships is spotty, many ships being registered outside their real home ports for tax reasons and crewed by citizens of a variety of national jurisdictions. Third, fog (dangerous enough to highway traffic) has long been a menace at sea; for contemporaries, the *Titanic* at her launch seemed a marvel of safety not only for her watertight compartments but for her advanced sound detection system. Sea ice was considered a lesser hazard, but when visibility was lost, captains stationed themselves in a special "fog chair" and maintained white-knuckle alertness. Fourth, the cyclical and risky financial environment of global shipping encourages owners to be risk takers, and national rivalries sometimes impede safety agreements. Fortunately, the shipwreck rate has declined from one ship lost each day when the sociologist Charles Perrow originally published his classic *Normal Accidents* in 1984 to fewer than half that number in 2016, but the high seas are still a throwback to buccaneering nineteenth-century entrepreneurship. In 2015, *The New York Times* even ran a series, "The Outlaw Ocean," on chaotic and exploitive conditions at sea. Perrow calls marine transport "an error-inducing system." There is no counterpart to the North American wilderness's "death by GPS" at sea, yet location systems do have common weaknesses. Radar, for example, encourages captains to order higher speed, yet as with travelers, their conduct under stress is sometimes mysteriously perverse. While radar gives ships, even in fog, a clear sense of other vessels in their neighborhood and ample time to avoid them, and while there are clear rules for such encounters, marine experts have long recognized the "radar-assisted collision," in which two ships converge despite all safeguards. According to a report later published by the U.S. National Academy of Sciences, newer location technologies like integrated charts have not changed the problem. Bad decisions at sea have much in common with those of GPS-equipped motorists. Each can become so reliant on the technological aid that its information (and new systems provide ever more of it) can interfere with perception of actual surroundings. In the absence of strong visual clues, and with the most advanced navigational apparatus, even nuclear submarines of the European allies France and the United Kingdom collided (although without serious damage) as recently as 2009.[21]

The sinking of one of the Mediterranean's largest cruise ships, the *Costa Concordia*, in 2012 showed how electronic navigation could—like conventional radar before it—make navigation riskier. The ship was only three hundred meters from the shore of an island where it was supposed to pass in a traditional salute when it struck a rock and sank, killing thirty-two passengers. As is often the case in disasters, there were multiple failures—especially of lifeboat evacuation as the ship listed—and the captain was sentenced to a sixteen-year prison term for manslaughter and other offenses. But the technology was also caught up in an organizational failure. The *Costa Concordia* had a required modern Electronic Chart Display and Information System (ECDIS) that tracked the ship's position against a digitized database of charts. Investigation revealed, however, that the underlying data of such systems may have been transferred from decades-old paper documents. ECDIS systems are designed to sound audible alarms when maneuvers take them into hazardous conditions. In some cases there are so many alarms that officers switch the system off, false positives being a side effect of efficient safety systems. (We will see this again in Chapter Five on medicine.) The result of this deliberate interruption resembled that of the Air France 447 crew during its autopilot's weather-related switch to manual mode: confusion among the crew. In the *Costa Concordia*'s case, the presence of multiple nationalities and the owner's alleged neglect of onboard training compounded the captain's mismanagement. And the point of the *Costa Concordia* is that digital equipment like ECDIS and the more advanced navigation systems now available depend on the analog skills of officers and crew working with paper charts and with direct observation. As in education, digital and analog are complementary, not antagonistic.[22]

The above lessons of flying and of seafaring bear directly on driving. Both the improved accuracy of GPS and its occasional spectacular failures appear to point to a new transportation paradigm, self-driving vehicles. Despite decades of school driver programs—which tend to increase the number of accidents by getting young motorists on the road sooner—and public service announcements by police forces, insurers, and motorist associations, the public's technical understanding of driving, and its level of skill, are remarkably low. I realized this when I spoke at a meeting of safety engineers and had a chance to hear professionals and even to try out a state-of-the-art driving simulator. I discovered that while corporate safety directors did not neglect what the public supposes to be their responsibility—equipment and training for hazardous jobs like maintaining shade trees with chainsaws and other potentially lethal equipment—much of their attention goes to road safety. The trip to and from the job can be more dangerous than the work itself. Charles Perrow has observed that even though fighter pilots have a nearly one-in-four chance of dying in peacetime flights in a twenty-year career, more of them die in automobile accidents just because of the many more hours they spend driving than flying. The U.S. military pays special attention to road safety programs; the air force has received a commendation for its "Alive at 25" defensive driving campaign for young service members.[23]

The risks of distracted driving, especially talking and texting on the road, are well known. Speakerphone conversations are legal almost everywhere in the U.S., even though research has shown them to be comparable in distraction to handheld calls. Severe laws have had limited success in reducing texting while driving, which can be even more distracting. But some of the most serious issues in road safety have little to do directly with new technology. The majority of drivers still do not consistently observe the two- to three-second following distance (or one car length per ten miles per hour) recommended by safety professionals. Yet as one of the other speakers at the safety engineering conference pointed out in his presentation, drivers' motivation for following too close is based on a misperception. They consider it "an insult to their manhood or womanhood," as the physicist and automotive safety expert Leonard Evans puts it, when another car passes them and cuts ahead. But according to the speaker, these drivers' mathematics are all wrong. Keeping a safe speed and a safe distance and letting others cut in has an almost imperceptible effect on the time needed for a journey, two seconds per occurrence according to Evans, or a total of a minute or two at most in an hour-long trip. Falling behind is only an illusion.[24]

I also learned what I never was told in my own driving lessons, how to adjust side mirrors to virtually eliminate the blind spots that are one of the longest-running problems in automotive safety design. The speaker showed how it is possible to align the side mirrors so that a car passing on the left begins to be visible in a side mirror as soon as it no longer appears in the rearview mirror. Until this happens the mirrors may seem to show nothing, but the image is there when it is really needed. Once in the simulator I realized how attentive a good driver needs to be, constantly scanning those mirrors, looking both ways when approaching intersections, and being alert for the unexpected entry of children and pets into the roadway. I had new respect for driving as a high-concentration task. At the same time, I understood how fatiguing it might be to keep up this attention on a long trip. And while we are warned about using smartphones and tablets, research also shows that even talking with passengers and listening to music may degrade performance slightly.

A recent generation of driver assists has been directed at common risks. Many automobiles now have lane departure warnings that issue a series of loud beeps when the car drifts across a line, potentially saving the lives of drowsy or daydreaming motorists and those around them. There are also blind-spot warnings, and automatic braking for pedestrians and other hazards as a backup. Yet with each new safety feature, the paradox of the road becomes more clear. Especially on congested roads, the driver is in a kind of pipeline, being carried along with the flow and unable to escape or affect its course, sometimes subject to mysterious jams caused by nothing more than a form of fluid dynamics once density passes a threshold. Trying to maintain a buffer zone around the car as a kind of air cushion, as some defensive driving authorities advise, means constantly being overtaken by sometimes hostile fellow drivers. While some trucks have proximity sensors to signal following too closely, the technology has reached few automobiles, and unlike their German counterparts, who can levy $450 fines for following too closely, U.S. highway police rarely ticket for tailgating despite a high rate of deaths from rear-end collisions. And in city driving, as Ari Schulman discovered, a combination of voice instructions, GPS or smartphone screen, and urban street conditions can be more stressful than driving without navigational devices.[25]

The self-driving vehicle is thus the outcome of trends long predating civilian global positioning; for example, the automatic transmission, which removed decisions about shift points. In 2017 an average new car had 100 million lines of code, more than twice the complexity of the Large Hadron Collider at CERN with which the Higgs boson was detected. With navigation and entertainment systems sharing an interface, with smooth automatic transmissions that often allow better mileage than remaining manual models, and with adaptive cruise control that not only maintains speed but automatically slows down when approaching vehicles ahead, the act of driving itself begins to seem anachronistic. Turning full operation over to the machine becomes an attractive alternative, even if the American driver's hallowed assumption that it is no crime to drive eight miles or so over any speed limit is abandoned to more literal controls. Why should the automobile not become the chauffeur? In the test phase, self-driving cars have a safety record superior to that of the average driver, but not radically so. In February 2016, Google had to acknowledge that one of its self-driving cars was at least partly responsible for a minor collision; there had been 17 accidents per 1.3 million miles Google's fleet had driven since 2009. This was actually higher than the official human driver rate of 0.38 reported accidents per 100,000 miles with property damage, but perhaps equal when unreported conventional minor accidents are taken into account. Autonomous cars are thus already comparable in safety to human drivers. Their sensors and algorithms can recognize even exceptional conditions, like police officers' hand-directing traffic. So isn't it more efficient for the car to take over? Isn't that where GPS has been leading us all along? Whether or not the founders of the transportation companies Uber and Lyft originally planned complete automation, they seem on the way to replace many human drivers with fully automated cars.[26]

There is an asterisk in Google's statistics. There probably would have been significantly more accidents if the human occupants of Google's cars had not been prompted by the system to take control—272 times in slightly more than one year, plus another 69 incidents in which the human driver switched to manual operation, preventing an accident (in his or her judgment) in 13 of those cases. The enthusiast owner of a luxury all-electric vehicle was killed while operating it in what the maker, Tesla, called Autopilot mode, with hands off the steering wheel. Tesla management said that despite the name, directions clearly warned against this practice, and announced that future software versions would not permit hands-free operation.[27]

The future of the self-driving car is a crux of algorithmic efficiency. On the side of its inevitability is the power of machine learning, the ability of programs to learn as people do from exposure to countless variations of objects in their surroundings until they are able to recognize, for example, dogs and cats. The achievement of mastery at Go, mentioned earlier, is one mark of the power of algorithms. On the other side is the ubiquity of bugs in all programs. Security experts estimate that 1,000 lines of software code contain between 15 and 50 defects; in the next decade, automobiles may have up to 200 million lines of code. The environment in which vehicles operate is also constantly changing, and the program probably can never include all possible configurations of vehicles, pedestrians, cyclists, and weather conditions. The Tesla fatality, for example, occurred with a white truck of certain dimensions that may not have been perceived accurately as such; Tesla and the supplier of its cameras and video processors, Mobileye, broke off their partnership amid disagreements about the cause of the accident. The paradox of efficiency, as in the other navigation systems we have seen, is that the smoother automatic loco-motion becomes, the rarer the need for user intervention will be. But this hands-off capability in turn will give drivers fewer opportunities to practice emergency skills, so that their efficiency as operators will decline and may not be adequate when electronic guidance fails.[28]

If drivers need to rely less and less often on their own judgment, if autonomous operation becomes a norm, dilemmas are likely to follow. When should automatic systems allow drivers to take over operations? If automobiles are designed as electronic entertainment cocoons rather than windows on their surroundings, detachment of drivers from the road might make it seem inadvisable to let them take over when equipment seems to be malfunctioning. Both permission and denial risk disaster.[29]

There are three other caveats to the apparent efficiency of self-driving automobiles. One is the extent of constant human interven-tion in the software. David A. Mindell, a professor of aeronautical and astronautical engineering and of the history of technology and manu-facturing, has underscored how cluttered the software of self-driving cars is with the fixes that engineers have made, adjusting thresholds for distinguishing signals from noise and adding countless fudge fac-tors. Under the hood, the vision of a self-correcting machine learn-ing turns out to be closer to the patchwork familiar to the users of desktop computer operating systems. One difference is that automo-tive guidance software must respond to an ever-changing landscape and unpredictable reactions of human drivers—or even of other mak-ers' algorithms. Seemingly autonomous code may be really, Mindell observes, "deeply humanly crafted."[30]

A second caveat might be called the democratization of local knowledge. If we have lived for a year or two in a place, we know how to avoid bottlenecks and use shortcuts. Some GPS receivers and apps are able to mimic this hard-won experience by real-time reporting of traffic. This can indeed help us use the capacity of the road sys-tem more efficiently. With time, motorists in congested areas learn that some back roads can be more efficient at peak hours—or even off-peak—than the highways designated by GPS and services like MapQuest and Google Maps. When these are suburban streets, occa-sional commuters were usually a small annoyance. A printed guide to Los Angeles road shortcuts published in 1990 led only to revision of some traffic signs and a ticketing offensive by police. All this changed when Google acquired an Israeli start-up called Waze. Waze began as an idealistic project to share road information freely via smartphones without paying the annual subscription fee that many commercial GPS makers charged for traffic updates. Acquired by Google in 2013, Waze is integrated with Google's base maps and now appears to fill the local-knowledge gap with both user-contributed information and data on actual user driving times. It may be the ultimate application of the collaborative web, with over twenty million users worldwide in 2015. On its face, Waze embodies the best of radical efficiency: getting full use out of the existing road grid rather than building additional highways, saving fuel, even automatically updating the lowest prices en route, and promoting carpooling and shared rides. The reality is more complex. Traffic does not necessarily flow smoothly through the so-called shortcuts. It is often congested and backed up. Google rightly points out that drivers have a legal right to use the public roads, yet once enough people pool their data to achieve new efficiency, they frustrate each other as well as the businesspeople and homeowners on their routes. Some of the residents vent their frustration by lying to Waze about construction and accidents in their neighborhoods. Google in turn tries to screen these out with new algorithms.[31]

As a Waze user since early 2017, I have not found any such controversy, at least in congested central New Jersey. I have received important safety warnings, especially regarding potholes, and contributed a few of my own. It is gratifying to be thanked by fellow Wazers. However, the Google Maps base data are in places seriously flawed. Taking a usual route, I was unexpectedly prompted to enter a warehouse complex I had not previously visited. Complying out of curiosity, I came to a busy intersection with not only a no-left-turn sign, but a triangular island all but preventing the turn. Waze prompted me to turn left anyway. Worst of all, when I tried to edit the map online, I found I did not have such privileges yet. Waze also sometimes tempts drivers with the distraction of entering information. Further, the program does not appear to learn a driver's preferred route automatically, though it occasionally shows glimmers of empathy. It mistakes my home location by the equivalent of a city block.

My own experience with GPS suggests that the extremely detailed maps needed for autonomous or even semiautonomous navigation will take years and much human labor to produce, and because of inevitable changes will never be completely up-to-date. There are four million miles of roads in the United States, and they all will have to be mapped to a tolerance of four inches, an order of magnitude greater than the present accuracy of several yards. Mapping and automobile companies say that although equipment for capturing such detailed images costs $100,000 today, the vehicles of the future will compile huge image files as they are driven, data that can be built into new, super-detailed base maps. But countless details can never be gathered so efficiently—for example, houses in gated communities and on other private roads, as well as buildings in apartment complexes that do not follow conventional street numbering systems. (That is why Waze and Google Maps confuse my address.) While autonomous features can be lifesavers when fog and snow limit visibility, they have difficulty on mountain roads and in avoiding potholes and small animals.[32]

Even if conflicts over crowdsourced GPS services like Waze are settled, there is a third, social risk. The so-called ridesharing companies, Uber and Lyft, may try to persuade local authorities to hire them to replace public transportation by subsidizing individual rides; both companies are planning to convert to autonomous operation. While in principle this could replace low-traffic bus routes or supplement existing service, in practice, if left unchecked, it will probably increase the number of vehicles on the road and add to public budgets. Coupled with underinvestment in public transportation, ridesharing services actually seem to be increasing road congestion rather than reducing it, as their advocates once promised. In New York City, where surcharges on now declining yellow taxi rides helped fund the subway system, the rise of ridesharing apps has cost the Metropolitan Transit Authority $28 million since 2014. Deterioration of subway maintenance has in turn led more riders to turn to apps in a dangerous cycle of privatization. Reviewing a University of California at Davis study of transportation in American cities that confirmed the negative effects of ridesharing apps on urban life, the *New York Times* writer Emily Badger pointed out that while these services may make travel more efficient for individuals, they make public transportation less efficient for cities and can actually encourage additional trips when people give up private cars. There is also a shortage of funds to modernize outmoded subway signaling systems and replace decades-old rolling stock, even in the booming real estate markets of New York City and Washington, D.C. Conferences on the "smart" networked cities of tomorrow seem to coincide with hellish hour-long equipment breakdowns in the cities of today.[33]

In addition, Waze, Uber, and Lyft are all hostage to the fragility of both the Global Positioning System and the vehicular software that depends on it. Cheap GPS jammers have been traded openly on the web and used for years by automobile thieves thwarting tracking devices and by supervision-shy truck drivers as well. The U.S. military is sufficiently alarmed by the possibility of GPS disruption by hostile powers or terrorists that it is developing alternative geolocation networks. Jeeps and Teslas have already been hacked while in motion. Waze and similar platforms are even vulnerable to devices that can create multiple supposedly reliable data sources influential enough to distort the system's information. And nature itself may be hazardous to GPS-controlled vehicles. Seldom mentioned in journalists' encomia to autonomous cars is the growing understanding of the threat of extreme solar weather. The most extreme solar flares propel material called coronal mass ejections (CMEs) capable of disrupting satellite transmissions; in fact, one such disturbance is thought to have interrupted railroad traffic in England as early as 1841, when movement on one line was suspended briefly after telegraphic instruments went haywire. In 1967 a solar storm disabled American missile-tracking equipment, risking confrontation when the Soviet Union was initially suspected of jamming. (Fortunately, the air force's solar observatories soon disclosed the real cause.) The U.S. National Oceanic and Atmospheric Administration (NOAA) is using new satellite technology to present more detailed images of potential threats and to predict them more accurately, but prevention remains out of the question. To all these threats, the technological policies of the U.S. authorities so far have thus been contradictory. On one hand, the government repeatedly recognizes the serious risk of interruption. On the other hand, its guidelines acknowledge this but do not set clear security standards, if that is indeed possible. The "Federal Automotive Vehicles Policy" publication is a thoughtful beginning, but its summary acknowledges that it is "guidance rather than rulemaking," deferring the hardest questions. While I can offer no concrete answers either, I will argue later that the devices and software of the autonomous car movement can genuinely improve efficiency if used rightly.[34]

So far we have considered navigation and orientation, and the risks as well as the undoubted advantages of the efficiency of satellite signals and algorithms in finding our way. But more is at stake than moving from point A to point B—or even avoiding pitfalls while doing so. We have also seen how the printed map provides an understanding of a place that the electronic map—despite its flexibility and specificity—cannot. And we have seen evidence that the better a location technology is, the greater the chance that skills, essential if that technology ever fails, will be compromised.

There is still more than wayfinding to understanding both familiar and unfamiliar surroundings. We have an ability to form a total understanding of a space, richer than what can be shown on any electronic or paper map, including features that have not yet been identified as such. We may never consciously have noticed a sign on the road, yet we can tell when it has been replaced. I have noticed even the replacement of a small traffic camera at a busy intersection with a larger one, probably because I often wait at that intersection and the old style became lodged in my memory without my being able to recall it if asked. There is usually no economic payoff in noticing small things like that, except perhaps for detectives and spies. Much of what we call "sixth sense" and "street smarts" consists of unconsciously absorbing countless details and becoming alert to changes. This elusive form of knowledge is not usually associated with efficiency, but it should be, because it can alert us to opportunities as well as dangers.

A series of scholars have explored the history, sociology, politics, and aesthetics of the environment. With practice, we get to see what maps and GPS screens are unable to render: the present as a series of layers, of streets, buildings, and other features like streetlights and manhole covers that have been built up over time and that are often in the course of further evolution. For those who have learned to look, there is often a vestige, if only the foundation of a long-removed gate. While observation is essential, online resources can help us develop that way of looking. On Broadway in Washington Heights, near Manhattan's northernmost point, stands a graffiti-encrusted marble arch inset into an automobile shop, or rather, the shop was constructed without the expense of demolishing the arch. It was once the inhabited gatehouse of a magnificent hillside estate long displaced by apartment buildings. To some this will signify our disrespect (or grudging respect) for the past, to others the city's capacity for endless renewal, and to still others some grander principle in nature. But it surely helps in the business of real estate to have an understanding of such changes. They are part of an ongoing process.[35]

John Brinckerhoff Jackson, John Stilgoe, and other critics and historians of architecture and landscape have described how our familiar world was formed. But the real revolutionary in understanding American places—someone as acute in his vision as South Sea navigators and Inuit hunters—was the journalist Grady Clay. Clay came to the urban landscape during its great upheaval in the 1960s with the fresh eye of a journalist. He perceived and named phenomena hidden in plain sight, "patterns and clues waiting to be organized." Drawing on the personality theory of the psychologist George A. Kelly, he realized the world is not just something we perceive but something we construct actively in our own minds. The mental pictures that we build help us predict and change things.[36]

Clay's *Close-Up: How to Read the American City* shows us how our environment was built in layers, the typical American community taking its shape from a path along a riverfront, supplemented by parallel roads as communities grew, attracted to the river but also endangered by flooding. But it is no textbook or manual and does not pretend to be an economic or political study of urban development. Clay's book is really a call to the exercise of our visual understanding, of our ability to construct a new kind of mental map of our surroundings, something that the most advanced geographic systems alone cannot do. We all know some of them, like "gentrifying neighborhood." Others were already established planners' jargon like TOADS ("temporary, obsolete, abandoned, derelict sites"), LULUs ("locally unwanted land uses"), and Lighting Districts (downtown zones where cities, utilities, and merchants subsidize enhanced illumination to stimulate flagging sales and deter crime). Most of us have passed abandoned farms; Clay explains why they were cultivated in the first place and why it is uneconomical to resume growing (boom-and-bust price cycles). Clay also coined apt terms of his own, like Drop Zone, a liminal area of declining land values and productive wealth. Neither mainstream paper maps nor consumer electronic databases identify such areas, yet they are often the first thing a traveler notices. They are also indications of underlying political and economic challenges. How many maps or GPS systems, for example, contain codes not just for traffic volume but for road surface conditions? Not that efficient representation of data is always a good thing for society. In 2012, Microsoft patented a feature for pedestrian GPS that would warn users of high-crime areas—reinforcing racism and segregation, according to critics. The problem is that while genuinely useful for individuals, electronic mapping also reinforces stigma and can be part of a self-fulfilling prophecy. And there is a sad precedent. Federal mortgage guarantee programs of the New Deal era and their associated (paper) maps institutionalized racial discrimination in housing long before modern geographic information systems became available, beginning in the 1930s and lasting into the 1960s.[37]

Geographic discovery goes even beyond the features described by Clay and other explorers of urban and rural spaces, the edges of knowledge. A surprising portion of the world is still unmapped, according to geographers and cartographers. Whole neighborhoods of major cities in Latin America are excluded from Google Street View. Even for the United States, only a few maps are up to the highest European standards for displaying features like the elevation of cities. As the creator of some of the most acclaimed recent U.S. maps, the cartographer Dave Imus, has observed, "so many maps are difficult to understand, forcing the eye and mind to work overtime trying to perceive what it's looking at." With GPS directions, "you're no more connected with your surroundings than looking for the next turn."[38]

The limits of all representations of geographic reality bring us to the complementary skill of wayfinding, which might be called way-*losing*. Waylosing is productive and instructive disorientation, distraction, wild-goose chases, dead ends. Silicon Valley culture still glorifies profiting from failure—even if in practice resilience often demands a network of well-off friends and family members. Google Maps and Google Street View can still be used for exploration, but the Google mission statement, "organize the world's information and make it universally accessible and useful," says nothing about randomness or curiosity or the value of occasionally disorganized information. As Ari Schulman has noted, the conditioning of our expectations by representations did not begin with electronic maps or online image sharing. Even in the heyday of print, it was a challenge to visit sites like the Grand Canyon without having the experience diminished by the familiarity of guidebooks.[39]

It might not be a bad thing that GPS directions sometimes take us out of our way, but there is nothing like the "lost art of getting lost," as an often-repeated phrase puts it. Part of the enjoyment of the old-style road trip, as celebrated in books and films, was encountering people and sights that were not described on any map or in any guide. The goal of Silicon Valley seems to be creation of a personalized, dynamic, ultimate guidebook to the world. Even its definition of serendipity is another description for accessing useful existing knowledge. Consider the scenario envisioned in 2010 by Eric Schmidt, the CEO of Google, who imagines walking down the streets of a foreign city and having information searched automatically: "'Did you know? Did you know? . . . This occurred here. This occurred there.' Because it knows who I am. It knows what I care about. It knows roughly where I am." And he continues that "autonomous search—this ability to tell me things I didn't know but am probably very interested in is the next great stage . . . of search." That autonomous search can now be implemented by so-called augmented reality, the overlaying of images, video, GPS, and other information in real time on images of places as displayed by cameras on the screens of smartphones and other devices. Some applications, like the Pokémon Go game, a virtual treasure hunt for Pokémon characters, may help people get productively lost if they are not too single-minded about it. On the other hand, in their quest for the characters, players often seem riveted on the screen rather than the surroundings through which the game takes them.[40]

Old-style waylosing was different. You could misread a map or take a wrong turn; or a bridge on a carefully planned routing might be unexpectedly closed without good detour signs. Today there is almost a getting-lost industry. The art is a subject of a book by the writer Rebecca Solnit, of a conference by the New America Foundation, and of frequent articles and blog posts. Most people seem to be able to recall a productive incident. Yet being lost is not so easy. As Solnit observes, today's urban and suburban hikers and campers no longer have the same familiarity with nature and wilderness skills as nineteenth-century people who had grown up in the countryside. Getting productively lost on road trips and in cities also needs preparation—not in the sense of finding one's way back but in being able to notice unexpected features and to meet people unaccustomed to travelers. There is a special thrill in seeing something not famous in guidebooks.[41]

If travel means ticking off a bucket list of sights efficiently, getting lost can be only a distraction. But many of the most memorable sights are those unfamiliar from the books. When I was an exchange student in Heidelberg in the late 1960s, I saw the castle and other landmarks and lived in a converted patrician house in the center of town across from the historic university center. But what I remember most vividly was a side trip to have a pair of shoes repaired. It was a visit to another century, down a back alley and up a flight of stairs, where I met a small, bent, elderly man who removed the heels and saw that to save money on rubber the manufacturer had filled them with wooden inserts. I was mildly humiliated when the cobbler cackled "Ami, Ami," using the Germans' semi-insulting word for Americans, the equivalent of "Kraut"—perhaps a foretaste of the approaching decline of U.S. shoe manufacturing. Yet in writing my dissertation on nineteenth-century German history, I discovered that the shoe repairer and his little shop and the balcony in a centuries-old courtyard made the artisans I was studying much more vivid.

Waylosing is thus efficient in its inefficiency, just as conventional travel has become inefficiently efficient. There are now not only conventional guidebooks but audiotours and smartphone guides in almost all major museums. Yet the experience—like the first encounter with often-reproduced monuments like the Grand Canyon—can be anticlimactic because of saturated exposure. For centuries seeing an original work in a foreign museum was a privilege of affluent travelers who had probably seen at best a black-and-white engraving; now mass airline travel fills the great collections. The paradox is that because of crowds equipped with smartphones and digital cameras, and because of the demands of conservation and security, it can be hard to appreciate a work at close range. On the other hand, color art photography and reproduction have improved immensely; a growing number of museum collections are available freely as high-definition images online. These images are often made with lighting apparatus that would damage the objects with regular use but that is allowed for a single session. Museum website viewers can also enlarge details of objects beyond the capability of a normal magnifying glass. And as one art museum director observed to me as we toured an exhibition, younger visitors are seeing the objects only through the devices they are using to record them—even though none of these images will approach the quality achieved by the museum's professional photographers.[42]

The inefficient wanderer, on the other hand, will be using his or her time more efficiently by discovering what is less documented, or even undocumented. Those will often be the memories that persist longest. Schulman quotes the geographer Yi-Fu Tuan's comment that when we at last encounter the canonical sites, "the data of the senses are pushed under in favor of what one is taught to see." And self-driving cars would make it especially difficult to get lost. A human driver can take a turn on a hunch, can slow down in time to visit an unusual sight. It is not clear how well autonomous vehicles will be able to react to spontaneous directions. Will a traveler be able to say "pull over at the antiques shop with the red sign"? And autonomous vehicles will not have the local knowledge of taxi and limousine drivers whose personalities and interactions are wonderfully unpredictable.[43]

The Silicon Valley philosophy fails because private life cannot be run as a business, and even businesses can benefit from un-businesslike accidents. The algorithmic approach to life can be helpful because the future is often like the past, yet reality has not lost its power to surprise us in ways that enhanced reality can never anticipate.

Global Positioning Systems need not be a threat to real efficiency. The next generation, which will combine signals from land stations with those of satellites to achieve accuracy of inches rather than yards, will make devices more useful than ever. For users of maps and atlases, it is much more efficient to know coordinates instantly than to have to thumb through indexes. GPS might be abused by some hikers and climbers, but it is still a godsend for others.

One problem of Silicon Valley, as of some of its critics, is a binary outlook that appears to require a choice between old and new. This is understandable on both sides. The industry, with its high failure rate, needs a vision of change that will sweep away the old. Some opponents of technocracy, conversely, are reluctant to concede any real net benefit. A pragmatic view is to see information technology as a series of complementary layers and adding to our capabilities. It is not only Inuit elders who understand this. The United States military, which took the lead in developing satellite navigation during the Cold War, is also recognizing it. The U.S. Naval Academy, which discontinued teaching celestial navigation in 1998 after a curriculum review, restored it to the course of study in 2010. While even the present GPS is more accurate than traditional methods by orders of magnitude—sextant readings can err by a mile and a half—the risk of disrupted GPS, including defensive disabling of the system in case of enemy attack, is too great to abandon a backup capability, navy senior officers have concluded.[44]

Our challenge is to combine preindustrial wayfinding, classical printed maps, and the newest navigational technology to realize the best of each mode. The science of geography, which has studied these technological transitions, is a potentially ideal guide, but it has long faced challenges in the United States. Harvard's decision to abolish geography as a program in 1948 was the beginning of the discipline's troubles. Not that it initially seemed a great loss to the field. Harvard's program, in truth, was small, its faculty not top ranking, and its teaching (according to at least one former graduate student's account) mediocre. Harvard's president, James B. Conant, made a show of inviting an assessment by one of the giants of the field at the time, Isaiah Bowman of the Johns Hopkins University. But instead of following Bowman's recommendations to recast the department along Bowman's own lines, Conant shut it down, having played one faction against another. Conant, though a strong geography student himself in his high school days, did not believe the field was "a university subject." It was a prejudice, not a conclusion of a systematic review. But the decision—followed a few years later by the abolition of geography departments at Yale and Columbia—did lasting damage to geography's image nationally. Harvard partly reversed its decision in establishing a Center for Geographic Analysis, though not a department, in 2006.[45]

Geography has also been politically fractured from the start. Its nineteenth-century pioneers included both anarchists (the Russian prince Peter Kropotkin) and imperialists (the German founder of geopolitics and teacher of Rudolf Hess, Karl Haushofer). On a visit to Harvard, Ronald Reagan's secretary of defense, Caspar Weinberger, once called for a revival of the field. Yet some of the most influential recent Marxist thinkers have been geographers rather than sociologists or economists: David Harvey and his student Neil Smith. Geographic information systems (GIS) are among the most technologically sophisticated tools of social science, but humanistic geographers like Yi-Fu Tuan and David Lowenthal form a strong qualitative tradition. So geographers often seem to have more in common with their colleagues in economics, environmental sciences, sociology, and history than with each other. This has not helped geographic education at the pre-college or college levels. U.S. presidents have had boards of economic advisors, and some historians have suggested a council of their own. But the public seems to share Conant's stereotype, seeing the field as the description of boundaries, cities, and resources, rather than the analysis of relationships and trends. It is an old problem. "We don't do rivers and mountains anymore," a junior Harvard professor replied to Conant's fond memories of his high school days. Perhaps there should have been more old-style political geography after all; President George W. Bush, educated at Andover and Yale, confused (among other nations) Slovakia and Slovenia. Donald J. Trump, a Wharton School alumnus whose First Lady was born in Slovenia, astonished Israeli hosts and his own staff alike when he announced in Jerusalem, after a visit to Saudi Arabia, that he had "just got back from the Middle East." Paradoxically, Trump's upset Electoral College victory in the 2016 presidential election underscored the power of political maps as few recent events have.[46]

Geography, as the professional study of the spatial dimension of society and human relationships, is thus one of the best illustrations of Robert K. Merton's concept of obliteration by incorporation, cited in Chapter Three. It invigorated sister disciplines so much that they annexed much of its territory. In 1955, the University of Chicago Department of Geography made history with an ambitious published symposium volume, *Man's Role in Changing the Face of the Earth*, a landmark in environmental studies. Only twenty years later, the department, the oldest of its kind at a U.S. university, was abolished, although Chicago now once again has geography professorships and a Committee on Geographical Studies. One of the reasons for the field's rebirth is the rise of satellite imagery and geographic information systems; while traditional (and elegant) cartography was a prominent part of the French social history movement centered on the journal *Annales*, few English-speaking scholars followed in the 1960s or 1970s.[47]

This apparently discouraging situation is really an opportunity. A revival of interest in spatial literacy, from the earliest school years through graduate studies, is long overdue. And it does not have to wait for a national commission, multimillion-dollar planning grants, curricular guidelines, and the rest of the apparatus of educational change. Teaching can certainly help in spatial awareness, but the skills of wayfinding and waylosing are within everybody's reach. It begins with the family. Even a shopping trip to a supermarket can be, with a little preparation, a highly educational experience. Why are food stores located where they are? Why is produce nearly always near the entrance, and milk far from it? We are all instinctively geographers. We don't learn to navigate space efficiently. It often takes trial and error.

It is an encouraging sign that more parents are choosing to raise their children in cities. Observing the city, learning about its layout, the zones of its economic activities, its transportation, can be a visual education it itself. But suburbs—especially older ones—have stories of their own to be discovered.[48]

An ordinary automobile or bus ride can be packed with information. The automotive industry has promoted back-seat entertainment systems to keep children occupied, and there is nothing necessarily wrong with them, but children (and adults) should experience their world more and tunnel through it less. There is an in-car gaming system called Mileys with location-sensitive features. It isn't hard to imagine that GPS-equipped software could be used to help children learn more about what they are seeing on a trip, and to involve parents.[49]

There is also much to be said for lower-speed transportation. As a visitor to France, I have admired the TGV railroad lines that now travel at up to 320 km/200 miles per hour. Given airport congestion and security delays, they are often effectively faster than flying. But they change the experience of travel. When I first took a TGV, I noticed two things. First, to sustain the extra-high speeds, the lines had been cut through the countryside as directly as possible, avoiding the natural contours and roads usually paralleled by conventional railroads of the nineteenth and twentieth centuries. This is a long-standing trend. In the Princeton, New Jersey, area, the main line between New York and Philadelphia originally followed the sometimes meandering route of its predecessor, the Delaware and Raritan Canal. During the Civil War, the present, direct right-of-way was laid out to the east. A new human landscape of factories and cities grew up around it (John Stilgoe has described the landscape in his book *Metropolitan Corridor*), and enough remains to record that history. The TGV, with far fewer stops and even straighter layout than nineteenth-century express lines, loses in sightseeing efficiency what it gains in destination efficiency. The first-time traveler, trying to focus out the window at the usual distance, sees only a blur; the view has to be extended outward at least a mile or so to prevent dizziness, so contact with surroundings is partially lost. In fact, when high-speed lines are built over new and more direct rights-of-way, they are likely to blight the beauty zones that travelers most want to see. This has not always been the case. The rescued Settle–Carlisle railroad line linking England and Scotland, built at prodigious expense in funds and human life for main line service in the Victorian era, was still indirect enough to enhance rather than harm the landscape of the Yorkshire Dales, but the planned H2 high-speed train is now feared as a threat to another natural wonder, the Chilterns.[50]

In considering travel and the natural and human landscape, we see the ambiguity of the idea of efficiency. One kind is measured by the directness and speed of a trip, so that the ultimate goal may be to eliminate any sense of a journey at all. Airlines flying above the clouds, interstate highways, and high-speed railways all began to break our connections with the landscapes through which we move. The supposed utopia of watching videos in a self-navigating vehicle is the outcome of a process at least a half century old.

As we have seen, though, there is more to efficiency than directness. Systems vulnerable to natural hazards or malicious attack with no human backup can hardly be considered efficient in the long run. Technology that leaves no place for human skills, that even reflects suspicion of them, is paradoxically dependent on the prowess of fallible programmers. Technology that isolates us from the environment does not let us use our travel time to our greatest advantage.

There is still reason to be optimistic about travel. Location-based mobile computing can help us avoid its frustrations. It can be pro-serendipitous, help us search for information about our surroundings (as opposed to receiving it passively) and share our discoveries. GPS can be skill-enhancing, not deskilling, but only if we retain our ability to navigate the old-fashioned, inefficient way without it. Technology, if used rightly, can exercise our built-in GPS rather than allow it to atrophy.

THE MANAGED BODY

WHY WE ARE STILL WAITING FOR ROBODOC

In the early twenty-first century, medicine—unlike commerce, media, education, and geography—is inherently inefficient. When the stakes are life and death, or health, and when norms consider access to good care a fundamental human right (whether or not laws or practice live up to this ideal), cost-benefit analysis is severely limited. Those who deplore the sums spent on end-of-life care dare not argue for systematic euthanasia of the terminally ill. In fact, even veterinarians—who traditionally have seen putting ailing animals out of their misery as both necessary and ethical—now often suffer emotionally when they do end a nonhuman patient's life. Many animal owners now regard their pets as family members, and some are willing to pay tens of thousands of dollars out of pocket for complex procedures like reconstructive surgery.[1]

It has not always been so. A hundred years ago, progressivism was associated not with animal rights but with an attack on individual human rights in the interest of social efficiency. The racist sociologist and "social efficiency" advocate Edward Ross, whom we encountered in the Preface, was not alone. In his book *Illiberal Reformers*, the economist Thomas C. Leonard has documented how some figures once revered as paragons of modernity—from Woodrow Wilson to Virginia Woolf and D. H. Lawrence—endorsed forced sterilization and even mass euthanasia of "defectives" in the interest of prosperity and healthy future generations. So did a number of heroes of the left, like the radical economist Scott Nearing. His more conservative Yale counterpart, Irving Fisher, who made and lost a fortune as an inventor of filing-card systems, even regarded eugenics as the basis of a future religion.[2]

In the postwar years, revelations of the horrors of National Socialist killings of mental patients, as well as those of the Holocaust, discredited at least older movements for what was once openly called "racial hygiene," especially once American influence on Nazi eugenics became notorious. The decades from 1945 to the 1970s were also the peak of physician-centered medicine, as antibiotics appeared to promise a germ-free future and the Salk polio vaccine removed the most dreaded viral threat. A generation of young doctors were taught to be scientist-clinicians. A growing proportion of the middle class, including many unionized workers, was covered by health insurance. The conquest of cancer seemed within reach when President Richard Nixon signed the National Cancer Act in 1971. The popular metaphor of a war on cancer, like the war on drugs, implied that—as in the Second World War—the stakes were so high that a quick and successful conclusion outweighed economical use of resources. Medicine in general was becoming increasingly costly even allowing for inflation, but its inefficiency was implicitly thought inevitable, just as the expense and delay of litigation seemed the price of giving all parties every opportunity to make their case. In 1952 an attorney in the federal civil service and a popular legal writer, William Seagle, even provoked academic wrath with his book *Law: The Science of Inefficiency*. Only arbitrary and dictatorial bodies, like the Tudor monarchs' infamous Court of the Star Chamber, Seagle argued, have avoided the inefficient tangles of the common law.[3]

The West reached a turning point in the 1980s as voters endorsed the cost-cutting brand of efficiency that Margaret Thatcher, Ronald Reagan, and other politicians praised as "free market," under fire from progressives then and now. The U.S. private insurance industry promoted Health Maintenance Organizations that limited choice to participating doctors and hospitals agreeing to negotiated rates. Prescription costs could be controlled by restricting reimbursement according to schedules of preferred drugs and favoring generic medications. The burden of additional paperwork encouraged the consolidation of group practices.

What has happened since the 1980s falls into five categories:

1. The rise of the electronic medical record with detailed standardized procedure codes, as a key to efficient medicine, at the cost of some efficiency.
2. The exploitation of the evidence-based medicine movement by pharmaceutical manufacturers who can shape statistics to control evidence.
3. The promise of precision (personalized) medicine based on sequencing individual genomes, which potentially can save lives but also introduces new sources of inefficiency.
4. The rise of the quantified self and health monitoring devices, which in turn help make enhanced communication with health care providers possible, but may also complicate patient-provider relations.
5. The proliferation of false positives, overdiagnoses, and alarms—the result of more sophisticated tests and medical hardware—leading to caregiver fatigue, unnecessary patient stress, and sometimes adverse outcomes.

None of these technological trends is intrinsically harmful. In net results we are better off with current technology than we would have been by avoiding it. On the other hand, the nature of medicine—like that of education—makes it impossible to measure everything of value. An examination for a scientific or engineering degree can determine whether or not a candidate has mastered essential knowledge and formulas. Employers' initial satisfaction with the preparation of new professional staff, salary records, and the like, are also eminently quantifiable. Much more elusive are the qualities that make people efficient later in their careers, especially when efficiency means resolving unexpected, messy problems that don't generally appear on examinations. The point is not to disparage quantification but to understand its biases and limits.

In principle, electronic medical records have been the obvious answer to one of medicine's most glaring and sometimes fatal inefficiencies, the notoriously illegible handwriting of many physicians, and the challenge of communication among primary care doctors, specialists, nurses, and pharmacists. Well into the twentieth century, library schools taught a standardized hand for writing catalog entries on index cards. But while librarians have always strived for uniformity and legibility, physicians until recently had a professional tradition of autonomous practice that has impeded sharing. The consequences of such inefficiency have been tragic. In 1999 a U.S. Institute of Medicine report estimated that seven thousand patients in the United States died annually as a result of errors in reading prescriptions. It estimated the cost of all prescription errors at $77 billion annually. In one British survey published in 2002, fully 15 percent of medical records examined were found to be illegible. Beginning in the early 2000s, new electronic prescription systems began to replace paper documents. While an improvement, they were no panacea. According to another report of the Institute of Medicine published in 2007, issues of "usability, readability, training, and suboptimal system safeguards" continued to result in errors. One study found twenty-two distinct kinds of mistakes resulting from electronic systems.[4]

Such reservations are not arguments against new technology or for the restoration of paper. They are reminders of what we have seen about educational technology. Efficiency is difficult to implement efficiently. It takes more time, money, and failures than advocates expect. And electronic prescribing is only the beginning of a much more complex set of challenges, the electronic medical record, an idea that sounds clear enough but introduces a new real world of complications.

We can start with data entry. The electronic record is not just a word-processing-style document with some embedded test results and images but a standardized unit of an increasingly national system. To make medicine more efficient for the government agencies and private insurers who manage payments, conditions and procedures must be standardized. Rationalized medicine is managed with tables of detailed codes. These are not entirely computer-age innovations. Those who have seen Billy Wilder's masterpiece *Double Indemnity* will recall Edward G. Robinson, as the Pacific All-Risk crack claims investigator Barton Keyes, challenging his boss's attempt to portray the victim's death as a suicide, rattling off all the subcategories of suicide in his actuarial tables and pointing out that there were no cases of jumping from moving trains. In fact, statistical standardization of medicine was already almost ninety years old in 1944 when the film appeared; the government of France's Emperor Napoleon III had introduced the first such list in 1855. After repeated delays, American physicians and hospitals finally accepted the latest version of the codebook, the ICD [International Classification of Diseases]-10, in October 2015.[5]

Medical managers have welcomed the change. On the positive side, the additional training needed to learn the system is just part of the inefficiency needed to become more efficient. If all physicians could simply get on with diagnosing and treating patients, and leave the administrative details to office and hospital staff (including America's 168,000 professional medical coders in 2014), there would be little controversial about the change. Some of the categories inspired mirthful newspaper reporting and even Twitter feeds. There is not only a code for bird bites, but individual codes for species; for example, an initial medical encounter after a macaw bite. (We might wonder whether ICD-11 will further subdivide macaws into blue-and-gold, Spix's, and so forth, or consolidate the psittacine categories.) There is another for an orca attack. A few are so bizarre and even apparently physically impossible, such as burns from a flaming water ski, that they might have been pranks by fatigued code experts or perhaps dummy entries to detect copyright infringement, just as dictionary and map publishers have been known to insert bogus words and places, respectively. (In fairness to the World Health Organization, which establishes the master list, many of the categories singled out by sarcastic journalists were added by U.S. health officials, and use of the more arcane subcategories is optional.)[6]

Whatever their potential long-term benefits for the quality of care, electronic medical records (EMRs) have not made physicians more efficient in the sense that most laypeople and business managers use the term. They have not reduced administrative overhead or freed time to see patients. While there seem to be no evaluations of practice before and after EMRs' implementation, they seem to have accomplished the reverse. One study of interns at the Johns Hopkins University medical school in 2013 discovered that they were devoting only 12 percent of their time to patients and over 40 percent to computer work. Another paper, published in the *Annals of Internal Medicine* in September 2016, confirmed this impression among practicing doctors. With EMRs, it revealed, physicians spend far more time on administrative tasks than most patients realize. For every hour of direct contact, doctors spend two hours at the office filling out EMR forms and completing other paperwork. Those who kept home diaries reported one to two hours each day of additional work at home. These findings were not surprising. They confirmed a number of recent letters to medical journals and the lay press about grunt work, and supported studies of the increasing rate of medical burnout. Some senior medical administrators agree with this impression. Robert W. Brenner, the chief physician of a hospital network using EMRs, told a conference that "I've seen physicians at their wits' end, absolutely panic-stricken about how they're going to see patients and do what they have to do." Emergency room physicians may need to perform four thousand mouse clicks during a ten-hour shift, according to one study, or an average of one every ten seconds. Potential abuses compound the problem. A minority of doctors do abuse incentives. For example, in some plans that pay physicians according to the degree of risk rather than by the procedure there is a serious incidence of "upcoding," exaggerating the risk of cases for higher reimbursement. Safeguards against such practices only add to the complexity of claims and reviews. Of course, there are positive effects of electronic record-keeping, too. It can build checklists into medical practice, alerting doctors to recommendations and possible side effects, and if used wisely it can monitor quality of care, even as it also risks diminishing that quality. Since ICD-11 was still under development when this book went to press, it is difficult to say whether it will be a net gain or loss for the efficiency and the effectiveness of medicine.[7]

The increasing power of information technology in analyzing medical data and diffusing the results to professionals began in the 1990s as a means to control spending on unnecessary medications. The prospective double-blind study, in which neither investigators nor patients are aware of which doses contain the active ingredient and which are placebos, seemed to guarantee rigorous evaluation. The out-of-pocket cost of the series of animal and human tests needed to achieve approval by the U.S. Food and Drug Administration (FDA), not to mention other national and transnational authorities, has been estimated at $1.4 billion by the Tufts Center for the Study of Drug Development, an amount to which the center adds $1.2 billion in losses of other uses of that money plus additional research after the drug has been approved. (Critics of the pharmaceutical industry consider these costs inflated, but however they are defined, there seems little doubt that despite improvements in the efficiency of research tools since 2003, expenses have increased by 145 percent.)[8]

Drug regulation is inefficient even compared to other regulatory processes, and deliberately so. The chances are much higher that a new chemical will be ineffective or even harmful than that it will be a milestone in healing, so procedures have been correspondingly cautious since the early 1960s, when lax policies on preapproval testing of the sedative Thalidomide resulted in an epidemic of birth defects. Since 1962, pharmaceutical manufacturers have had to demonstrate not only the safety but the effectiveness of new drugs, with some later exceptions for the experimental treatment of terminally ill patients.[9]

While the FDA's official historical pamphlet notes the increased efficiency of electronic transmission of research data since 2000, the process still has a high price in time and money. And the development of new drugs demands especially qualified and highly paid scientists, making expenses so far impossible to reduce. As equipment becomes more sophisticated and generates more data, the results take increasing skill to analyze; efficient instruments create a demand for elite analysts. We already saw in Chapter Three that advanced online courses and individualized learning are costly to deliver for similar reasons. The economist William Baumol identified this paradox in the arts and education as well as medicine. It is commonly called Baumol's cost disease, although Baumol pointed out that the growth of overall wealth will make spending increasing proportions of GDP on health less painful than we imagine.[10]

In the 1990s, a breakthrough in pharmacology seemed on the horizon: rational drug design, using knowledge of the basic mechanism of molecular biology to create molecules targeted for specific diseases, with fewer side effects and more rapid development and testing. The movement is still alive and may yet achieve its promise. But so far, like the majority of potential efficiency breakthroughs in all fields of technology, rational drug design faces unexpected obstacles of nature, complexity that sometimes can be discovered only in trying to implement a new principle. The chemist and *Scientific American* blogger Ashutosh Jogalekar has penetratingly summarized its problems. Nature, rather than corporate greed or the patent system, makes innovation hard. It can take extensive work to determine which proteins are responsible for disease, and even once that is known, the structure of some proteins makes it difficult to design molecules that can click into place and bond to them. Even if these succeed, other proteins (especially those responsible for the spread of cancer) may adapt to take their place, just as bacteria evolve under the selective pressure of antibiotics. Once a target protein has been identified, millions of natural and synthetic molecules may be tried to determine which is a "hit," one that still can only potentially be modified to become an effective therapy. Finally, our bodies' cells have evolved to keep foreign substances out, and their structure will repel both water- and fat-soluble molecules, so that a delicate balance must be achieved. Half of all new drugs are still derived from naturally occurring substances that have been collected painstakingly and screened. As Jogalekar acknowledges, even rational drug design still has a large element of serendipity because of all the obstacles nature has put in our way.[11]

Biomedical researchers and pharmaceutical companies have thus been in a challenging position. It is increasingly easy to acquire and analyze mountains of data and to test unprecedented numbers of possible molecules for their match with proteins that cause disease. Someday new artificial techniques may or may not create a far more efficient way to design drugs. Meanwhile, publication and testing have concentrated on the improvement of known families of molecules and their extension to other conditions. Sildenafil citrate, trademarked by Pfizer as Viagra, originally was approved as a heart medication, then became a blockbuster after its role in treating erectile dysfunction was discovered (and marketed brilliantly), and then was prescribed as heart medication for a condition affecting mainly women. In fact, according to one recent study, a quarter of all "transformative" drugs introduced since 1984, defined as both innovative and having a major impact on patient care, have been repurposed, often from government- and philanthropically funded research on rare diseases.[12]

While the efficiency of data analysis may eventually lead to new transformative treatments, evidence so far has been discouraging. After all the information technology breakthroughs of the 1990s, only four of the twenty-six transformative drugs—about 15 percent—were approved after 2000. So far data analysis has been used, according to critics of biomedical research, to exaggerate the value of small changes benefiting mainly marketing and patent protection. In fact, skeptics say, information technology can make biomedical science much less efficient by padding the literature with questionable results.[13]

How efficient is today's biomedical research? Thanks in part to technological changes that have shifted scientific publication to digital formats in which the marginal cost of distributing additional copies approaches zero, scientific journals and papers have been burgeoning. From 1996 to 2011 alone, 25 million papers were published by 15 million scientists around the world. Yet academics who have studied the quality of results have reached alarming conclusions. Eighty-five percent of those papers, they believe, are worthless. Many influential results have failed to be replicated. This is not due to the structural inefficiency we noted above, a consequence of the obstacles that reality puts in researchers' way. In fact, critics would be happy if more negative findings were published. The real problem is that papers make exaggerated claims for the validity of their results.[14]

Authorities encouraged the health care efficiency movement of the 1990s, evidence-based medicine (EBM), as a reaction to the exaggerated claims of pharmaceutical salespeople. Hard data, it was hoped, would curb waste. The replication crisis is the unintended result of this crackdown. It is possible, without breaking any conventional ethical rule, to design medical experiments and analyze their results to maximize the appearance of effectiveness even when a careful examination of the data reveals faults like a small sample size or statistical measures of significance that are not as meaningful as they usually seem. As we have seen earlier, the late-twentieth- and early-twenty-first-century faith in metrics can distort the quality of what is being measured. Remember the rise of the quantitative study of the researchers' productivity and influence, in Chapter Two, and especially the rise of citation analysis. From the very beginning of the movement, the professionals who developed it were careful to point out its limits, just as pharmaceutical companies disclose side effects in their package inserts and in those disconcerting, rapidly recited lists at the close of their television commercials, oral fine print. To the pharmaceutical industry's critics within the medical profession, the EBM movement has been hijacked by a proliferation of questionable studies.[15]

One important check on the limits of papers has been systematic reviews and meta-analyses, which study data and conclusions from multiple papers to achieve stronger validity. But the epidemiologist John Ioannidis, who first called broad attention to problems of replicating scientific findings in 2005, has discovered that in practice reviews and meta-analyses have compounded the problem. Since these genres are cited more often than the majority of papers themselves, they have become a favorite means of professional advancement, especially in China. "Instead of promoting evidence-based medicine and health care," Ioannidis summarized in his "policy points," "these instruments [systematic reviews and meta-analyses] often serve mostly as easily produced publishable units or marketing tools."[16]

Even when industry has the best intentions, the number of publications may help neutralize them. As the study of transformative drugs has shown, pharmaceutical makers rely heavily on academic rather than internal research, and the explosion of papers by researchers seeking tenure and promotion means that there may be thousands related to a single disease, where an industry research manager may have to follow a half dozen diseases. Conventional reporting about science takes the sheer number of papers to be a measure of the product of knowledge. But since many authors are under pressure for quantity as well as quality, numbers can also signify a strategy that journal editors call salami slicing—the division of results that could appear in a single paper into multiple ones. Editors consider this strategy marginally ethical, and some discourage it by requiring authors to disclose other papers in press or submitted. But salami slicing is also institutionalized and rationalized in academic science. An anonymous dean, writing in *The Chronicle of Higher Education*, has even suggested that the "least publishable unit," as slices are called, has the virtue of building a young faculty member's self-confidence and writing skills. Less positively, the writer acknowledged that many of his fellow administrators are incorrigible bean counters who will never be persuaded to pay more attention to quality than to quantity. Their policy may be less effective, but it is more efficient in the use of their own time. This efficiency unfortunately makes the larger academic and publication system less efficient by promoting information overload, and burdens academic libraries with spiraling costs for journals, disproportionate to the growth of significant results.[17]

A cure for the cycle of journal price increases and subscription cancellations seemed to appear with the rise of open access, generally online-only, journals, available without charge on the web. Authors (or more usually their institutions) pay charges up front to support peer review, editing, and website costs—a far more efficient way to launch a new journal than to pay heavy up-front costs and hope for enough paying subscribers. In fact, such publications may be too efficient. With minimal barriers to access and pressure from a growing number of scientists around the world to publish, the number of open access journals has exploded. According to the Open Access Directory project, there were 9,156 peer-reviewed titles in October 2016 and over 2.32 million articles. Of these journals, as many as 10 percent could be fraudulent, according to a librarian and researcher, Jeffrey Beall, who posted a list of over three hundred suspect publishers on the web. Other whistle-blowers wrote nonsense articles that were accepted and were able to join editorial boards with dubious aliases and made-up credentials. Yet despite these scandals, it has proved impossible to draw a bright line between legitimate and exploitive journals, just as it is not always easy to distinguish real from fake news. There is a gray area of opportunism and relaxed standards that falls short of fraud. Some open access advocates insist that only about one percent of journals are founded in bad faith. Confronted with challenges to his methods and threats of litigation, Beall retracted his list in January 2017. In a European biochemistry journal later that year, he explained that he had withdrawn the list specifically to end an aggressive campaign directed at his superiors at the University of Colorado. An anonymous and highly personal anti-Beall site has nonetheless remained, claiming to represent "a group of librarians around the world" united for open access against the alleged "predatory blogger."[18]

In 2017 the Federal Trade Commission (FTC) applied for a preliminary injunction against one of the most prominent open access journals concerns, the Bangalore, India, Omics International, accusing it of misleading researchers into spending $26.6 million or more on publication and conference registration fees. Omics has countered that the charges are "fake news" inspired by Beall's discontinued blog, defended its reviewing procedures, and blamed the legal action on FTC bias toward traditional subscription-based publishing. Whatever the merits of the case, a *Bloomberg Businessweek* report revealed that Omics's contributors and conference participants did not all fit the stereotype of struggling researchers in marginal institutions. They included some of the largest U.S. pharmaceutical companies, which the article alleges use open access to avoid the rigorous review standards of leading conventional journals in promoting new products. (Some companies did not comment, while others considered Omics's open access journals appropriate for at least some kinds of studies.)[19]

The efficiency of publishing, and of measuring the quantity and quality of researchers' output in biomedical sciences, would be no problem if demand for and supply of researchers were in balance. But it is not. Even in the relatively fortunate U.S., over 85 percent of new biomedical PhDs will not find tenure track academic positions. As Gina Kolata wrote in *The New York Times* about prolonged postdoctoral fellowships at 1990s pay scales that can last until researchers' forties, "biomedical scientists in academia are essentially apprentices until middle age."[20]

. . .

Given the obstacles to streamlining medical practice without burdening and demoralizing physicians, and the use of information technology to accelerate pharmaceutical breakthroughs, at least one other path to medical efficiency appears to be open: personalized medicine based on sequencing of individual patients' genomes. The statistical studies in clinical trials draw on relatively small samples of patients; some important side effects are not discovered until after a drug is widely used. This is not the fault of information technology. To the contrary, the most efficient way to reduce risks is to use massive databases of prescriptions and results, especially since neither animal nor clinical studies can deal with the range of possible interactions among drugs. Russ Altman, a professor of bioengineering, has pointed out that the *average* seventy-year-old takes no fewer than seven prescription medications. (Their necessity, and their contribution to longevity and well-being, are another issue.) Altman's graduate student Nicholas Tatonetti found a way to look beyond the FDA's Adverse Event Reporting System to a more precise analysis. Tatonetti and Altman were able to isolate populations within the database that were similar in variables like age and gender but differed in whether a single drug, like one for hypertension, was prescribed. Those not receiving the drug were a natural control group. If adverse events like headaches or vomiting occurred more often in those taking the drug, there was a good chance that it was responsible. Patients could also be sorted according to pairs of drugs. The results showed that there were many more side effects than package inserts had disclosed, an average of 329 versus the average of 68 acknowledged by drug manufacturers. And there were over 1,300 adverse effects from combinations of two drugs (in a database of 1,332) that could not be attributed to a single one of the pair.[21]

Algorithms can thus help make medicine more efficient by identifying drugs that should be used with greater caution or even be removed from the marketplace, saving money as well as lives. But this form of efficiency has a limit. It can interpret only after the fact, not predict results. And sometimes drugs must continue to be used despite known serious side effects. Thus from the 1990s the project for the sequencing of the human genome has been linked to the exciting prospect of a new model of medicine, in which the genetic markers for susceptibility to disease, and to adverse effects in treatment, can be established by sequencing the genome of every patient and tailoring therapy to his or her unique DNA. Precision medicine, also known as personalized medicine, is a twentieth-century development of an ancient idea—that each person has a distinctive constitution and needs customized remedies to bring his or her body into balance. (This was the basis of the Four Humors theory of Galenic medicine, and of India's Ayurvedic medicine, as well as of the nineteenth-century homeopathic movement. Homeopathy has survived partly because of this personalization, despite its contradiction of chemical laws that declare its medicines to be inert.) In the rapid expansion of the pharmaceutical industry after the Second World War, physicians and scientists began to study why some patients had adverse reactions while others did not. The geneticist Arnold Motulsky was the first to identity hereditary susceptibility to side effects of individual medications in 1957, inaugurating what became known as pharmacogenetics. By the late 1990s genetic information could be used to tailor treatment for some forms of breast cancer. When the human genome was first sequenced in 2003, it appeared that a new age of medicine would begin. By 2007 genetic testing became routine in decisions on prescribing the anticoagulant warfarin. In 2009 a new test allowed hospitals to examine patients' genes for mutations affecting drugs' effectiveness, and by 2014 the cost of sequencing an individual genome had declined to only $1,000. By 2016, major programs in the United Kingdom (the 100,000 Genomes Project focusing on rare diseases), the United States (the Precision Medicine Initiative involving a million volunteers), and China were set to compile large data sets. In principle, projecting further declines in the cost of sequencing and tests, precision medicine promises to be a breakthrough in efficiency as well as effectiveness.[22]

Yet precision medicine is still necessarily inefficient in the sense that most fundamental work is inefficient. It takes more time and effort than investigators realize when they start a project. Social psychologists usually see this as a regrettable negative tendency, the source of delays and cost overruns, and their negative name for it is the Planning Fallacy. Only after the genome was sequenced was the full complexity of gene expression realized. It became clear by about 2010 that the prospect, promoted by science writers if not by all the leading genomic scientists, was not succeeding. The science writer Stephen S. Hall, in a review in *Scientific American* in 2010, summed up the skepticism at a low point of the movement. The central problem was that the relatively easy scenario for genomic medicine, the search for common genetic variants—finding the DNA variants that tended to distinguish people with a disease from those unaffected by it—was a failure. Hall quoted one of the pioneers of genomics, Walter Bodmer, as acknowledging that the "vast majority" of those variants "have shed no light on the biology of diseases."[23]

The skeptics of precision medicine are no more able to prove their case in advance than advocates are. It is true that multiple genes control human development and health in combination, and also that gene expression is affected by environmental factors like hunger and stress, which in a few cases appear to have hereditary consequences. Even identical twins do not share these epigenetic influences exactly. Recent studies have suggested the role of the bacteria and other microbes in the human gut and small intestine in affecting a number of illnesses, and though the ratio of microbes to human cells in the body is now closer to 1.3 to 1 than 10 to 1, the composition and balance of the human microbiome is still a powerful though largely unexplored influence. It appears, for example, that breasts and possibly other organs have distinctive microbiomes that may affect the incidence of cancer. Precise therapy might have to rely on both genomic and microbial analyses and could thus be exponentially more complex. One prominent skeptic of precision medicine, the hematologist-oncologist Vinay Prasad, has written extensively on medical reversals: abandonment of well-established treatments, diet recommendations, and pharmaceuticals that turn out to be ineffective or harmful. Prasad has observed that in his own specialty, precision medicine successes in producing remission have been limited to a small number of "super-responders," and that the one controlled study of precision oncology showed an almost equally discouraging rate of progression-free survival in those receiving therapies based on their individual mutations as opposed to the control group treated according to their own physicians' judgment: 2.3 months versus 2.0 months for the control group. While recommending continued trials, he has called the movement "inspirational" rather than promising. And some internal medicine specialists, all too familiar with substance abuse, poor dietary choices, and other lifestyle issues, believe that environmental factors swamp the benefits that precision medicine might give to many of their patients.[24]

Some statisticians have also discovered previously hidden flaws in big data analysis, especially in medicine, notably Xiao-Li Meng in lectures at the Royal Statistical Society in London and at the University of Chicago. While Meng's analysis is technical, he summarized the problem of big data in general in an email: "Once we take into account data quality, a seemingly tiny defect would take an enormous sample size to compensate." The point is that big data can be valuable, but only with more skill and sophistication than many commentators assume.[25]

Genomic optimists have a strong case of their own, expressed by another oncologist (and best-selling writer), Siddhartha Mukherjee, who has warned against obsession with negative unintended consequences of innovation. His arguments recall Albert O. Hirschman's Hiding Hand concept, which we have already encountered: once we commit ourselves to a goal, we may discover surprising resources to reach it. Mukherjee has observed in *The Gene* that nature often turns out to be unexpectedly simple rather than monumentally complex. In the early 1950s each organism was thought to have such a distinctive, dauntingly complex genetic code that there could never be a theory for all life. The discovery of the double helix proved that nature was surprisingly simple, with a single molecule and a single code for all life, enabling modification of the genomes of all organisms and even, by 1980, making possible the production of mammalian proteins in bacterial cells and vice versa. The existence of "master regulatory genes" supports the hope of finding more simplicity behind the complexity of DNA. To extend Mukherjee's analysis, the genomic revolution did for biology what the scientific revolution of the seventeenth century had done for cosmology. Just as the stars and planets were known to be made of the same matter as earth (though this could not be truly confirmed before spectroscopy and space probes) rather than special substances, so a gene is a gene whether in a potato or a person. Behind the multiplicity of genomes are master regulatory genes that can determine the complex facts of anatomy and physiology. One of the most promising areas for precision medicine is not genes themselves but another component of DNA, the switches that turn them on and off and that are sometimes located on the genome far from the genes they control. A number of these switches may influence diseases like schizophrenia, multiple sclerosis, and diabetes, according to research by the molecular biologist and Broad Institute director Eric Lander and hundreds of colleagues in a federally funded program.[26]

Personalized medicine may yet become as revolutionary as antibiotics. Lander has observed that sixty years elapsed from the birth of the germ theory of medicine to the production of penicillin, and he has said that his position even at the height of enthusiasm in 2000 was that the project would really be for "our children's children." Even if we accept the skeptics' view of the odds against the prospect, it appears to be an excellent risk, even if after a generation the goals and techniques of precision medicine turn out to be significantly different from those of today. It accounts for less than one percent of the $34 billion budget of the U.S. National Institutes of Health (NIH) in fiscal year 2017. It is very possible that our grandchildren will have, as a result of the successes and failures of genomics, a very different idea of the gene itself than that of the 1990s, just as 1990s' ideas were radically different from those of the early 1950s. As Lander himself noted at a summit on gene editing, while there are four to five thousand genes affecting disease, they mainly affect probabilities, work in combination, and may also have positive roles, which could be why evolution has spared them. That is an argument against permanent germline genetic engineering, though, rather than individual gene therapy or tailoring treatments to individual genomes. The point in the context of efficiency, though, is that, like other groundbreaking work, it will be (as Lander's time scale suggests) inefficient, needing many false starts to find more productive concepts.[27]

What can we do while we're waiting for bespoke treatments? There are other ways to promote health by knowing ourselves, according to technology enthusiasts. One might be called Genomics Lite: genotyping for known genes rather than compiling a complete sequence of an individual's DNA. Even after the rapid drop in the price of sequencing, the latter is still a questionable expense given the lack of insurance reimbursement and of FDA-approved treatments that require knowing a full genome. Genotyping is limited to genes already known to affect health, disease, or even quirks like the ability to detect certain tastes. This procedure is now easy enough that the best-known genotyping company, 23andMe.com, offers the service for only $199 and has a million customers, according to its fact sheet. While the health information in 23andMe's reports was originally limited to risks of hereditary transmission of disease, in April 2017 the FDA authorized the company to sell tests that directly evaluated an individual's genetic risks. The private company's market capitalization exceeded $1 billion in 2016 and probably increased after the ruling. Yet despite this commercial and regulatory success, there are grounds to doubt whether people will actually use genetic information to change their lifestyle and reduce their risks.[28]

Until genotyping is more widely accepted, the most popular form of medical self-knowledge is likely to be self-monitoring through wearable technology. According to the information technology website Engadget.com, nearly twenty million devices like wristbands and smartwatches capable of recording motion and monitoring at least some vital signs were sold in the first quarter of 2016, an increase of more than two-thirds over the same period in 2015. The information technology consulting firm IDC estimates that the global market for "wearables," including wristbands, watches, clothing, eyeglasses, helmets, and other accessories, will reach 216.3 million units by 2020. An April 2016 report by the consulting giant PwC shows how popular the concept has become. In 2014, over 20 percent of PwC's survey sample owned at least one wearable; by 2016 the proportion stood at 49 percent; 36 percent owned more than one. Health was the most important reason for purchase. The number of respondents declaring themselves excited by wearables had grown from 41 percent in 2014 to fully 57 percent. The report also notes, though, the continuing skepticism of nonwearers, suggesting to me that technological attitudes may become increasingly polarized, as political identities have.[29]

Wearables promise healthier living, then—and possibly insurance savings—to many or most of their users. Self-monitoring appears to be a logical development in the movement for more efficient living. But there is more than one side to efficiency. The same technology that empowers people through self-surveillance and voluntary sharing of personal data with friends and family members has another potential: monitoring by employers and possibly even by governments. For many information technology enthusiasts, this may be not a bug but a feature, an opening for a benevolent paternalism that can combat deadly trends toward obesity and sedentary living, reduce health care costs, and increase longevity. Other studies cited by PwC estimate that there were already 75 million wearables in the workplace by 2016, and that by 2020 fully 8 million people would be required to wear them as a condition of employment. About half of respondents saw efficiency as the prime benefit of wearables. And far from resisting Big Brother, participants also expected his helping hand. Two-thirds thought that employers should pay for or at least subsidize monitoring devices. Thirty-seven percent thought their companies should adopt cutting-edge technology even if it did not improve productivity. There was even greater enthusiasm about wearables in the home. Parents were 50 percent more likely than nonparents to own a mobile device. And they saw benefits ranging from health (85 percent) through productivity and parenting (in the 70s) to relationships and stress levels (in the 60s). If the report is representative, self-monitoring is on the way to becoming a domestic rite. Whether it can add ten years to users' lives, as 70 percent of respondents now believe, remains to be seen.[30]

One surprise of the PwC report is that privacy is not only declining as a concern despite the increasing possibilities for networking, surveillance, and hacking, but ranks low in reasons for nonadoption. Still, there are signs of resentment that concern some advocates. When companies promote fitness contests, monitoring steps and other physical activity, some employees unscrupulously attach their devices to hamster wheels, power drills, and even family dogs, a recurring problem of measurement as an incentive. Perhaps inspired by such evasion, researchers at MIT (as though to confirm long-standing leftist suspicions that the entire institution is a corporate conspiracy) have developed badges that monitor employees' social interactions as well as vital signs. The idea behind the project is not panoptic or Orwellian scrutiny, according to the founders' description. Supervisors do not have access to the data of individual staff members, though the latter can view their own information. Rather, the aggregated data provide insights into what distinguishes strong from weak performers; members of lower-scoring groups, for example, communicate with each other less often. Earlier versions of the badges have also revealed how financial traders—who have yet to be replaced by algorithms—respond to losses and other stress physiologically. The software might help at least some traders retain their balance. The profits of the vendor, a Boston-based company called Humanyze, come not from sales of hardware and software but from use of the data.[31]

Stripping data of links to individuals does not guarantee privacy. Security specialists have shown that it is often possible to reidentify people who have been de-identified for their protection. It is not certain, though, that employers or others would have either the motivation or the means for unauthorized snooping, apart from any legal consequences. The more serious problem of employer-sponsored and self-directed activity monitoring alike is different. It is that the efficiency of gathering data about people's activities in the short term does not make the technology necessarily an efficient or effective means to fitness in the long run.

The unintended consequences of self-monitoring technology were revealed in a study by a professor of marketing, Jordan Etkin. Etkin performed a series of six experiments with undergraduate and adult subjects (web-based, using Amazon's Mechanical Turk program for payment) engaging in a variety of activities: not only walking (using a pedometer rather than a more advanced device) but coloring shapes and reading texts. The performance of some of the participants was measured and reported to them; control groups had no such feedback. Etkin's findings were consistent with years of social psychology research on intrinsic and extrinsic rewards, a line of research challenging B. F. Skinner's idea, which we encountered in Chapter Three, that all behavior can be positively shaped by carefully administered rewards. Later psychologists have discovered that when people receive external rewards for something that gives them pleasure, they enjoy it less. (In fact, the educational critic Alfie Kohn has even argued, in his book *Punished by Rewards*, that positive reinforcement can be as harmful as the old punitive ideas that Skinner thought society should overcome. Writing more than a decade before the rise of wearable computing, he saw all forms of incentives as conservative techniques for social control.) Those whose steps were tracked by the pedometers lost interest in walking and walked less—in fact, less than control group members whose activity was never measured. Measurement, Etkin found, even reduced participants' overall sense of happiness and well-being.[32]

While there are enthusiastic wearables users who scoff at such findings, other anecdotal evidence confirms them. Two writers have shed light on the problem. Cari Romm, in her *New York* magazine blog, even describes the "existential angst" of stopping measurement of her steps by Fitbit. Paul Ford, in *The New Republic*, relates how he developed a program in pre-wearables days to track food and exercise to reduce his obesity. He ended his self-devised and temporarily successful program, regaining his weight, unable to bear the self-monitoring regime. "Weight loss—the self-improvement industry in general," he wrote in his diary, "is a kind of natural, physical postmodernism. You become the text you are editing, rewrite your feelings, the body." He saw his friends' Fitbits and other wearables as unsustainable. Romm's and Ford's experiences, and those of others, show how self-monitoring can begin as an exciting and rewarding project and become an onerous duty. Depending on the activity, it can take weeks for pleasure to return. It is possible that this is a minority response, despite Etkin's findings. After all, as we have seen, many experiments in medical and behavioral sciences cannot be replicated. On the other side, a number of other social psychologists have reported similar findings, and numerous other papers report the disadvantages of extrinsic motivation.[33]

Is it possible that people using activity trackers under medical supervision with goals of weight loss will benefit even if exercise enthusiasts may not? At least one experiment suggests the opposite. Young people seeking to shed weight were assigned to groups after receiving diet and exercise advice. One recorded their food and activity on a website; the other wore devices that measured their movements. The experimenters originally believed that the second would be more motivated by the efficiency of receiving automatic feedback on progress toward their goals. In reality, their loss of an average of 8 pounds was significantly less than that of the control group, at 13 pounds. They may have just rebelled against self-surveillance as many other users have. But the researchers also believe that feedback showing they were falling short of their activity goals discouraged rather than prodded them. It is possible that the quantified-self movement is highly successful for some people who believe in it especially strongly, making its use an intrinsic feature rather than a means to an end, while others are correspondingly resentful. All this does not negate the value of activity trackers for those who respond positively to them in the long run. It just means that, overall, they do not seem to help reduce weight or increase exercise or fitness.[34]

(A positive unexpected result of information technology for health was revealed by a study of users of Microsoft's Band activity tracker. Those users who appeared to be playing Pokémon Go—an augmented reality game for mobile devices in which a user's real location allows his or her avatar, or symbolic virtual self, to interact with the stylized creatures of the Japanese game, who can be spotted and captured in real-world settings as seen through the back cameras of smartphones and tablets—engaged in a high-technology treasure hunt that deliberately challenged them to walk as far as possible. At least in the first months of adoption, tracking did encourage an unforeseen boom in activity by users, according to the study. Players increased their number of steps by 25 percent in the month studied, regardless of sex, age, or weight. If the entire U.S. population of players was responding similarly, the game added 144 billion steps to American activity in that month. Of course, the players studied were already motivated to exercise, and the study did not try to measure the persistence of behavior. It did suggest, though, that the best way to motivate people is not to subject them to self-surveillance on meeting goals but to offer activities enjoyable for their own sake.)[35]

Some people with life- or health-threatening conditions may benefit from monitoring, and their loss of enjoyment might be considered a mild side effect—unless, of course, it induces them to relax their vital activity routines. In 2016 I could find no medical study of positive and negative consequences. This absence may have been intentional. Makers of activity monitoring so far have made no claims for use in diagnosis or treatment of disease. The Food and Drug Administration, which has the authority to classify and regulate them as medical devices, has explicitly declined to do so as long as the trackers are not sold as therapeutic technology. The FDA considers existing wearables as "low risk general fitness devices." Yet the regulatory status of wearables is complicated. First, communities of users online—without manufacturers' authorization—may make and promote health claims. Even if they do not, a technology can still become a de facto medical treatment by word of mouth and popular practices. Google is so widely used for self-diagnosis—despite obvious privacy issues, 80 percent of the U.S. public searches for symptoms online, according to one report—that its developers have produced a symptom search feature to help make answers more accurate and to encourage medical attention when appropriate. The skepticism of many medical researchers about the value of vitamins and other dietary supplements has not significantly diminished the $36.7 billion (2014) market. Second, information technology media report that some wearables manufacturers are developing versions that could be approved as medical devices. If they are, effects on motivation might be deemed side effects to be noted among issues on the package insert.[36]

The widespread use of professional-grade monitoring devices for broader categories of patients raises other questions that may not fall within the scope of the FDA. We have already seen that many physicians feel overtaxed by the reporting burdens of government agencies and private insurers. Patient ratings are a form of consumer feedback that may improve the efficiency of care, but can also distort it with conflicting incentives. A doctor may improve outcomes by taking additional time to diagnose one patient, for example, but may lose points when his or her conscientiousness keeps other patients waiting—even if the more careful diagnosis saves a life. Big data, even on the patient level, thus have hidden costs beyond the immediate technical challenge of storage and migration to new devices. There is also the possible additional burden on physicians' time for learning to interpret the flood of data from wearables.

The potential inefficiency of the quantified self goes beyond activity trackers to other devices, especially those in the gray area between recreation and therapy that has been such a challenge to regulate. Critics inside and outside the medical profession, from the philosopher Ivan Illich to the psychiatrist Arthur J. Barsky, have long observed that health consciousness can become unhealthy and even pathological. The philosopher of science Ian Hacking has introduced the idea of looping: laypeople internalizing the medical profession's definitions of illnesses and thus choosing and conforming to labels. Search engines can help amplify this behavior, leading to what has been called cyberchondria. Preoccupation with treating even a real illness or discomfort can focus such attention on it that visits to a succession of doctors in a search for a cure can become a worse source of stress than the underlying symptom. Insomnia can fall into this troublesome zone. A guest editorial in the *Journal of Sleep Research* (of the European Sleep Research Society) by the communication scholar Jan Van den Bulck points to one self-monitoring device, the Sony SWR10 SmartBand, that awakens a sleeper whose level has changed from deep to light, since there is evidence that spending too much time in the latter state will make the sleeper groggy if he or she wakes up naturally. In addition to such dedicated devices there are an estimated 100,000 health-related smartphone apps, some of which are associated with sensors or other monitoring devices exchanging data with the user's smartphone. While there are other problems associated with this technology—such as manufacturers going bankrupt and leaving devices unsupported in new smartphone operating systems and thus useless—Van den Bulck is most concerned about what has become known as "orthorexia," a passion for healthy living that has become, like the extreme dieting consciousness that inspired the name, a menace to health. Applied to sleep, this preoccupation might even be called "chronorexia." An excessive quest for efficient living can lead to its opposite.[37]

The most radical manifestation of the quantified self in health may be not sleep but sexual apps. Some of them are mainly mobile-era adaptations of medical advice for promoting fertility. Other apps, especially those marketed to men, treat sexual life as a form of competitive performance and let subscribers compare their own statistics of partners and acts with those of other users in their area. Part of the spirit of the quantified self is sharing data, and some of the apps even let subscribers in nearby locations make contact with each other, yet another variation on computer dating. While Deborah Lupton, the Australian sociologist who has written about such programs, did not investigate the number of actual users and contacts made, she has pointed out the values underpinning the technology. Many men and women, skeptical about people, have come to believe that it is more beneficial to rely on data and the algorithms that interpret them than to trust individuals. Revelations on the extent of surveillance programs by the National Security Agency (NSA) and other intelligence organizations, and the tactics of confidence swindlers and identity thieves, may have limited the popularity of sharing, but they have not killed it.[38]

Some people thus feel that the pursuit of personal efficiency by gathering, analyzing, and comparing one's own data is a liberating experience. Others find that goals and comparisons of data are the opposite, a burdensome form of self-monitoring. As the historian Sarah E. Igo has shown in her book *The Averaged American*, self-comparison with collective social science data goes back at least to the early and mid-twentieth century, to best sellers like the sociologists Robert and Helen Lynd's books on "typical" Middletown and the statistics in the Kinsey reports on human sexuality. The mobile technology revolution's great innovation is to make both data gathering and comparison possible in real time; significantly the phrase "quantified self" first appeared in *Wired* magazine in 2007, the year of the iPhone's introduction. But it remains to be seen who is made more self-confident and competent by the new technology, and who becomes more anxious and dissatisfied.[39]

We have already seen that sequencing the human genome is only the beginning of a decades-long process of untangling the many interactions of genes and life circumstances. But with or without genetic information, diagnosis remains more challenging than most laypeople recognize. According to a study by the neurologists David E. Newman-Toker and Ali S. Saber Tehrani of a U.S. national practitioner database, of 350,000 claims of malpractice between 1986 and 2010, the largest category (29 percent) was for diagnoses that were overlooked, mistaken, or delayed. Contrary to popular impressions, this was greater than errors in treatment (27 percent) or in surgical procedures (24 percent). According to the authors, malpractice allegations regarding diagnoses understate the problem. Autopsies suggest that 10 to 20 percent of deaths resulted from conditions not identified during the patients' lifetimes. Fully half these deaths were preventable.[40]

Can artificial intelligence reduce suffering and needless deaths? The IBM supercomputer Watson, which won the game show *Jeopardy!* against the strongest human contestants in 2011, has more recently been tutored in genomics and oncology at major cancer centers and has been trained to assimilate the findings of medical journals and research panels as soon as they appear—one possible answer to the flood of data noted earlier in this chapter and in Chapter Two. Watson learned to think like an oncologist and matched the judgment of human experts of the Molecular Tumor Board of the University of North Carolina at Chapel Hill in 99 percent of cases. In 30 percent of the cases, Watson was able to make a suggestion overlooked by the doctors. Watson and other supercomputers might be the future of personalized genomic medicine. Already it has found successful treatments for rare conditions that even elite physicians had overlooked.[41]

This record seems impressive. Yet artificial intelligence, while it can be highly effective, can hardly be called efficient. The Watson supercomputer that won *Jeopardy!* needed 85,000 watts of power; the human brains that it defeated, only 20 watts. It is yet another piece of expensive advanced medical apparatus, and one that has been subsidized by both IBM and its medical partners. In other words, while highly effective in challenging cases, it is not a miracle for public health. It has been mainly a public relations triumph in search of profitable applications. It does promise at least one genuine contribution to medical efficiency: earlier recognition of "rare" diseases, defined by the National Institutes of Health as those affecting under 200,000 people in the United States; about 6,800 of such ailments are known.

For the 10 percent of the population suffering from one or more, diagnosis takes an average of over 7.5 years, visits to eight physicians, two or three misdiagnoses, and often severe financial stress. Artificial intelligence assistance in spotting these unusual cases can bring big gains to health care, even if most rare diseases have no known treatment. And obstacles to extending Watson's power to the desktop suggest that medical supercomputers of its type are likely to remain niche services.[42]

In September 2017 an investigative report by the medical news site STAT underscored the gap between IBM's bold marketing of its Watson for Oncology program, and the initiative's more modest results. Watson, it concluded, is really "Memorial Sloan Kettering Cancer Center in a portable box. Its treatment recommendations are based entirely on the training provided by doctors, who determine what information Watson needs to devise its guidance as well as what those recommendations should be." It has access to outside articles selected by the same physicians but does not analyze them independently. While Sloan Kettering is one of the world's most prestigious hospitals, the report adds that its recommendations reflect the biases of U.S. medicine, according to some overseas physicians who have used the technology. Watson does have significant benefits in providing reliable guidance more rapidly than committees of staff doctors, and in giving junior doctors a greater say in decisions. And it may yet achieve IBM's goal of significant improvement of outcomes. The report also sees promise in some competing projects for artificial intelligence in medicine. They key lesson in medicine, as in education, is that making an efficient automated system usually needs more extensive skilled work than its planners expect.[43]

The artificial intelligence available to most physicians is far more modest and affordable. It can be both efficient and lifesaving by helping professionals adhere to checklists and spot warning signs they might otherwise have overlooked. But it has neither Watson's near-universal medical journal database nor the benefit of Watson's extensive coaching. Harvard Medical School researchers published the first review of these programs in 2016, and their results cooled earlier expectations that software running on off-the-shelf computers could exceed the diagnostic skills of professionals. Instead, the doctors prevailed. Two hundred thirty-four internal medicine specialists were presented not with live patients but with "vignettes" of forty-five clinical cases, each reviewed by at least twenty physicians. Each proposed the most likely diagnosis followed by two alternatives. The same questions were asked of the programs. On the first choice, the doctors were right more than twice as often as the programs, 72 percent versus only 34 percent. When alternates were included, 84 percent of the doctors listed the correct diagnosis among the top three; the electronic symptom checkers scored barely above half at 51 percent. The programs fared relatively better with common diagnoses and worse when conditions were more unusual. This may suggest that experienced doctors have acquired not only rules but the ability to identify more complex issues: tacit knowledge that they might not be able to describe in advance when developing an algorithm but that they can exercise in practice.[44]

The quantified self and diagnostic artificial intelligence share obstacles to true efficiency that are two of the most troublesome issues in medical technology: false positives (with their consequences, over-diagnoses) and toxic uncertainty. The simplest case of the former may be alarm fatigue. In *Why Things Bite Back* I pointed to the epidemic of erroneous electronic detection of home burglaries and automobile theft. Nearly fifteen years later, in 2010, the problem had not changed. Even a representative of the security alarm industry acknowledged that eight out of ten police calls proved groundless, and many police departments were still levying fines for excess calls. Efforts to make alarm technology more discriminating while avoiding false negatives have evidently been slow. Car alarms, on the other hand, have ceased to be the urban plague they were in the early 1990s thanks to improved electronic key security and reprogramming to suppress alarms from innocent sources of vibration.[45]

In medicine there is no equivalent of the electronic key fob. And there are strong incentives for manufacturers of electronic devices to issue alerts for every possible risk to the patient; if one is disregarded because there are too many, hospital staff, not the device manufacturer, will be held responsible. The efficiency of medical equipment in notifying doctors and nurses of potential problems predictably makes care less efficient. In his book *The Digital Doctor*, the professor of medicine and pioneer of modern patient safety studies Robert M. Wachter cites a lawsuit that dramatized what has become known as alarm fatigue. An eighty-nine-year-old man at one of America's premier hospitals, Massachusetts General, died from cardiac arrest even though ten nurses had been aware of beeps at a central station and warnings displayed on signs in the hallway. A loud bedside alarm indicating a slowing heartbeat had been switched off by an unknown hand. Mass General settled the case for $850,000. *The Boston Globe*, investigating the event, discovered that between June 2005 and June 2010, at least 216 patients had died because alarms failed or because medical staff were fatigued by false warnings. A *Globe* reporter found that in Boston Children's Hospital, alarms were triggered by a child pumping his legs in bed, and by everyday activities like eating, burping, and working on a paper craft project. At Dr. Wachter's own hospital at the University of California at San Francisco, there was an average of one alarm every eight minutes for each of the 66 or so intensive care patients, a total of 15,000 each day and 381,560 each month for only one of five alarm systems; together there were at least 2.5 million alerts each month in intensive care.[46]

Serious as the hospital alarm problem has been, it is actually one of the more tractable unintended consequences of efficiency. The aviation industry has confronted false signals for decades and has developed a systematic hierarchy of warnings along with rigorous training in responding to them, as Dr. Wachter discovered in interviewing the hero pilot Chesley Sullenberger and taking controls of a simulator. Because only a few giant corporations build the majority of long-distance commercial aircraft, alarms are not a patchwork of signals from many vendors but a single integrated and layered program. It starts with the most urgent visual, voice, and stick-shaking signals when a plane is about to stall and crash. A second level notifies pilots of conditions that require immediate action but don't threaten the flight path; the color red is never used at this level. There are 40 of those "warnings." Below them are 150 or so "cautions" that demand immediate attention but do not yet require any response. These signals are amber, without any audible alarm. Finally, "advisories" disclose problems that will need attention later but that do not threaten safety because other redundant systems will take their place. Through experience, Boeing engineers have identified the sensors that are most likely to create false alarms, and thus to be ignored or even disabled, and have devised more accurate alternatives.[47]

We saw in Chapter Four that even the most carefully structured system of aviation alerts can lead to panicked reactions if automatic operation leaves pilots unprepared. In hospitals there is no autopilot, and there are many more situations to monitor. The staff are often required to balance multiple activities, and multitasking is known to degrade performance. Wachter cites a study of 98 nurses in Australia preparing and administering over 4,200 medications. Each interruption made a drug error 13 percent more likely; four successive interruptions doubled the chance of death or serious harm. While some technology enthusiasts are proud of their ability to multitask, considering it a sign of superior efficiency, few people can switch their attention repeatedly without degrading their performance.[48]

Alarm fatigue is not limited to the signals of devices. It also applies to the warnings besetting hospital pharmaceutical managers. Electronic medical records, for all their advantages over previous chaotic paper-based systems, are not only burdensome for doctors as we noted earlier, but also are all too efficient at producing warnings—and as a result may not be so efficient at all. Early studies of electronic medical records and related technology like bar coding of prescriptions suggest that they can reduce adverse events. But they also create obstacles to staff efficiency. In Dr. Wachter's hospital, which was able to benefit from the experience of other hospitals that had installed its information technology system, pharmacists received pop-up alerts on almost half the approximately 350,000 medication orders issued each month. Even physicians had to deal with a total of 17,000 alerts monthly. This means that the gains in principle from the efficiency of monitoring doses and warning of possible adverse reactions might be neutralized by fatigue; at least one study suggests there are considerable differences in adverse effect reports between institutions adopting systems from the same vendors. Fatigue can increase the risk of entry errors. In one case described in detail by Dr. Wachter, a young patient received a dose of the antibiotic Septra that was forty times what the pediatric resident intended when she entered the order into the system. Senior residents, responding to repeated warnings, had developed a culture of ignoring alarms; they had transmitted this attitude to their new colleague. Fortunately, the patient was saved without permanent injury, but the dose could have been fatal. When such potential disasters occur despite multiple precautions, risk analysts call the result the Swiss cheese effect; in most cases one of the safeguards will prevail, but every so often all the gaps will line up as the holes of assorted cheese slices will if you put them together.[49]

There is every reason to hope that alarm fatigue can be mitigated if medicine follows the aerospace model. Already, Robert Wachter reports that adjusting thresholds and delaying notifications that are not urgent and may be the result of transient conditions can reduce the mental load of medical personnel. There is another kind of warning signal that is not so easily managed, leading to two of the most serious criticisms of the efficiency and sensitivity of today's testing equipment: overdiagnosis and overtreatment. These are not exclusively technological issues; they go back to the heyday of medical bleeding. (George Washington's doctors treated his laryngitis by drawing over two liters of blood, hastening if not causing Washington's death the following day. And the distinguished Philadelphia physician and patriot Benjamin Rush prescribed the same cure for himself, claiming the procedure had saved him from yellow fever.) An Australian health studies scholar with a background in journalism, Ray Moynihan, and his colleagues have noted how economic and social pressures as well as technological change have led to the unnecessary classification and treatment of people as sick. Professional panels have been defining the threshold measurements for diseases downward, even creating new categories like pre-diabetes, supposedly in the interest of early detection and prevention but sometimes to the benefit of pharmaceutical manufacturers rather than patients. Up to 80 percent of people with high cholesterol receiving lifetime drug treatment may not need it, and 30 percent of people diagnosed with asthma do not benefit from their treatment, according to the studies Moynihan cites. Of course, some doctors and patients have always believed in aggressive treatment, and others have been more conservative. One major difference today is the efficiency of newer medical technology in detecting "abnormalities" that might have been missed—and often would not have affected health during a typical lifetime. Autopsies reveal not only the diseases that should have been treated but cancers that were best left alone. Improved imaging leads to what are called "incidentalomas," abnormalities unrelated to the original symptoms or tests and that may in turn lead to further testing. Scans of the pelvis, head, neck, and chest may reveal these in up to 40 percent of patients. Moynihan observes, as evidence of overtreatment, that while the rate of cancer detection has risen, death rates from cancer have remained relatively stable.[50]

The efficiency of gathering health information through tests and scans contrasts with the complexity of deciding on what treatment, if any, to apply. We have already seen that at least in the second decade of the twenty-first century, electronic health recordkeeping may have increased rather than reduced the administrative load on physicians, making it even harder for them to find time to explain and weigh options with patients. In some cases, personalized genetics may simplify a choice, but the more we learn about genes and disease, the more physician and patient enter a maze of probabilities. For example, one specialist in biomedical informatics—a hybrid discipline of medical information and computer science devoted to organization of, and access to, health care knowledge and records—at Columbia told a *New Scientist* writer that because of the expansion of medical literature, "dozens of conditions that are being missed . . . could easily be diagnosed by a machine." Through machine learning, he suggested, an algorithm might find bits of evidence suggesting a risk for developing multiple sclerosis, perhaps 0.5 or 5 percent, according to the reporter. The researcher hopes to develop software that will "spit out warnings or recommendations." Even if early treatment can prevent progression of multiple sclerosis or other diseases, what of adverse effects of treatment on the majority of patients at the 5 percent level who never would have developed the disease? And since anxiety may itself be a determinant of health, might not fear lead to complications of its own? The same article reports that Microsoft has published an algorithm using web searches to identify people who may have pancreatic cancer, and Google's DeepMind, a London artificial intelligence unit, is analyzing British National Health Service records to help ophthalmologists identify people at early stages of eye disease. In these cases, as with more conventional screening, early detection may prevent death in some instances, but it also may be harmful to health care in others if not properly evaluated. While protecting privacy is vital, it is even more important to do no harm in treatment. As Moynihan emphasizes, seconded by the editor of *BMJ*, overdiagnosis and overtreatment use medical resources that are needed for those who are undertreated. The efficiency and sensitivity of testing and of algorithmic analysis of medical records of individuals may actually make health care systems less efficient and less effective in promoting the well-being of the entire population.[51]

In extreme cases, this anxiety can lead to what the writer Charles Siebert called toxic uncertainty, a painful consciousness of being at risk and not being able to make clear-cut decisions. Newspapers regularly report such cases. In one, another writer at risk, Patricia Fall, recounted how a routine $99 consumer genetic test by 23andMe .com revealed a positive result for a gene mutation associated with an elevated rate of breast cancer. This was confirmed by a further $4,000 professional test for breast cancer genes, and followed by a three-year series of MRIs, mammograms, sonograms, and biopsies, including frequent false positives. Patricia Fall's insurance company refused to cover some of these costs. Without an actual diagnosis of cancer, she had scheduled and canceled preventive removal of her ovaries three times and preventive double mastectomies twice. The efficiency of generating information and data led not to clearer decision making but to an agony of choice. The FDA has since limited the genetic information that mass-market genotyping companies can supply, but the toxic uncertainty issue will not go away. If more and more people and their physicians learn of probabilities of developing multiple sclerosis and other diseases, health anxiety may become an epidemic in its own right.[52]

Summing up, technology has been creating modern medical practice since at least the invention of the stethoscope by the French physician R. T. H. Laennec in the early nineteenth century. Laennec's invention, as the physician and historian of medicine Jacalyn Duffin has written, helped bring about a revolution that has freed diagnosis from heavy reliance on the patient's subjective reports and has substituted the examining physician's observations of the body's hidden functioning, once detectable only after death. Today's genetic analysis and imaging technology are taking this trend to new levels; the stethoscope itself, dependent on the sensitivity and training of the doctor's hearing, retains its ritual power as the white coat does, but risks becoming a museum piece. There is no denying the benefits of new and more efficient tools. Imaging can diagnose conditions and can often improve outcomes and reduce costs by helping physicians select the most effective and best tolerated medication when several choices are available. Artificial intelligence can reduce the often harrowing search for correct diagnoses of rare diseases, and it may be able to help find cures. Electronic medical records properly implemented may yet fulfill their promise if the burden on physicians—and the corresponding risk of efficiency-sapping burnout—can be reduced. Nobody wants to return to the sometimes tragic handwriting errors that helped motivate the computerization of medical records.[53]

We have seen that there are significant risks to health, and even to the efficiency of medicine, in using new resources indiscriminately. We should not idealize the soft side of medicine; many intuitions of doctors have been proved wrong in double-blind clinical trials. But we also should not ignore the evidence that physicians' empathy can be therapeutic. Dr. Vikas Saini, head of the health care reform organization the Lown Institute, has quoted its founder, the cardiologist and inventor Dr. Bernard Lown, winner of the Nobel Peace Prize, as observing that "the usual rules of efficiency are inverted in medicine. The more time a physician spends with patients, the more efficient he or she becomes. Listening costs next to nothing, and so is infinitely more cost-effective than drugs and devices." Listening is the key to the most effective and economical use of medical technology, and to avoidance of overtreatment. Limited as the stethoscope is, it also represents what research is beginning to recognize as the therapeutic power of touch. Deborah Lupton, in her studies of the quantified self movement, has noted the tension between data and "embodied knowledge." Medicine is most efficient and effective when it bridges the two.[54]

Better statistical understanding can help. In his book *Gut Feelings*, the cognitive psychologist Gerd Gigerenzer shows that there need be no opposition between data and intuition. The introduction of a formal system for deciding whether or not a patient should be admitted to a coronary unit, using data tables and a calculator, improved doctors' decisions significantly over intuition alone. Yet when these aids were removed, it turned out that doctors continued to achieve their higher level of accuracy. Their experience using the data-based system had permanently improved their intuition. A further step was to make a simplified flow chart with a limited number of decision points—a "fast and frugal decision tree," as Gigerenzer calls it. It needed no database or calculator, and its results were best of all.[55]

Reforms of malpractice law and insurance, Gigerenzer suggests, are needed to remove incentives for overdiagnosis and overtreatment that can lead to serious health consequences. In medicine, analog thinking and information technology must go together. Institutions can also affect doctors' ability to understand each patient's case in depth. In health care systems like Belgium's and Switzerland's, where patients have a greater choice of primary care doctors and specialists, the average appointment lasts fifteen minutes rather than five, as it does in the United States. The quality of medical care may depend more on culture than on technology.[56]

We might compare medical decision making to computer chess. With some chess software and on some chess websites, a player (outside a tournament setting, of course) can see the probability that a given opening or early mid-game move—databases store each move of over eight million games dating back centuries—will result in a win. But the historically stronger move might not be the right one in a particular match. A master or grandmaster will study an opponent's games and understand his or her psychology and style. So a doctor with uncertain information needs not only statistics about outcomes but an understanding of the values and priorities of the patient.

Finally, real medical efficiency needs attention to what lies beyond the patient: the environment and community. Surroundings can be more important than anything measured in a physician's office or hospital. So-called nonmedical determinants of health and public health measures—diet, environmental protection, sanitation, and immunizations—have played a large if contested part in the continued extension of the average human lifespan. In the 1970s, revisionist historians of medicine took a radical point of view in casting doubt on the effectiveness of medications and surgery in prolonging life. While some of their work had serious methodological errors and gaps, they had a point that is still recognized. At best, medicine has accounted for only half the gain in longevity in modern times. One recent review by the epidemiologist John P. Bunker cites a Scottish study that estimated the combined impact of medical prevention and treatment services accounts for 5 or 5.5 years of the 30 years of additional lifespan since 1900, and half the 7 or 7.5 additional years since 1950. This is an impressive contribution, to which must be added medicine's relief of suffering and improvement of quality of life. But as the rise of opioid abuse since the 1990s has tragically shown, treatments for the relief of pain can result in still more pain and premature death—the result not just of aggressive promotion by the pharmaceutical industry in the twenty-first century's first decade but of patients' belief in the power of medications and doctors' limited time for explaining risks. While the efficiency of electronic medical records is helping doctors cooperate in treating abuse in high-risk blue-collar regions, big data also amplified overprescription by enabling the manufacturer of the most controversial pill, OxyContin, to identify doctors with the greatest number of pain-management patients for further marketing efforts.[57]

Among the most intriguing factors promoting health are family and community ties, and the continued participation of older people in the fabric of life. One of the so-called Blue Zones with a high concentration of centenarians is on the Greek island of Ikaria, where boiled Greek coffee is a staple; another is in Loma Linda, California, a center of Seventh-day Adventists who shun caffeine and the other Mediterranean favorite, wine. To balance genetically oriented studies, demographers point to the Italian American immigrant community of Roseto in northeastern Pennsylvania, which had lower rates of heart disease than neighboring towns despite its residents' attachment to potent stogie cigars and copious wine, salami, cheese, and meatballs fried in lard. They toiled in malodorous, hazardous slate quarries. Yet in their isolation from hostile Protestant neighbors in nearby towns, they avoided competition and conspicuous consumption among themselves. Ironically, once their children began to achieve the prosperity they had hoped for and became part of American suburban society, the new generation's sickness and mortality rates rose and made the Rosetans hard to distinguish from residents of nearby communities.[58]

If we had to identify what could reduce morbidity and mortality rates most efficiently in the long run, it would probably be learning from traditional, ostensibly inefficient lifestyles. The sad reality of technologically driven health care is that so much of it should be necessary.

CONCLUSION

INSPIRED INEFFICIENCY

HOW TO BALANCE ALGORITHM AND INTUITION

The new efficiency of the platform society has brought remarkable benefits—and inevitable drawbacks. Electronic bill paying saves trees and postage, but it also endangers support for postal carriers, whom many people find indispensable in their communities. Social media promotion and digital advertising promise to target consumers more precisely, but they also drain resources from reporting and editing. Auction sites and digital marketplaces bring buyers and sellers together with zero or minimal direct cost, but they have decimated once profitable classified advertising sections, not to mention the always struggling secondhand bookstores that do so much for serendipitous discovery. Consumers are better informed about airline fares through travel sites, but the carriers' software and fee structure always seems to be a jump ahead. Mobile devices liberate people from the office, but they also allow employers unprecedented power to preempt free time—and increasingly often even to monitor their physical activities, as we saw in the last chapter. Ridesharing services may make private cars unnecessary for many city dwellers, but they may also undermine public transportation and leave riders vulnerable to price gouging once competition from transit and medallion taxis declines. Electronic securities markets promised lower transaction costs but have encouraged so much rapid trading that the cost of the financial system as a component of GDP has increased. An explosion of efficiency has in many ways made the world less efficient.

This inefficiency of extreme efficiency receives less attention than other challenges of information technology: generation of electronic waste, exploitation of workers in developing countries from silicon and graphite miners to device recyclers, destruction of jobs in the developed world by automation, state surveillance, harms to reputation, unaccountability to democratic decision making, amplification of inequality, damage to human relationships, disruption of childhood, and vulnerability to fraud, terrorism, and power interruptions. The leading platform companies are aware of these issues. They are studying how to address them with safeguards, if only in their own interest. Each problem, if it goes far enough, may impair efficiency. If the possibility of hacking electronic voting saps confidence in election results—and so far there is no evidence that intruders have changed any actual election results—hand counting paper ballots may be more efficient for political life than electronic tabulation. (At least that was the decision of Netherlands officials in 2017.) Even if screen reading is more efficient than paper—and we have seen that in some ways it is—it may obstruct children's learning if it disrupts sleep patterns, as evidence suggests it can. If computer fraud and identity theft continue to increase, they may reduce confidence in web transactions. The same is true if the collection of personal data results in advertising that consumers find excessively personal. One possible remedy is more transparency about the algorithms that platform companies use. But the decisions made by machine-learning programs may be opaque to the programmers themselves. Even when rules are explicit, revealing them might distort behavior. According to Campbell's Law, once a criterion is known, people will begin gaming the system—for example, by teaching to the test rather than for long-term understanding. If the formulas behind credit scores were explained fully, people would use tricks to raise their ratings without actually becoming more solvent.[1]

In 1917 the largest U.S. corporations were the giants of railroads, steel, and petroleum, which had flourished with continuous production. In 2017 the top companies in market capitalization were Apple, Alphabet (Google's parent corporation), Microsoft, Amazon, and Facebook. Critics' warnings—of a new Gilded Age of oligarchic power—may actually be understatements. In 1899 the Pennsylvania Railroad, America's largest public corporation, had a market capitalization of $373 million, or about $10.3 billion in today's money. The privately owned web-based transportation service Uber had in August 2017 an estimated market capitalization of almost $70 billion despite multiple scandals. In the 1890s, the Pennsy had over 8,000 miles of track in twelve states and the District of Columbia, over 3,000 locomotives, as many passenger cars and more than 12,000 freight cars, and at least 100,000 employees. In November 1900 it declared a semiannual dividend of 2.5 percent plus an extra dividend of one percent. According to sources referenced by Wikipedia in February 2017, Uber had only 6,700 salaried employees and was estimated to have lost $3 billion in the previous year. Such is the sway of the platform model of web-based efficiency (someday) generating profit with a relatively small number of employees. Since 2007 or so, mobile computing, together with the accurate consumer GPS permitted since 2000, has potentially extended this model to nearly all of the United States, Europe, and parts of many other countries. The so-called sharing society, the idea that web-enabled rentals can make ownership a luxury or an investment, has replaced the early-twentieth-century cult of production that inspired both American capitalists and Soviet planners. In the platform society, electronic media licensing services like the Apple Store and the Google Store, streaming media services, virtual online courses, automobiles (autonomous and conventional), and medical imaging devices and monitors will be in constant touch with powerful analytic engines. Machine learning will allow these services to become ever more attuned to customers' wishes and tastes, according to the services' advocates.[2]

Even philanthropy reflects efficiency consciousness. Today's technology billionaires, who enjoy even more post-inflationary wealth than most of the robber barons, believe their methods can transform all of society. As Evgeny Morozov has observed, their largesse is often self-interested in a way that the charity of early-twentieth-century capitalists like John D. Rockefeller and Andrew Carnegie was not. While many of the Bill and Melinda Gates Foundation's health grants are in the classic public health tradition, we saw in Chapter Three how it also has cherished a belief in the power of big data in transforming education—whether aggregating countless details of student activity and performance or measuring engagement with galvanic wrist monitors. Unlike the early-twentieth-century Taylorists, the Gates grantees are seeking not a single Best Way but customization of instruction for the needs of each student. Yet the interaction of students and teachers in real-world classroom settings is probably too complex to be modeled by big data. It depends heavily on local knowledge difficult to capture in such settings.[3]

The Gates Foundation's galvanic skin response grant failed, we noted, because of concerns about student privacy. But it also—regardless of the good intentions of the foundation and grantee—seemed disturbingly like a high-tech version of Frederick Winslow Taylor's time-and-motion studies. While bracelet readings do not measure output directly—students might be engaged without necessarily mastering the subject—their use is based on the same assumption that monitoring can improve people's performance. Instead of a stopwatch, the wristband and its physiological data are hoped to bring teachers and students into harmony, just as Taylor's incentives were intended to align the interests of workers and owners. Earlier, in 2008, sharp-eyed journalists at *The Times* of London had discovered a Microsoft patent application for a wireless system for monitoring employees' heart rate, body temperature, movement, facial expression, and blood pressure, as well as the good old galvanic skin response. The idea seems to have been abandoned after a media and labor union uproar, but the gap between the 1910s and the 2010s may not be as wide as we had thought.[4]

Despite the success of specialized computers using machine learning in highly structured, formalized domains like *Jeopardy!*, Go, and even poker, even some enthusiasts of artificial intelligence recognize that while today's information technology can learn from data, it still cannot do so efficiently. As the writer Alex Hern reported in *The Guardian* on a conference on machine learning, artificial intelligence still does not have the equivalent of James Watt's condensation chamber, the late-eighteenth-century breakthrough that made the coal-burning steam engine the motive power of the Industrial Revolution. Platform companies' quest for efficiency may require using resources extravagantly. The massive energy consumption of IBM's Watson, which we saw in the last chapter, and the location of Google's data centers near sources of cheap hydropower and abundant water cooling actually reflect the limits as well as the capability of computing. Google has recently changed its energy strategy, contracting for renewable power with a goal of 100 percent renewable sources. The DeepMind artificial intelligence system that Google acquired in 2014 has reduced its data systems' power consumption by up to 15 percent, at least according to one measure. Still, Google's and other "green" data centers must remain connected to the grid rather than directly to wind or solar sources (which may be distant from the centers), and data center energy consumption continues to grow, though at a far slower rate than in the first decade of the twenty-first century.[5]

The optimism of mogul-evangelists like Bill Gates, Eric Schmidt, and Mark Zuckerberg for a truly efficient connected world has been at the very least premature. We need new approaches, beyond familiar (and often justified) critiques of technological millennialism. We should start, paradoxically, by tolerating hype rather than condemning it outright. Exaggerated claims for innovation are necessary, going back to the European settlement of the New World, as we have seen, and probably even further. (The legendary Pied Piper of Hamelin may be based on the actual fast-talking medieval recruiters, called "locators," who enticed young people to settle the new cities and frontier countryside of Eastern Europe. Their successors were still serving the Habsburgs well into the eighteenth century.) The boosters who promoted America's Western cities two centuries later sincerely believed they were telling the truth about future prosperity amid an often shabby present; if enough accepted their vision, they could be right. Silicon Valley utopianism, like the imagery that lured America's pilgrims and pioneers, is necessary. One has only to read the disclosures in today's initial public offering prospectuses. Most things fail. While caveats protect entrepreneurs from litigation and even prosecution by presenting risk candidly, the dream of owning part of the next Google or Facebook can be intoxicating, just as fantasies of the next Xerox or the next Microsoft once were. All these companies were once obscure challengers to older, entrenched organizations. Grandiose visions of transformation are coin of the realm. We should neither condemn them nor take them at face value, just as we should treat the forecasts of doomsayers and stagnationists, who are also selling a point of view.[6]

Having recognized the virtues of technological promotion, we can also see how innovation can sometimes undermine itself. The extravagant expected returns on investments in so-called unicorns—billion-dollar companies like Uber still losing money before going public—are competing for capital with "market-creating" innovation (to use Clayton Christensen's phrase) that could not only reduce costs but create jobs. We have seen that excessive efficiency can lead to shadow work and efficiency-sapping fatigue. Electronic medical records, while a welcome alternative to the perils of notoriously illegible handwriting, have imposed more rather than less clerical work on physicians. Newspaper publishers lay off actual writers but hire staff to promote "reader engagement" and decipher social media algorithms. Meanwhile, social media sites are torn between charges of bias against human curators versus protests over misinformation when algorithms alone decide.[7]

The substitution of data points for the physical presence of people creates inefficiencies of its own. Without constant practice, if only on simulators, automated control tends to degrade operator skills over time, an alarming prospect since self-driving automobile networks will never be immune from the hacking and denial of service attacks that are endemic to the Internet of Things. Medicine reduced to tests and measurements ignores the benefits of the touch of physicians. Even without multitasking and email, a classroom dominated by students' devices may be less efficient for learning than a traditional one. In fact, Silicon Valley itself has become one of the world's most expensive places for housing because its corporations still believe that physical presence and interaction are more efficient in collaborative work, even if a growing number of workers are arranging telecommuting. Apple has spent $5 billion on its new twelve-thousand-employee circular headquarters Campus 2 in Cupertino to inspire staff members with the aesthetic vision of the company's leader, Steve Jobs. In the words of the company's design head, Jonathan Ive, it is "a building where so many people can connect and collaborate and walk and talk." (Despite all its technical and environmental innovations, the structure's reversion to the self-contained ideal of twentieth-century corporate technology complexes led the *Los Angeles Times* architecture critic to call it a "retrograde cocoon.") In May 2017, IBM reacted to declining earnings by abruptly ending the liberal telework policies that it had not only practiced but recommended to other companies. An unspecified number of its 360,000 employees were notified to move to a work center, apply for a new IBM position, or resign. Whether or not Apple's new building will engender a fresh burst of creativity, whether or not IBM's ultimatum will make the company newly competitive, both moves reflect a revival of face-to-face thinking and new misgivings about virtual presence.[8]

The major current dream of Silicon Valley, the autonomous car that does not need driver attention, could if successful make the driver a more engaged observer of his or her surroundings, as we saw in Chapter Four. Yet Ford Motor Company has patented a movie screen covering the windshield, protecting the driver from any visual contact with other vehicles or life along the road, a kind of Plato's cave on wheels. Ford's CEO has declared that his corporation is metamorphosing "from . . . an auto company to an auto and a mobility company." Ford vehicles, he assures us, will be "able to use analytics to anticipate people's needs, as opposed to people trying to tell us what they want." Among those needs may be orders from Amazon, Ford's partner in artificial intelligence, so when not watching movies we'll be able to buy what Amazon's algorithms have decided we desire. Evidently, even the ancient philosophical aphorism "Know Thyself" is now ripe for outsourcing.[9]

Fortunately, we do not have to choose between digital and analog lifestyles. Even in Silicon Valley people are not doing so. I doubt that many of its gourmet corporate cafeterias proudly serve genetically modified cuisine. Many information technology professionals' children, as we have seen, attend schools that offer spirituality rather than a head start in coding. High school and college students may not buy or read printed newspapers, but much of the news they do read online is made possible by the remaining print news market. The ratio of electronic to print books appears to be stabilizing. The U.S. Navy is reviving instruction in celestial navigation and use of the sextant. Technology journalists are often closer to their high-level industry sources than to technical people in the trenches or to their pragmatic fellow citizens outside the media.

Balancing algorithm and intuition to achieve inspired inefficiency needs six strategies. First is the *perfect 5* concept developed by David Mindell, citing the work of his joint thesis advisor and colleague in aeronautical and astronautical engineering, Tom Sheridan. Sheridan, who had studied behavioral psychology with B. F. Skinner and analyzed the Three Mile Island nuclear power plant meltdown, originated the idea of the spectrum of automation, from the purely human to the entirely robotic. If the scale runs from one to ten, Mindell, like Sheridan, believes the optimum is at five, in the middle. Turning all decisions over to a completely automated system means not eliminating human error, but unleashing the inevitable bugs that engineers and programmers unavoidably introduce into their design despite the most diligent efforts. Automation works best under the control of well-prepared human operators, on the model of NASA astronauts in the Apollo program, who deliberately were given extensive powers over Apollo's onboard computer. The principle has not changed even after more than half a century. Not only for vehicles but for all other systems controlled by algorithms, a caveat from a 2012 Department of Defense report applies: "There are no fully autonomous systems just as there are no fully autonomous soldiers, sailors, airmen or Marines." It seems more efficient to make processes autonomous rather than to recruit and train skilled people, whether truck drivers or editors, but in the long run the robot and the human are best able to correct each other's weaknesses.[10]

One foundation of the perfect 5 strategy is the underrated resources of our own minds. The new efficiency movement often cites research on human irrationality in decision making to support the outsourcing of thought to algorithms. But as the sociologist Harry

Collins showed in his book *Artificial Experts*, we all have an immense fund of tacit knowledge about the real world that can never be programmed into a computer as chess openings, for example, can. It is doubtful that even IBM's Watson, with its vast databases and multiple algorithms, can interpret the meaning of a proverb not already explained in its memory as a first-grade schoolchild probably could just on the basis of experience in his or her short life. Tacit knowledge, especially anticipation of human feelings and reactions, helps us respond creatively to unfamiliar challenges. As Collins put it, "we know more than we can say" because we have learned from social interactions, not just from the kinds of instructions that are programmed into devices. (A corollary is that even machine learning is not like human learning because it occurs outside social interaction.) Our intuitions also draw on a capacity for unconscious understanding more flexible than machine logic. In the words of Gerd Gigerenzer, "Often what looks like a reasoning error from a purely logical perspective turns out to be a highly intelligent social judgment in the real world."[11]

Relying on our intuition does not mean surrendering to it unchecked. To the contrary, electronic memory, algorithms, and automated decision making may free us for more creative activities as pioneers of computer science like Norbert Wiener advocated in the 1950s. As the mathematician-philosopher Alfred North Whitehead foresaw as early as 1911: "Civilization advances by extending the number of important operations which we can perform without thinking about them."[12]

Second of the six strategies for balance is *physical presence*. Face-to-face communication is usually less efficient than electronic exchanges in terms of time spent, but it offers a far more efficient way to convey shades of meaning, gauge responses, and adjust words to avoid misunderstandings and reach agreements. That is why technology companies are, as we have just seen, still investing in offices designed to foster both collaboration and creativity. Emoji are a visually intriguing but limited way to convey the same nuances. While there is a place for video and telephone medicine, there is no substitute for the presence of a patient. In education the most crucial resource is still not information technologies but enthusiastic teachers trained to engage students in classrooms. Finland's school reform yielded some of the highest scores on international tests, yet Finland has largely avoided testing, ranking, and tracking. This style of teaching is labor-intensive; teaching is treated as the equivalent of the legal and medical professions, with high salaries, and is a coveted choice. As a result, Finland has become far more competitive economically in the half century since its school reforms—by not being obsessed with measurement and competitiveness.[13]

Part of physical presence is the sense of terrain, the mapping of people and objects in real space. Think of the difference between a supermarket or specialty store and a catalog or website, or between GPS directions and a paper map, and in turn between a printed map and actual presence in a place. A printed book is a kind of terrain, the paragraphs of each page and illustrations having their own shape. In medicine a patient's body, as opposed to data, is also terrain that complements other information. Geographers and cognitive psychologists have long recognized the importance of the mental maps we make; there is even special software to diagram ideas and products. Because of the limits to practical monitor size, there is still no substitute for an old-fashioned storyboard with push pins and cards for an overview of large projects and coordination of complex schedules. Even the comedy film editor Brent White, who has four large monitors at the workstation in his studio, used a storyboard for an overview of the scenes in the film *Spy* that he edited with the latest electronic equipment and software.[14]

(Of course, there is no law that a physical representation is better to work with than a virtual one. In chess, there seems to be no evidence that either beginners or experts play better with three dimensional pieces on a board or with virtual boards on computer screens. There is no doubt, though, that if playing through the master games is the only way to proficiency, reviewing them with computer software packs more practice into less time than old-style moves on a three-dimensional board—and is thus more genuinely efficient.)[15]

Physical presence also applies to economic life. The rationale of Amazon's acquisition of the Whole Foods supermarket chain in June 2017 is still unfolding, but at least part of it seems related to its decision to open its own unorthodox style of retail bookstore. A bricks-and-mortar store is also a laboratory of consumer behavior that complements the massive data of online shopping habits. Another measure of the persistence of the physical is resistance to the idea of the cashless society. The threat of this movement, which has gained support in Europe and India as a way to combat crime, is not only that even more theft and fraud will be electronic. It is not even the obvious danger to privacy. It is rather an even more serious issue of personal data that might be called asymmetric efficiency. Even without prying into individuals' lives, the owners of proprietary databases and software know far more about our aggregate behavior than they publish. We have some techniques of our own, like price- and fare-tracking software, but consumers and even academic researchers are like club players trying to defeat supercomputers. While cash, like electronic funds systems, can be abused, it also helps reduce the imbalance between big data and little people.[16]

The third strategy for balance is *creative waste*. Regarding loss, Silicon Valley has a mind divided against itself. It celebrates the positive role of failure and how insights from it can lead to ultimate success. But it also promotes the idea that algorithms, especially enhanced by machine learning, can approach perfection just as computers have prevailed in games, even though the reality of most human enterprises is far more complex than games on a limited board with well-defined rules. Hollywood studios may not have used artificial intelligence algorithms to program their films in the early 2010s, but they did expect that a small number of big-budget blockbuster sequels featuring familiar stars and plot lines would sustain them. A Harvard Business School professor, Linda Elberse, championed this strategy. But by the summer of 2016, some of the largest studios were reporting declining or nonexistent profits, and the $150 million *Ben-Hur* sequel failed to earn a tenth of its production cost. Recalling a warning of the doyen of directors, the anthropologist of mass culture Grant McCracken concluded "Spielberg 1, Harvard 0." That might be an exaggeration; in the long term Elberse may indeed be correct that blockbusters are the main drivers of profit in today's environment, and her work has rightly dampened enthusiasm for Chris Anderson's "long tail" of individually modest but collectively profitable sales. The real problem is that blockbuster economics stands in the way of experimentation, which can be a source of future blockbusters. Steven

Spielberg had called for "new paradigms," yet these usually can be discovered only by the inefficient process of trial and error. Algorithms for predicting fiction and nonfiction best sellers, based on big data on readers' habits, have also appeared and present the same problem. By efficiently identifying what has worked in the past and fostering more of it, they are courting consumer fatigue. Of course, human acquisition editors, as I once was, often stay with the familiar, too, which is why some of the greatest commercial successes—most recently J. K. Rowling's original *Harry Potter and the Philosopher's Stone*—were rejected by a dozen or more houses. The strength of intuitive decision making is not in the gifts of any single editor but in the variety of outlook and tastes across publishing as a whole, corporate and independent. It has on balance recognized talent efficiently as a system (as opposed to individual editors' judgments) in part because it is inevitably wasteful.[17]

In Chapter Two we saw that competition for citations and for publication in so-called high-impact journals had a chilling effect on innovation, no matter how much lip service is paid to it. The peer review of grant approval makes it difficult for a dissenting proposal to be approved. It is efficient to go with established laboratories and lines of research rather than dissenters who are likely to fail.

The fourth strategy is *analog serendipity*. The web originally was digitally serendipitous, offering hyperlinks that could branch in unexpected directions. In the twenty-first century the rise of mobile computing with its smaller screens and influence of social media tailored web use more to individual tastes while risking the creation of filter bubbles of like-minded comment. The better the algorithms of platform companies become, the more tailored to the user's existing patterns of browsing and the lower the chances of productive surprises, even if most people see more diverse sources of information than the filter bubble hypothesis implies. As we saw in Chapter Two, some programs have been designed to foster serendipity, and there are apps that deliver articles curated in a serendipitous spirit. Analog media have more than an aesthetic appeal. Because they are not just screen representations but occupy three-dimensional space, they access our imagination in ways that digital media can complement but never completely replace, just as digital media uniquely lend themselves to efficient search and quantitative analysis. Print information on too large a scale is unwieldy. When I had a fellowship in Washington, I sometimes thought of applying for a pass to use the Library of Congress stacks but realized that the number of volumes and the distance between volumes would defeat serendipity. At the other extreme, the collections of the historical "seminar" when I was a visiting scholar at the University of Heidelberg contained a carefully selected library of noncirculating standard and current works, eminently browsable. The 52,000-volume reference collection of the New York Public Library's Rose Main Reading Room includes not just encyclopedias and dictionaries but standard scholarly works. High school and college teachers should take heart from students' continued recognition of the value of print textbooks, as we saw in Chapter Three. As Ann E. Michael, a college writing teacher who encourages students to explore older print resources, has noted, the stacks can be unexpected sources of inspiration. The poet Stanley Kunitz said his life was changed by finding a book of Gerard Manley Hopkins's poems in his college library while looking for a thesis topic and encountering "God's Grandeur" in this volume that he had picked at random.[18]

Silicon Valley executives and researchers, aware of the serendipity issue, have taken steps to design for productive accidental encounters. To some, the idea of engineered serendipity may be an oxymoron, like studied sincerity. Yet the moguls themselves do not seem to get the idea. In an interview with *Time* magazine on the occasion of his winning Person of the Year, Mark Zuckerberg, CEO of Facebook, praised serendipity as an "awesome" force but went on to define it as the recognition of what we already know. No longer, he explained, will we miss seeing friends who happen to be at the opposite corner of a restaurant; indeed, since then Facebook has been able to show consenting contacts' real-time locations. But I suspect that for most people, serendipity means either rediscovering in person an old friend or acquaintance who is probably not a Facebook Friend, or becoming friends with a stranger at the next table. In Chapter Four we encountered Eric Schmidt's vision of a context-sensitive smartphone guidebook that could tell us all about the background of a city. But what of surprises that are not in the GPS database, which will probably be cluttered by advertising? Managed and domesticated serendipity so far is a hollow representation of the real thing.[19]

Fifth is *desirable difficulty*, which we encountered in Chapter Three. It is not just that we learn more by taking handwritten notes than by using a device with a keyboard, or that slightly harder-to-read fonts promote comprehension. It is also that sometimes an inefficient connection results in our assimilating information more efficiently. The psychologist Adrian Ward found that simulating a slow web connection made students more likely to consider new information critically during searches instead of regarding it as something they already knew. There is even a Slow Web movement seeking a return to the deliberative speed of the obsolescent dial-up modem. While I don't consider that era a golden age, the feeling is still worth experiencing, as I noted in Chapter Four about the view from European ultra-high-speed trains, or for that matter the taste of steel-cut slow-cooking Irish oatmeal as opposed to its mass-market rolled counterpart.[20]

In general, we may appreciate something more deeply when we get it less conveniently, and thus get more for our money. There are other reasons, too, of course; even more than ninety years after the great inflation of the 1920s, Germans still prefer paying with cash to using credit cards, if only to protect privacy and avoid overspending. Thrift can be an important form of efficiency. But even for credit card spenders, inefficiency can actually help us enjoy our purchases more. Silicon Valley, true to the "friction-free" creed, is constantly finding new ways to shorten delivery times, whether through more automated distribution centers or through experimental technology like robots and drones. Amazon's Echo home speaker is a triumph of artificial intelligence, not only playing music on request but making possible ordering by a simple command using the company's Alexa Voice Service, an idea that must appall traditionalist Germans. But it is not necessary to reject electronic commerce to see an advantage in delayed delivery. Social psychologists have found that people interpret longer delivery times as reduction of their ultimate enjoyment of a product, which is why Amazon's one-click ordering feature, and its Prime program guaranteeing free two-day delivery for many of its items in return for an annual membership fee, have been so popular. Most purchases are not urgent, though. It turns out that waiting makes using the product more enjoyable, according to other psychological experiments. There is a positive value in anticipation. The catch is that the next time they order, people generally do not remember how waiting enhanced their enjoyment, just as students might not be aware of how writing rather than typing notes on a laptop keyboard helped their understanding. Consumers don't learn the benefits of deferred enjoyment, and vendors have no incentive to teach them. But most people who have been on a long waiting list for a product or experience they have really wanted probably will recall some excitement of expectation. Buyers of bespoke luxury products or of custom-built houses might become impatient, but it is more likely that they will see the delay as further evidence of the quality of their purchase.[21]

The sixth and final strategy, as we saw in Chapter Three, is *cognitive bootstrapping*. The more one knows about something, the more powerful the algorithms of search engines can be. We can recognize from a list of results the sources that we know from experience are most reliable and discard others that the software has promoted. Repeated practice lets us distinguish serious from fake facts, and lets us identify contrasting opinions and their advocates. Bootstrapping is the art of learning to begin with one query and using the results to find new and more precise search terms. It would be better, as I suggested in Chapter Two, if search engines could be programmed to be more selective. In fact, they already can, but this slower search would take more time for the user, accustomed to almost instantaneous answers, and more processing expense for the search engine provider. Bootstrapping is a more economical alternative, using options that search engines already have built into them; for example, limiting searches to generic top-level domains like .gov, .edu, and .org, which may initially exclude some excellent sites and include dubious ones but helps find more academically authoritative ones if scientific credentials are important. As in other activities it is only in deliberate practice, analyzing our last search for information and looking for ways to improve it, that we can develop expertise.

The new challenge of the digital world is the illusion that we can outsource our skills and judgment to algorithms. The founders of Silicon Valley did not think that way. Originally most properly saw computing as a means to relieve people of repetitive and mind-numbing tasks to exercise uniquely human creativity. The web's original hypertext was serendipity incarnate. In the early twenty-first century that dream is not dead, but it is fading. Just as economic inequality has been growing—in part because of the effects of new technology—the price gap between entry-level mobile devices and desktop computers designed for professional and semiprofessional content creation has been widening, even if high-end smartphones cost more than low-end laptops.

If the web is to achieve its promise, inspired inefficiency implies a critical view of all its convenient results, especially search engine queries and social media feeds. Some social scientists and popular writers have seized on popular irrationality, supposed indifference to facts, and uncritical acceptance of partisan statements. Yet elites are in no position to look down on anybody. Historically in the twentieth century, some of the best educated people in the United States and Europe were seduced by Lenin, Stalin, Mussolini, and Hitler. Stage magicians, who earn their livelihoods fooling people, claim that brilliant audiences are the easiest to deceive. The playing-card wizard and historian of magic Ricky Jay told the writer Paul Hoffman that the ideal believers would be Nobel Laureates because the egos of brilliant people make them feel impervious to deception. Penn Jillette of Penn & Teller explained that brilliant scientists are used to accepting counterintuitive ideas like black holes and string theory. Bernie Madoff's Ponzi scheme fooled not only highly sophisticated elite investors but many respected investment advisors. One of his victims, Stephen Greenspan, was a professor of psychology specializing in gullibility.[22]

I have found that academic friends at the top of their fields, while not gullible, never needed to acquire the general search skills that I was compelled to develop as an editor and writer. In fact, even in the 1980s at the dawn of end-user electronic databases in libraries, one prominent social scientist had never heard of the standard electronic bibliography in his field, probably because he did not need it. He knew the colleagues, journals, and papers necessary in his own work. Cognitive boostrapping through search is a skill that can and should be taught, but that like music and sports needs hours of practice. With enough experience, a search intuition can begin to form; reference librarians become information athletes who find ways to elusive sources using a variety of search terms, limits, and other techniques.

Teachers at all levels, from elementary school to graduate school, as well as librarians have an exceptional opportunity to show a new generation why too much efficiency can be inefficient, and why more skilled effort can in the long run be more efficient, just as singers are taught optimal ways to breathe even though most normal breathing is unconscious.

Even if schools and colleges, faced with so many financial and curricular pressures, do not create new programs for search, it is a skill that individuals can develop on their own through practice and through use of resources provided by Google and other search engine companies. The right kind of search—not always the most efficient in the short run—can improve investments, purchases, travel, and health decisions.

I hope this book has shown how new and old technologies alike can be right for some uses and wrong for others. It is an obvious point, but we sometimes need to be reminded of the obvious. Utopianism and dystopianism are useful together in imagining futures but unsatisfactory as programs. Analog experience can enhance digital efficacy. Digital tools can improve analog access. We don't have to choose between the two. We should choose not to choose.

ACKNOWLEDGMENTS

I owe this project first of all to my original editor at Alfred A. Knopf, Ashbel Green (1928–2012), an inspiring publisher, whose encouragement (and shared interests in technology and Ivy League lore) in the 1990s made it possible for me to begin and sustain a new life as a writer, and who sponsored the original contract for this book. In the turbulent environment of the years since 2008, the project went through a number of incarnations. My editor after Ash Green's retirement, Andrew Miller, helped me give the book its present shape as a study of the ironies of the twenty-first-century web of mobile computing, platforms, and algorithms. His comments have been indispensable. My agent, Peter L. Ginsberg, president of Curtis Brown, Ltd., has been equally essential as advocate and critic for more than thirty years. I have been most fortunate in working with all three.

As an independent scholar, I also am indebted to the colleagues and institutions who have helped support the writing of this book. These include Stanley N. Katz and Paul DiMaggio of the Center for Arts and Cultural Policy Studies in the Woodrow Wilson School of Princeton University; Arthur Molella, now director emeritus of the Lemelson Center for the Study of Invention and Innovation at the National Museum of American History, Smithsonian Institution, and his successor, Arthur Daemmrich; Ruth Schwartz Cowan, who as chair of the Department of the History and Sociology of Science at the University of Pennsylvania sponsored me as a visiting scholar there; and Jackson Lears of the Rutgers University Department of History, where I now am a visiting scholar and contributor to the *Raritan Quarterly Review*. Thanks are also due to Edward Felten, who made possible a visiting position in the Princeton Center for

Information Technology Policy, and David Robinson, then administrator of the Center. I am especially grateful to Stephen Ferguson of the Princeton University Library, and the library's excellent reference and acquisition staffs. Virginia Baeckler, now retired as director of the Plainsboro Public Library, encouraged me to develop my ideas on critical web search for the library's public lecture series.

I explored many of the issues in this book as a contributor to *The Wilson Quarterly;* as columnist for *Technology Review;* as a contributor to, and blogger for, *The Atlantic;* and as a writer for the American Enterprise Institute's online magazine, *The American.* I appreciated the encouragement of, respectively, Jay Tolson and Steven Lagerfeld, Jason Pontin, James Gibney, and Nick Schulz and Eleanor Bartow.

Among my friends, Barbie and Robert Freidin deserve special thanks. I also appreciate the help of other friends and colleagues: Daniel Akst, John M. Darley, James Dickinson, Peter Dougherty, Gary A. Fine, Benjamin Friedman, Jerilou Hammett, William H. Janeway, Landon Y. Jones, Emile Karafiol, James E. Katz, Stephen Kotkin, Russell C. Maulitz, Xiao-Li Meng, Richard K. Rein, Philip Scranton, Robert Sedgewick, and Preston Torbert.

NOTES

PREFACE

THE SEVEN DEADLY SINS OF EFFICIENCY

1. "Newspapers: Fact Sheet," http://www.journalism.org/2015/04/29/news papers-fact-sheet/.

2. Ray Kurzweil, *The Age of Spiritual Machines: When Computers Exceed Human Intelligence* (New York: Penguin, 2000), 105; Ray Kurzweil, "The Coming Merging of Mind and Machine," *Scientific American*, March 23, 2009 (originally published in 2008), https://www.scientificamerican.com/article/merging-of-mind-and-machine/.

3. Edward A. Ross quoted in Herbert M. Kliebard, *The Struggle for the American Curriculum, 1893–1958* (New York: Routledge Falmer, 2004), 76–78; Yoram Bauman, "Solow's 'Computer Age' Quote: A Definitive Citation," July 14, 2010, http://standupeconomist.com/solows-computer-age-quote-a-definitive-citation/.

4. "Jules Verne Accurately Predicts What the 20th Century Will Look Like in His Lost Novel, Paris in the Twentieth Century (1863)," *Open Culture*, January 25, 2016, http://www.openculture.com/2016/01/jules-verne-accurately-predicts-what-the-20th-century-will-look-like.html.

5. Robert J. Michaels, "Energy Efficiency and Climate Policy: The Rebound Dilemma," http://www.instituteforenergyresearch.org/wp-content/uploads/2012/07/NJI_IER_MichaelsStudy_WEB_20120706_v5.pdf.

6. Mick Hamer, "Horse Power Beats Diesel," *New Scientist*, July 13, 2002, 11; Michael Pollan, *The Botany of Desire* (New York: Random House, 2001), 230–31.

7. Dave Rosenberg, "Silicon Valley Techies Turn Back Time," *San Francisco*

Chronicle, March 9, 2013; see also Matt Richtel, "A Silicon Valley School That Doesn't Compute," *New York Times*, October 23, 2011.

8. Nelson D. Schwartz, "The Middle Class Is Steadily Eroding. Ask the Business World," *New York Times*, February 3, 2014; David K. Randall, "Only the Store Is Gone," *New York Times*, February 19, 2006; Arthur M. Okun, *Equality and Efficiency: The Big Tradeoff* (Washington, D.C.: Brookings Institution Press, 2015); Fred Hirsch, *Social Limits to Growth* (Cambridge, Mass.: Harvard University Press, 1978).

9. Evgeny Morozov, *To Save Everything, Click Here: The Folly of Technological Solutionism* (New York: PublicAffairs, 2013), 313–14.

10. Mike Isaac, "Uber's Culture of Gutsiness Under Review," *New York Times*, February 23, 2017.

11. https://en.wikipedia.org/wiki/Category:Books_about_the_Internet.

12. Arnold Bennett, *A Man from the North* (New York: George H. Doran Co., 1911), 69, cited in Roy Porter, "Reading Is Bad for Your Health," *History Today* 48, no. 3 (March 1998): 11–16.

13. See my reviews of the optimistic Kevin Kelly's *What Technology Wants*, *Issues in Science and Technology* 27, no. 1 (Fall 2010), ("Technophilia's Big Tent"), http://issues.org/27-1/br_tenner-2/; and the skeptical David Edgerton's *The Shock of the Old* in the *London Review of Books*, May 10, 2007 ("A Place for Hype"); Raffi Khatchadourian, "The Doomsday Invention," *New Yorker*, November 23, 2015.

14. Morozov, *To Save Everything*, 6. Morozov's use of "solutionism" reflects a curious gap in the English language. For all the influence of the efficiency movement in the late nineteenth and early twentieth centuries, there was no word for efficiency as a movement, except Taylorism, which was only one facet of it. The movement had its critics, but few dared call themselves anti-efficient.

15. Ibid., 171.

16. David Carr, *The Glass Cage: How Computers Are Changing Us* (New York: W. W. Norton, 2014), 211–24.

17. James R. Blackaby, "How the Workbench Changed the Nature of Work," *Invention and Technology* 2, no. 2 (Fall 1986): 27–30; Henry Petroski, "Slide Rules: Gone but Not Forgotten," *American Scientist* 105, no. 3 (May–June 2017): 148ff; Jeremy Hastings, "The Russian Peasant's Workout," *New York Times*, June 12, 2016; Liana Vardi, "Imagining the Harvest in Early Modern Europe," *American Historical Review* 101, no. 5 (December 1996): 1364–66; Morozov, *To Save Everything*, 20–21.

18. Cathy O'Neil, *Weapons of Math Destruction: How Big Data Increases Inequality and Threatens Democracy* (New York: Crown, 2016), esp. 199–218; Will Knight, "The Dark Secret at the Heart of AI," *Technology Review* 20, no. 3 (May–June 2017): 54–63; Stephen J. Dubner, "Why Uber Is an Economist's Dream," (including transcript of National Public Radio interview), September 7, 2016, http://freakonomics.com/podcast/uber-economists-dream/.

19. Frank Pasquale, *The Black Box Society: The Secret Algorithms That Control Money and Information* (Cambridge, Mass.: Harvard University Press, 2015); examples of deleted stories from Daniel Shuchman, review of Floyd Abrams, *The Soul of the First Amendment*, in *Wall Street Journal*, May 8, 2017.

20. David Sax, *The Revenge of Analog: Real Things and Why They Matter* (New York: PublicAffairs, 2016).

21. Paul Krugman, "Why Don't All Jobs Matter?," *New York Times*, April 17, 2017; Sax, *The Revenge of Analog;* on the state of retailing, see Christopher Mims, "Three Difficult Lessons for Traditional Retailers," *Wall Street Journal*, April 30, 2017.

22. Tim Harford, *Messy: The Power of Disorder to Transform Our Lives* (New York: Penguin, 2016); Moshe Levy, "Investing Is More Luck Than Talent," *Nautilus*, issue 44 (January 19, 2017).

23. Michael Shermer, "Surviving Statistics," *Scientific American* 311, no. 3 (September 2014): 94; Karen Damato, "When It Comes to Fund Performance, History Is Often Written by the Winners," *Wall Street Journal*, August 6, 2012; James B. Stewart, "Case Study in Chaos: How Management Experts Grade a Trump White House," *New York Times*, February 3, 2017; David A. Graham, "Trump's Dangerous Love of Improvisation," *Atlantic*, August 9, 2017; Bryan Burrough, "The Seat-of-the-Pants Presidency," review of Nigel Hamilton, *Bill Clinton: Mastering the Presidency*, *Washington Post*, July 15, 2007.

24. Francesca Gino, "Leaders Say They Want Nonconformist Employees. They Sure Don't Act Like It," *Wall Street Journal*, May 17, 2017; Matthew Hutson, "The Power of the Hoodie-Wearing C.E.O.," *New Yorker*, December 17, 2013; "FTAdvantage," http://www.fttoolkit.com/d/.

25. Jonathan Taplin, *Move Fast and Break Things: How Facebook, Google, and Amazon Cornered Culture and Undermined Democracy* (New York: Little, Brown, 2017); Franklin Foer, *World Without Mind: The Existential Threat of Big Tech* (New York: Penguin, 2017); Fred Campbell, "Trump Should

Break Up Google's Media Monopoly," *Breitbart*, June 21, 2017. My comments on Foer are based on his acute analysis of the technology industry mentality at *The New Republic* in "When Silicon Valley Took Over Journalism," *Atlantic*, September 2017, 28–31, which I cite in Chapter Two.

26. Joel Winston, "Ancestry.com Takes DNA Ownership Rights from Customers and Their Relatives," May 17, 2017, https://thinkprogress.org/ancestry-com-takes-dna-ownership-rights-from-customers-and-their-relatives-dbafeedo2b9e.

27. Elisabeth Rosenthal, "The Code Rush," *New York Times Magazine*, April 2, 2017, 42ff.

28. Steven Pearlstein, "Consumer Conformity: Why We Like Thick Clam Chowder (and Other Inferior Products)," *Washington Post*, July 25, 2011.

29. See her site, http://www.kanarinka.com/.

CHAPTER I
FROM MILL TO PLATFORM

1. Siegfried Giedion, *Mechanization Takes Command: A Contribution to Anonymous History* (New York: W. W. Norton, [1948] 1969); Daniel J. Boorstin, *The Americans: The Democratic Experience* (New York: Random House, 1973), 340–45.

2. Adrienne LaFrance, "The Mark Zuckerberg Manifesto Is a Blueprint for Destroying Journalism," *Atlantic*, February 17, 2017.

3. Kelly Clancy, "Nature, the IT Wizard: Nature Manages Information, the Currency of Life, with Exquisite Efficiency," *Nautilus*, issue 7 (November 21, 2013).

4. Richard A. Gabriel, *Man and Wound in the Ancient World: A History of Military Medicine from Sumer to the Fall of Constantinople* (Washington, D.C.: Potomac Books, 2012), 176.

5. On recent trends, see Pamela O. Long, "The Craft of Premodern European History of Technology: Past and Future Practice," *Technology and Culture* 51, no. 3 (July 2010): 698–714; Kevin Greene, "Technological Innovation and Economic Progress in the Ancient World: M. I. Finley Reconsidered," *Economic History Review*, new series, vol. 53, no. 1 (February 2000): 29–59; Peter Thonemann, "Who Made the Amphora Mountain?," *TLS*, August 9, 2013, citing Finley; Paul Saenger, *Space Between Words: The Origins of Silent Reading* (Stanford: Stanford Univer-

sity Press, 1997) and my review in the *Wilson Quarterly* 22, no. 2 (Spring 1998): 102.

6. Nicholas Horsfall, "Rome Without Spectacles," *Greece & Rome*, second series, vol. 42, no. 1 (April 1995): 49–56.

7. Hamid Hosseini, "Seeking the Roots of Adam Smith's Division of Labor in Medieval Persia," *History of Political Economy* 30, no. 4 (1998): 655–79.

8. Jacques Ellul, *The Technological Society*, trans. John Wilkinson (New York: Vintage, 1964), 72–73.

9. Charles Coulston Gillispie, *A Diderot Pictorial Encyclopedia of Trades and Industry*, 2 vols. (New York: Dover, 1993).

10. Giedion, *Mechanization Takes Command*, 79–86.

11. Mark Kurlansky, *Paper: Paging Through History* (New York: W. W. Norton, 2016), 240–41.

12. Matthew Blair, *The Paisley Thread Industry and the Men Who Created and Developed It* (Paisley, Scotland: Alexander Gardner, 1907), 38; Thomas J. Misa, *A Nation of Steel: The Making of Modern America, 1865–1925* (Baltimore: Johns Hopkins University Press, 1998), 243.

13. Edward Tenner, "Steel into Gold," *Humanities* 33, no. 5 (September–October 2012).

14. On the North Atlantic "steam lanes" delineated in the mid-nineteenth century to reduce the likelihood of collisions, see William H. Flayhart, *Disaster at Sea: Shipwrecks, Storms, and Collisions on the Atlantic* (New York: W. W. Norton, 2005), 38.

15. Cited in Fred R. Shapiro, ed., *Yale Book of Quotations* (New Haven, Conn.: Yale University Press, 2006), 418. The historian of science Theodore M. Porter has observed that Kelvin was really criticizing the physicist William Clerk Maxwell's equations (which still work without being understood) and undoubtedly would have thought even less of those of economists. See *Trust in Numbers: The Pursuit of Objectivity in Science and Public Life* (Princeton, N.J.: Princeton University Press, 1995), 71–72.

16. Giedion, *Mechanization Takes Command*, 118–21.

17. Burton J. Bledstein, *The Culture of Professionalism: The Middle Class and the Development of Higher Education in America* (New York: W. W. Norton, 1978); Paul Israel, *Edison: A Life of Invention* (New York: John Wiley & Sons, 1988), 397–98; Jeffrey Haydu, *Between Craft and Class: Skilled Workers and Factory Politics in the United States and Britain, 1890–1922* (Berkeley: University of California Press, 1991), 38.

18. Michael Froio, "Why Document the Pennsylvania Railroad?," October 16, 2013, http://michaelfroio.com/blog/2013/10/16/why-document-the-pennsylvania-railroad.

19. David Weil, *The Fissured Workplace: Why Work Became So Bad for So Many and What Can Be Done to Improve It* (Cambridge, Mass.: Harvard University Press, 2014), 28–42.

20. Kevin Maney, *The Maverick and His Machine: Thomas Watson, Sr. and the Making of IBM* (New York: John Wiley & Sons, 2003), 137–56; Christophe Lécuyer, *Making Silicon Valley: Innovation and the Growth of High Tech, 1930–1970* (Philadelphia: Chemical Heritage Foundation, 2006), 243.

21. Samuel Haber, *Efficiency and Uplift: Scientific Management in the Progressive Era, 1890–1920* (Chicago: University of Chicago Press, 1964); Thomas C. Leonard, *Illiberal Reformers: Race, Eugenics, and American Economics in the Progressive Era* (Princeton, N.J.: Princeton University Press, 2016).

22. Jack Quinan, *Frank Lloyd Wright's Larkin Building: Myth and Fact* (Chicago: University of Chicago Press, 2006).

23. Peter Drucker, *The Age of Discontinuity: Guidelines to Our Changing Society* (New York: Random House, 1966), 225.

24. Stalin quoted in Thomas P. Hughes, *American Genesis: A Century of Invention and Technological Enthusiasm, 1870–1970* (Chicago: University of Chicago Press, 2004), 251; Slava Gerovitch, "InterNyet: Why the Soviet Union Did Not Build a Nationwide Computer Network," *History and Technology* 24, no. 4 (December 2008): 337.

25. Stephen Kotkin, *Magnetic Mountain: Stalinism as a Civilization* (Berkeley: University of California Press, 1997), 43. On waste and environmental issues at the end of the Soviet era, see Kotkin's earlier *Steeltown, USSR: Soviet Society in the Gorbachev Era* (Berkeley: University of California Press, 1992), 279.

26. Peter Drucker, *The Unseen Revolution: How Pension Fund Socialism Came to America* (New York: Harper & Row, 1976).

27. Raghuram Rajan and Julie Wulf, *The Flattening Firm: Evidence from Panel Data on the Changing Nature of Corporate Hierarchies*, NBER Working Paper No. 9633, issued in April 2003.

28. Quoted in U.S. National Park Service, "Ford River Rouge Complex," n.d., https://www.nps.gov/nr/travel/detroit/d38.htm; James Hoopes, *False*

Prophets: The Gurus Who Created Modern Management and Why Their Ideas Are Bad for Business Today (New York: Basic Books, 2003), 255.

29. For a contemporary view of alienation and contracts, see Theodore R. Jacobs, review of William Serrin, *The "Civilized Relationship" of the General Motors Corporation and the United Automobile Workers*, in *New York Times Book Review*, March 18, 1973, 37–38.

30. Frederic D Schwarz, "A Message to Garcia," *American Heritage* 49, no. 2 (April 1998): 114ff; Emily Martin, *Flexible Bodies: Tracking Immunity in American Culture from the Days of Polio to the Age of AIDS* (Boston: Beacon Press, 1994), 143–59.

31. Jon Gertner, *The Idea Factory: Bell Labs and the Great Age of American Innovation* (New York: Penguin, 2012), 112; Katie Hafner, "Edgar F. Codd, 79, Dies; Key Theorist of Databases," *New York Times*, April 23, 2003.

32. Carla Lazzareschi, "MCI Founder McGowan Is Dead at 64," *Los Angeles Times*, June 9, 1992.

33. Daniel Gross, "Born to Run Things," review of Mark Mizruchi, *The Fracturing of the Corporate Elite*, *Bookforum*, July–August 2013.

34. Michael Rapoport, "Some Companies Alter the Bonus Playbook," *Wall Street Journal* (online), February 26, 2014.

35. Mark Hulbert, "Investing in a 'Winner Takes All' Economy," *Wall Street Journal*, April 10, 2017; Rakesh Khurana, *From Higher Aims to Hired Hands: The Social Transformation of American Business Schools and the Unfulfilled Promise of Management as a Profession* (Princeton, N.J.: Princeton University Press, 2007), 317–19; Joseph L. Bower and Clayton M. Christensen, "Disruptive Technologies: Catching the Wave," *Harvard Business Review*, January–February 1995, 43–53; Clayton M. Christensen, *The Innovator's Dilemma: When New Technologies Cause Great Firms to Fail* (Cambridge, Mass.: Harvard Business Review Press, 1997); Jill Lepore, "The Disruption Machine," *New Yorker*, January 23, 2014, 30–36.

36. John Herrman, "Stage Craft," *New York Times Magazine*, December 18, 2016, 15–18; David S. Evans, Andrei Hagiu, and Richard Schmalensee, *Invisible Engines: How Software Platforms Drive Innovation and Transform Industries* (Cambridge, Mass.: MIT Press, 1996); Martin Kenney and John Zysman, "The Rise of the Platform Economy," *Issues in Science and Technology* 32, no. 3 (Spring 2016): 62–69. On the role of academic consultants in promoting the platform concept uncritically, see Jonathan A.

Knee, "Review: The Rise of the 'Matchmakers' of the Digital Economy," *New York Times* (online), May 20, 2016.

37. See John MacCormick, *Nine Algorithms That Changed the Future: The Ingenious Ideas That Drive Today's Computers* (Princeton, N.J.: Princeton University Press, 2012).

38. Stephen Witt, *How Music Got Free: A Story of Obsession and Invention* (New York: Viking, 2015), 79.

39. Michael Lewis, *Moneyball: The Art of Winning an Unfair Game* (New York: W. W. Norton, 2003); William Davies, "The Age of Post-Truth Politics," *New York Times*, August 24, 2016; William Davies, "How Statistics Lost Their Power—And Why We Should Fear What Comes Next," *Guardian*, January 19, 2017; Rebecca Wexler, "Computers Are Harming Justice," *New York Times*, June 13, 2017.

40. Barry Schwartz, "Google Reaffirms 15% of Searches Are New, Never Been Searched Before," April 25, 2017, http://searchengineland.com/google-reaffirms-15-searches-new-never-searched-273786; W. Russell Neuman et al., "Tracking the Flow of Information into the Home," *International Journal of Communication* 6 (2012): 1022–41; W. Russell Neuman, *The Digital Difference: Media Technology and the Theory of Communication Effects* (Cambridge, Mass.: Harvard University Press, 2016), 1–2, 10–12, 43, 133–34.

41. "Google's Ad Revenue from 2001 to 2016," n.d., http://www.statista.com/statistics/266249/advertising-revenue-of-google/.

42. "Amazon Profit Crushes Estimates as Cloud-Service Revenue Soars," April 28, 2016, http://www.reuters.com/article/us-amazon-results-idUS KCN0XP2WD. On the idea of dematerialization, see Jesse H. Ausubel and Paul E. Waggoner, "Dematerialization: Variety, Caution, and Persistence," *PNAS* 105, no. 35 (September 2, 2008): 12774–79.

43. United States, Census Bureau, "Computer and Internet Use in the United States," 2013, https://www.census.gov/prod/2013pubs/p20-569 .pdf; "Smartphone Penetration Rate as Share of the Population in the United States from 2010 to 2021" (abstract), http://www.statista.com/statistics/201183/forecast-of-smartphone-penetration-in-the-us/; "U.S. Smartphone Use in 2015," http://www.pewinternet.org/2015/04/01/us-smartphone-use-in-2015/; Sherry Turkle, "Always-On/Always-On-You: The Tethered Self," in James E. Katz, ed., *Handbook of Mobile Communication Studies* (Cambridge, Mass.: MIT Press, 2008), 121–37.

44. Lucinda Shen, "How Mark Zuckerberg Gets $9 Billion Wealthier Every Year," *Fortune*, May 18, 2017; "Number of Facebook Employees from 2004 to 2016 (Full-Time)," https://www.statista.com/statistics/273563/number-of-facebook-employees/; https://www-03.ibm.com/press/us/en/pressrelease/51464.wss; "IBM Reports 2016 Fourth-Quarter and Full-Year Results," January 19, 2017, https://www.ibm.com/investor/att/pdf/IBM-4Q16-Earnings-Press-Release.pdf.

45. Tracey Lien, "Uber's Bad Month Keeps Getting Worse," *Los Angeles Times*, February 24, 2017; Chris Isidore, "Tesla's Market Cap Is Closing in on Ford's," CNN, February 22, 2017, http://money.cnn.com/2017/02/21/technology/tesla-ford/; Mike Isaac, "Expedia Leader Emerges as Pick For Uber's Chief," *New York Times*, August 28, 2017.

46. Noam Scheiber, "How Uber Pushes Drivers' Buttons," *New York Times*, April 3, 2017.

47. Clayton M. Christensen and Derek van Bever, "The Capitalist's Dilemma," *Harvard Business Review* 92, no. 6 (June 2014): 60–68; Bryan C. Mezue, Clayton M. Christensen, and Derek van Bever, "The Power of Market Creation: How Innovation Can Spur Development," *Foreign Affairs* 94, no. 1 (January–February 2015): 69–76.

48. Wiebe E. Bijker, *Of Bicycles, Bakelites, and Bulbs: Toward a Theory of Sociotechnical Change* (Cambridge, Mass.: MIT Press, 1995), 19–100; David Owen, *Copies in Seconds* (New York: Simon & Schuster, 2008), 253.

49. Coral Davenport and Eric Lipton, "How G.O.P. Shifted on Climate Science," *New York Times*, June 4, 2017; Philip Scranton, "Urgency, Uncertainty, and Innovation: Building Jet Engines in Postwar America," *Management & Organizational History* 1, no. 2 (2006): 149; Edward Tenner, "The Mother of All Invention," *Atlantic*, July–August 2010, 32; Owen, *Copies in Seconds*, 326; Tim Moynihan, "Samsung Finally Reveals Why the Note 7 Kept Exploding," *Wired*, January 22, 2017; "Why Lithium Batteries Keep Catching Fire," *Economist*, January 27, 2014; Joe Nocera, "The Hard Problem of Batteries," *New York Times*, February 10, 2015.

50. Jamie Condliffe, "An AI Poker Bot Has Whipped the Pros," *Wired*, January 31, 2017.

51. Sharon Gaudin, "Intel: Chips in Brains Will Control Computers by 2020," *Computerworld*, November 19, 2009.

52. Sarah Halzack, "Looking for the Lowest Prices on Amazon? You

May Have to Dig a Little," *Washington Post*, June 11, 2016; Thorin Klosowski, "How Web Sites Vary Prices Based on Your Information (and What You Can Do About It)," January 7, 2013, http://lifehacker .com/5973689/how-web-sites-vary-prices-based-on-your-information -and-what-you-can-do-about-it; Linda M. Khan, "Amazon's Growing Monopoly," *New York Times*, June 21, 2017.

53. Scott McCartney, "No, Really, This Is a Travel Agency," *Wall Street Journal*, February 16, 2017.

54. David Streitfeld, "It's Written in the Stars," *New York Times*, June 9, 2016; David Streitfeld, "The Best Book Reviews Money Can Buy," *New York Times*, August 26, 2012; David Streitfeld, "In a Race to Out-Rave, 5-Star Web Reviews Go for $5," *New York Times*, August 19, 2011; Sinan Aral, "The Problem with Online Ratings," *MIT Sloan Management Review* 55, no. 2 (Winter 2014): 47–52.

55. On the use of scholarly anti-forgery techniques to construct more sophisticated frauds, see Anthony Grafton, *Forgers and Critics: Creativity and Duplicity in Western Scholarship* (Princeton, N.J.: Princeton University Press, 1990).

56. Barney Jopson, "Toys R Us Boss Hits at Online Shopping," *Financial Times*, November 12, 2012; "Maybe Online Shopping Isn't So Green after All," *Conservation Magazine*, February 2016, (as reported by *The Guardian*); Matt Richtel, "A Convenient Truth," *New York Times*, February 16, 2016; Jim Gorey, "Why Planning Ahead Is Dead," *Boston Globe Magazine*, June 12, 2016.

57. Thomas Philippon, "Has the US Finance Industry Become Less Efficient? On the Theory and Measurement of Financial Intermediation," *American Economic Review* 105, no. 4 (2015): 1408–38.

58. Nathaniel Popper, "Stock Exchange Prices Grow So Convoluted Even Traders Are Confused," *New York Times*, March 2, 2016.

59. Andy Clarke, "The Index Fund: A Monster of Efficiency," *Vanguard Blog*, August 3, 2016, https://vanguardblog.com/2016/08/03/the-index -fund-a-monster-of-efficiency/; Norm Alster, "The Ease of Index Funds Comes with Risk," *New York Times*, October 11, 2015; James Mackintosh, "Let's Prevent Index Funds from Eating the Economy," *Wall Street Journal*, August 18, 2017; Frank Partnoy, "Are Index Funds Evil?," *Atlantic*, September 2017, 24–26.

60. Pawel H. Dembinski, *Finance: Servant or Deceiver? Financialization at the*

Crossroads, trans. Kevin Cook (Basingstoke, England, and New York: Observatoire de la Finance and Palgrave Macmillan, 2009), 11–32, 54–71.

61. Gerald F. Davis, *Managed by the Markets: How Finance Reshaped America* (New York: Oxford University Press, 2009).

62. Kristin Wong, "Most Americans Lack Reserve Cash to Cover $500 Emergency: Survey," nbcnews.com, February 12, 2017, https://www .nbcnews.com/better/money/most-americans-lack-reserve-cash-cover -500-emergency-survey-n493096.

63. James Surowiecki, "Why Startups Are Struggling," *Technology Review*, June 15, 2016; Patricia Cohen, "More Work for Less Pay," *New York Times*, March 9, 2017; Theo Francis, "Why You Probably Work for a Giant Company, in 20 Charts," *Wall Street Journal*, April 6, 2017; Mike Isaac, "Twitter Still Struggles Despite Wide Influence," *New York Times*, February 10, 2017; Shira Ovide, "Microsoft's Bing Isn't a Joke Anymore," *Bloomberg Gadfly*, July 19, 2016.

64. Ava Seave, "Fast Followers Not First Movers Are the Real Winners," *Forbes*, October 14, 2014; Farnsworth Fowle, "Joseph C. Wilson of Xerox Dies at 61," *New York Times*, November 23, 1971; Rana Foroohar, *Makers and Takers: How Wall Street Destroyed Main Street* (New York: Crown, 2016), 87.

65. Tyler Cowen, *The Great Stagnation: How America Ate All the Low-Hanging Fruit of Modern History, Got Sick, and Will (Eventually) Feel Better* (New York: Dutton, 2011); Robert J Gordon, *The Rise and Fall of American Growth: The U.S. Standard of Living Since the Civil War* (Princeton, N.J.: Princeton University Press, 2016); G. Paschal Zachary, "The Search for a Better Battery," *IEEE Spectrum*, April 25, 2016; Joel Mokyr, "The Next Age of Invention: Technology's Future Is Brighter than Pessimists Allow," *City Journal*, Winter 2014, 14–20.

66. Brian Hindo, "At 3M, a Struggle Between Efficiency and Creativity," Bloomberg.com, June 11, 2007, http://www.bloomberg.com/news/ articles/2007-06-10/at-3m-a-struggle-between-efficiency-and -creativity; Ryan Huang, "Six Sigma 'Killed' Innovation in 3M," *ZDNet*, March 14, 2013, http://www.zdnet.com/article/six-sigma-killed -innovation-in-3m/.

67. Nick Bilton, "'Smart' Home Suffers a Brain Freeze," *New York Times*, January 14, 2016; John Markoff, "Hackers Have New Entries with the

Internet of Things," *New York Times*, November 3, 2016; Alexandra Sifferlin, "Fidgeting Can Cancel Out the Bad Effects of Sitting All Day," *Time*, September 22, 2015; Carina Storrs, "Stand Up, Sit Less and Move More, Researchers Say; Here's How to Do It," CNN, August 6, 2015, http://www.cnn.com/2015/08/06/health/how-to-move-more/index .html.

68. Albert O. Hirschman, *Development Projects Observed* (Washington, D.C.: Brookings Institution, 1967), 9–34; Anthony F. C. Wallace, "The Perception of Risk in Nineteenth Century Anthracite Mining Operations, *Proceedings of the American Philosophical Society* 127, no. 2 (April 20, 1983): 99–106; Jeff Faust, "Weighing the Risks of Human Spaceflight," *Space Review*, July 21, 2003.

69. Jessica Stillman, "How Amazon's Jeff Bezos Made One of the Toughest Decisions of His Career," *Inc.*, June 13, 2016; https://www.inc.com/ jessica-stillman/jeff-bezos-this-is-how-to-avoid-regret.html.

CHAPTER 2
THE FAILED PROMISE OF THE INFORMATION EXPLOSION

1. Jeffrey Dastin and Anya George Tharakan, "Amazon Revenue Soars as Cloud, Retail Businesses Dominate," Reuters, April 27, 2017; Carl Shapiro and Hal R. Varian, *Information Rules: A Strategic Guide to the Network Economy* (Cambridge, Mass.: Harvard Business Press, 1999).

2. Jay Ritter, "Google's IPO, 10 Years Later," *Forbes*, August 7, 2014.

3. W. Russell Neuman, "Appraising Information Abundance," *Chronicle of Higher Education (Chronicle Review)*, January 31, 2010; W. Russell Neuman, Yong Jin Park, and Elliot Panek, "An Empirical Assessment of the Digital Revolution in the United States, 1960–2005," *International Journal of Communication* 6 (2012): 1022–41. See also David Weinberger, *Too Big to Know: Rethinking Knowledge Now That the Facts Aren't the Facts, Experts Are Everywhere, and the Smartest Person in the Room Is the Room* (New York: Basic Books, 2012).

4. Peter Bright, "Yahoo Killing Off Yahoo After 20 Years of Hierarchical Organization, *Ars Technica*, September 26, 2014.

5. See Bryan Pfaffenberger, *Democratizing Information: Online Databases and the Rise of End-User Searching* (Boston: G. K. Hall, 1990).

6. David Weinberger, *Everything Is Miscellaneous: The Power of the New Digi-*

tal Disorder (New York: Times Books, 2007), 46–63; Vindu Goel, "When Yahoo Ruled the Valley," *New York Times*, July 17, 2016.

7. Thomas P. Hughes, *Networks of Power: Electrification in Western Society, 1880–1930* (Baltimore: Johns Hopkins University Press, 1993), 79–105; "From Our Files: Arthur C. Clarke on Space Exploration," *Christian Science Monitor*, March 20, 2008. Clarke's landmark paper of 1945 explains the details of solar power but does not mention the reliability of vacuum tubes. It is reproduced here: "The 1945 Proposal by Arthur C. Clarke for Geostationary Satellite Communications," http://lakdiva.org/clarke/1945ww/.

8. Eugene Garfield, "The Evolution of the Science Citation Index," *International Microbiology* 10 (2007): 65–69.

9. Guy Gugliotta, "The Genius Index: One Scientist's Crusade to Rewrite Reputation Rules," *Wired*, May 22, 2009; Declan Butler, " 'Web of Science' to Be Sold to Private-Equity Firms," *Nature*, July 12, 2016.

10. "Method for Node Ranking in a Linked Database," U. S. Patent 6285999, https://www.google.com/patents/US6285999.

11. Behnak Yaltaghian and Mark Chignell, "How Good Is Search Engine Ranking? A Validation Study with Human Judges," *Proceedings of the Human Factors and Ergonomics Society Annual Meeting* 46, no. 14 (September 2002): 1276–80; Paul Marks, "Google Usability Chief: Ideas Have to Be Discoverable," *New Scientist*, November 23, 2011.

12. Nicholas Carr, *The Shallows: What the Internet Is Doing to Our Brains* (New York: W. W. Norton, 2010); William Poundstone, *Head in the Cloud: Why Knowing Things Still Matters When Facts Are So Easy to Look Up* (New York: Little, Brown, 2016).

13. Jessica Lee, "No. 1 Position in Google Gets 33% of Search Traffic [Study]," https://searchenginewatch.com/sew/study/2276184/no-1-position-in-google-gets-33-of-search-traffic-study; David Dunning, "We Are All Confident Idiots," *Pacific Standard*, October 27, 2014; Justin Kruger and David Dunning, "Unskilled and Unaware of It: How Difficulties in Recognizing One's Own Incompetence Lead to Inflated Self-Assessments," *Journal of Personality and Social Psychology* 77, no. 6 (1999): 121–34; Joe Keohane, "How Facts Backfire: Researchers Discover a Surprising Threat to Democracy: Our Brains," *Boston Globe*, July 11, 2010; Amanda Taub and Brendan Nyhan, "Why Objectively False Things Continue to Be Believed," *New York Times*, March 22, 2017.

14. Patrick Wintour, "Search Engines' Role in Radicalisation Must Be Challenged, Finds Study," *Guardian*, July 28, 2016; Farhad Manjoo, "Algorithms with Agendas and the Sway of Facebook," *New York Times*, May 12, 2016.

15. Caitlin Dewey, "The Story Behind Jar'Edo Wens, the Longest-Running Hoax in Wikipedia History," *Washington Post* (online), April 15, 2015.

16. Tom Simonite, "The Decline of Wikipedia," *Technology Review* 116, no. 6 (November–December 2013): 50–56; Andrew Lih, "Can Wikipedia Survive?," *New York Times*, June 21, 2015.

17. Michael Barthel, "Newspapers: Fact Sheet," http://www.journalism.org/ 2016/06/15/newspapers-fact-sheet/; Galen Stocking, "News Magazines: Fact Sheet," http://www.journalism.org/2016/06/15/news-magazines -fact-sheet/; David Carr, "A Newsroom Subsidized?," *New York Times*, October 19, 2009.

18. Paul Farhi, "A Bright Future for Newspapers," *American Journalism Review* 27, no. 3 (June–July 2005): 54–59; Adam Lashinsky, "Burning Sensation," *Fortune* 152, no. 12 (December 12, 2005): 55–58.

19. Andrew Ross Sorkin and Jeremy W. Peters, "Google to Acquire YouTube for $1.65 Billion," *New York Times*, October 9, 2006; Conor Dougherty, "In Earnings Debut, Google's Parent Sets Itself Up to Pass Apple in Value," *New York Times*, February 2, 2016.

20. James B. Stewart, "Facebook Time: 50 Minutes a Day," *New York Times*, May 6, 2016; Will Oremus, "Who Controls Your Facebook Feed?," January 3 2016, *Slate*, http://www.slate.com/articles/technology/cover _story/2016/01/how_facebook_s_news_feed_algorithm_works.html; Susan Pinker, "Does Facebook Make Us Unhappy and Unhealthy?," *Wall Street Journal*, June 3, 2017; Jack Nicas and Lukas J. Alpert, "Google to Protect Publisher Paywall," *Wall Street Journal*, September 13, 2017.

21. Joseph Lichterman, "The State of the News Media 2016: Mobile Continues Its Takeover," *Niemanlab*, June 15, 2016, http://www.niemanlab .org/2016/06/the-state-of-the-news-media-2016-mobile-continues-its -takeover/; Joseph Lichterman, "There Are Now More Americans Working in Internet Publishing than for Newspapers," *Niemanlab*, June 7, 2016, http://www.niemanlab.org/2016/06/there-are-now-more-americans -working-for-online-only-outlets-than-newspapers/; Bureau of Labor Statistics, U.S. Department of Labor, *The Economics Daily*, "Employment Trends in Newspaper Publishing and Other Media, 1990–2016,"

http://www.bls.gov/opub/ted/2016/employment-trends-in-newspaper -publishing-and-other-media-1990-2016.htm (visited August 16, 2016); John Herrman, "Faltering Ad Revenue and Traffic Bring Uncertainty to Online News," *New York Times*, April 18, 2016; Theodore Ross, "The Year Everyone Realized Digital Media Is Doomed," *New Republic*, December 13, 2016.

22. Rory Gallivan, "Amazon U.K. Taps Newspaper Distributor for Same-Day Deliveries," *Wall Street Journal*, October 16, 2014; Pew Research Center, *State of the News Media 2016*, https://assets.pewresearch.org/ wp-content/uploads/sites/13/2016/06/30143308/state-of-the-news -media-report-2016-final.pdf; Margaret Sullivan, "Is Global Expansion Good for Times Readers?," February 12, 2016, http://publiceditor.blogs .nytimes.com/2016/02/12/is-global-expansion-good-for-times-readers/.

23. Robert Darnton, "Writing News and Telling Stories," *Daedalus* 104, no. 2 (Spring 1975): 175–76.

24. Susannah Nesmith, "When 'Reader Engagement' Is More than a Buzz-word," *Columbia Journalism Review*, June 24, 2014.

25. John Agresto, "Art and Historical Truth: The Boston Massacre," *Journal of Communication* 29, no. 4 (December 1979): 170–74; Gary Scharnhorst with Jack Bales, *The Lost Life of Horatio Alger, Jr.* (Bloomington: Indiana University Press, 1985); on fake facts in the original *ANB*, see Gary Scharnhorst, "Alger, Horatio, Jr.," *American National Biography* online, February 2000, http://www.anb.org/articles/16/16-00028.html; Emilio Ferrara et al., "The Rise of Social Bots," *Communications of the ACM* 59, no. 7 (July 2016): 96–104.

26. Caitlin Dewey, "How Online Bots Conned Brexit Voters," *Washington Post*, June 27, 2016; Chris Baranuik, "Rise of the Ballot Bots," *New Scientist* 231, no. 3080 (July 2, 2016): 22; Katrin Bennhold, "Did Tabloids Cause 'Brexit'? It's Covered with Inky Fingerprints," *New York Times*, May 3, 2017; Arpan Bhattacharyya, "Fake News Did Not Affect the Election, Stanford-NYU Study Finds," *Big Think*, January 23, 2017; Hunt Allcott and Matthew Gentzkow, "Social Media and Fake News in the 2016 Election," *Journal of Economic Perspectives* 31, no. 2 (Spring 2017): 211–36.

27. Caitlin Dewey, "Facebook Fake-News Writer: 'I Think Donald Trump Is in the White House Because of Me,'" *Washington Post*, November 17, 2016; Abby Ohlheiser, "This Is How Facebook's Fake-News Writers

Make Money," *Washington Post*, November 18, 2016; Andrew Higgins et al., "Websites Hit a 'Gold Mine' in Fake News," *New York Times*, November 26, 2016; Erin Chack, "25 People Who Don't Realize The Onion Isn't a Real News Source," *BuzzFeed*, October 16, 2013, https://www.buzzfeed.com/erinchack/people-who-dont-realize-the-onion-isnt-a-real-news-source.

28. Geoffrey Kabaservice, "Our Failing President's Great Performance," *New York Times*, June 10, 2017; Edward Tenner, "What Really Bugs the Birthers," *Atlantic*, April 20, 2011.

29. Philip Bump, "Welcome to the Era of the 'Bot' as Political Boogeyman," *Washington Post*, June 12, 2017; Leonid Bershidsky, "No, Big Data Didn't Win the U.S. Election," *Bloomberg View*, December 8, 2016.

30. Shane Goldmacher, "Hillary Clinton's 'Invisible Guiding Hand,'" *Politico*, September 7, 2016, http://www.politico.com/magazine/story/2016/09/hillary-clinton-data-campaign-elan-kriegel-214215; David Auerbach, "Confirmation Bias: Did Big Data Sink the Clinton Campaign?," *n+1*, February 23, 2017, https://nplusonemag.com/online-only/online-only/confirmation-bias/; Edward-Isaac Dovere, "How Clinton Lost Michigan—and Blew the Election, *Politico*, December 14, 2016, http://www.politico.com/story/2016/12/michigan-hillary-clinton-trump-232547.

31. William Davies, "How Statistics Lost Their Power—and Why We Should Fear What Comes Next," *Guardian*, January 19, 2017.

32. Farhad Manjoo, "How Twitter Is Being Gamed to Feed Misinformation," *New York Times*, June 1, 2017; Philip Fernbach and Steven Sloman, "Why We Believe Obvious Untruths," *New York Times*, March 5, 2017; Sue Shellenbarger, "Most Students Don't Know When News Is Fake, Stanford Study Finds," *Wall Street Journal*, November 21, 2016; Alexios Mantzarlis, "Is This a 'Post-Truth' Election? Actually, NO," *Washington Post*, October 26, 2016; Barry Ritholtz, "Culturally Constructed Ignorance Wins the Day," *Bloomberg View*, June 27, 2016; Craig Silverman, "People Read News on Facebook but They Don't Really Trust It, a Survey Found," *BuzzFeed*, January 19, 2017, https://www.buzzfeed.com/craigsilverman/people-be-reading-but-not-trusting-news-on-facebook.

33. Jennifer Agiesta, "CNN Poll: 54% Say Russia-Backed Content on Social Media Moved 2016 Election," *CNN Wire Service*, September 22, 2017, via ProQuest Newsstand; Rebecca Ballhaus and Natalie Andrews, "The

Man on Trump's Digital Front," *Wall Street Journal*, October 14, 2017; Carole Cadwalladr [*sic*], "British Courts May Unlock Secrets of How Trump Campaign Profiled US Voters," *Observer*, September 30, 2017. The journalist Ari Berman has suggested that the real reason for Donald Trump's victory was voter suppression in Wisconsin and elsewhere: "Rigged," *Mother Jones*, December 2017, 24–31.

34. Dale Maharidge, "These Journalists Dedicated Their Lives to Telling Other People's Stories. What Happens When No One Wants to Print Their Words Anymore?," *Nation*, March 2, 2016; John Nichols, "Ben Bagdikian Knew That Journalism Must Serve the People—Not the Powerful," *Nation*, March 14, 2016; Alex T. Williams, "Employment Picture Darkens for Journalists at Digital Outlets," *Columbia Journalism Review*, September 27, 2016.

35. Pew Research Center, *State of the News Media 2016*, https://assets.pew research.org/wp-content/uploads/sites/13/2016/06/30143308/state-of -the-news-media-report-2016-final.pdf; Michael Schudson, *Advertising, The Uneasy Persuasion: Its Dubious Impact on American Society* (New York: Basic Books, 1984), 67–68.

36. Robert K. Merton, "The Matthew Effect in Science," *Science* 159, no. 3810 (January 5, 1968): 5663; Benjamin Carlson, "The Rise of the Professional Blogger," *Atlantic*, September 2009.

37. Jeremy W. Peters, "Web Focus Helps Revitalize *The Atlantic*," *New York Times*, December 13, 2010; Jason Mast, "Can the *Atlantic* Model Save Journalism?," *North by Northwestern*, March 1, 2016, http://north bynorthwestern.com/story/can-the-atlantic-model-save-journalism.

38. Mast, "Can the *Atlantic* Model Save Journalism?"; "Number of Magazines in the United States from 2002 to 2015," n.d., https://www.statista .com/statistics/238589/number-of-magazines-in-the-united-states/; Catherine Taibi, "Employment Rates Are Improving for Everyone but Journalism Majors," *Huffington Post*, February 23, 2015; Franklin Foer, "When Silicon Valley Took Over Journalism," *Atlantic*, September 2017, 28–31.

39. Matthew Dalton, "Fashion Ads, a Last Bastion of Print, Are Going Digital," *Wall Street Journal*, June 9, 2017; Stephanie Clifford, "Magazines Wink at a Wall," *New York Times*, April 7, 2009; Noah Waldman, "Study: 68% of Publishers Use Editorial Staff to Create Native Ads," August 16, 2016, https://contently.com/strategist/2016/08/16/study-68

-of-publishers-use-editorial-staff-to-create-native-ads/; Chantal Fernandez, "Behind the *WSJ Magazine*'s Biggest Issue Ever," August 14, 2014, https://www.businessoffashion.com/articles/news-bites/behind-the-wsj-magazines-biggest-issue-ever.

40. Sydney Ember and Michael M. Grynbaum, "Where the Future Isn't So Glossy," *New York Times*, September 24, 2017; Harry Mottram, "Industry Magazine Circulations: Trivia Down, Serious Up," *Print Monthly*, August 22, 2017; Graham Ruddick, "News Magazines Enjoy Circulation Boost While Celebrity Titles Suffer," *Guardian*, August 10, 2017.

41. Evgeny Morozov, review of Eli Pariser, *The Filter Bubble*, in *New York Times Sunday Book Review*, June 10, 2011; Will Rinehart, "Five Things We Know About the 'Filter Bubble' Thesis," https://medium.com/@willrinehart/five-things-we-know-about-the-filter-bubble-thesis-f34dfdc2789e#.htaofqvsi; Associated Press-NORC Center for Public Affairs Research, *How Millennials Get News: Inside the Habits of America's First Digital Generation* (2015), http://www.mediainsight.org/PDFs/Millennials/Millennials%20Report%20FINAL.pdf.

42. Zeynep Tufekci, "The Real Bias Built In at Facebook," *New York Times*, May 19, 2016; Davey Alba, "Defining "Hate Speech' Online Is an Imperfect Art," *Wired*, August 22, 2017.

43. Craig Lambert, "Our Unpaid, Extra Shadow Work," *New York Times*, October 30, 2011.

44. D. Qing Ke, Emilio Ferrara, Filippo Radicchi, and Alessandro Flammini, "Defining and Identifying Sleeping Beauties in Science," *PNAS* 112, no. 24 (June 16, 2015): 7426–31; David Galton; "Did Darwin Read Mendel?," *QJM* 102, no. 8 (2009): 587–89.

45. Oliver Sacks, "Scotoma: Forgetting and Neglect in Science," in Ernest B. Hook, ed., *Prematurity in Scientific Discovery: On Resistance and Neglect* (Berkeley: University of California Press, 2002), 70–84; Craig Prichard, "All the Lonely Papers, Where Do They All Belong?," *Organization* 20, no. 1 (2012): 143–150; Edward Tenner, "The 'Two Cultures' and the Decline of the Scientific Book," *Chronicle of Higher Education*, September 9, 1987, A48; Nicola Jones, "AI Science Search Engines Expand Their Reach," *Nature*, November 11, 2016; Stephann Makri et al., "'Making My Own Luck': Serendipity Strategies and How to Support Them in Digital Information Environments," *Journal of the Association for Information Science and Technology* 65 (2014): 2179–94; Ying Chen et al.,

"IBM Watson: How Cognitive Computing Can Be Applied to Big Data Challenges in Life Sciences Research," *Clinical Therapeutics; Bridgewater* 38, no. 4 (April 2016): 688–701; Genovefa Kefalidou and Sarah Sharples, "Encouraging Serendipity in Research: Designing Technologies to Support Connection-Making," *International Journal of Human-Computer Studies* 89 (May 2016): 1–23.

46. James A. Evans, "Electronic Publication and the Narrowing of Science and Scholarship," *Science* 321 (July 18, 2008): 395–99; Robert H. Frank and Philip J. Cook, *The Winner-Take-All Society* (New York: Free Press, 1995); Robert H. Frank, "Winners Take All (but We Can Dream)," *New York Times*, February 23, 2014.

47. Michelle Baddeley, "Herding, Social Influences and Behavioural Bias in Scientific Research," *EMBO Reports* 16, no. 8 (2015): 902–5.

48. Loet Leydesdorff, "Citations: Indicators of Quality? The Impact Fallacy," *Frontiers in Research Metrics and Analytics*, August 2, 2016; Matjaž Perc, "The Matthew Effect in Empirical Data," *Journal of the Royal Society, Interface* 11, no. 98 (September 6, 2014): 20140378.

49. Kornberg quoted in Ferric C. Fang and Arturo Casadevall, "NIH Peer Review Reform—Change We Need, or Lipstick on a Pig?" (editorial), *Infection and Immunity* 77, no. 3 (March 2009): 929–32; Konstantin Kakaes, "How Gobbledygook Ended Up in Respected Scientific Journals," slate.com, February 27, 2014, http://www.slate.com/blogs/future_tense/2014/02/27/how_nonsense_papers_ended_up_in_respected_scientific_journals.html.

50. Björn Brembs et al., "Deep Impact: Unintended Consequences of Journal Rank," *Frontiers in Human Neuroscience*, vol. 7, article 291 (June 2013): 1–12; Adam Marcus and Ivan Oransky, "What's Behind Big Science Frauds?," *New York Times*, May 23, 2015; Richard Monastersky, "The Number That's Devouring Science," *Chronicle of Higher Education*, October 14, 2005.

51. Joel Achenbach, "The Reproducibility Crisis," *Washington Post*, August 28, 2015.

52. Mark Sagoff, "Data Deluge and the Human Microbiome Project," *Issues in Science and Technology* 28, no. 4 (Summer 2012): 71–78; Robert Lee Hotz, "What Is Lurking in DNA? $50 Gift Cards, Old Movies," *Wall Street Journal*, March 3, 2017.

53. Steven Wiley, "Hypothesis-Free? No Such Thing," *The Scientist*, May 1,

2008; Tim Harford, "Big Data: Are We Making a Big Mistake?," *Financial Times*, March 29, 2014; "Thank You for Stopping By" [official notice that Google Flu Trends is inactive; last downloaded on September 3, 2017], https://www.google.org/flutrends/about/; Gianfranco Cervellin et al., "Is Google Trends a Reliable Tool for Digital Epidemiology? Insights from Different Clinical Settings," *Journal of Epidemiology and Global Health* 7, no. 3 (September 2017): 185–89.

54. Clay Shirky, *Cognitive Surplus: How Technology Makes Consumers into Collaborators* (New York: Penguin, 2010); Jaron Lanier, *You Are Not a Gadget: A Manifesto* (New York: Alfred A. Knopf, 2010), 79–80; Evgeny Morozov, *To Save Everything, Click Here: The Folly of Technological Solutionism* (New York: PublicAffairs, 2013), x.

55. M. E. J. Newman, "The First-Mover Advantage in Scientific Publication," *EPL* 86 (June 2009): 68001-p1-p6.

56. Duncan J. Watts, "Is Justin Timberlake a Product of Cumulative Advantage?," *New York Times Magazine*, April 15, 2007; Matthew J. Salganik, Peter Sheridan Dodds, and Duncan J. Watts, "Experimental Study of Inequality and Unpredictability in an Artificial Cultural Market," *Science* 311, no. 854 (February 10, 2006): 854–56; Schudson, *Advertising, the Uneasy Persuasion*, 94–99.

57. Robert H. Frank, "Will the Skillful Win? They Should Be So Lucky," *New York Times*, August 5, 2012; Daniel J. Boorstin, *The Image: A Guide to Pseudo-Events in America* (New York: Harper & Row, 1964), 60.

58. Umberto Eco, *The Infinity of Lists*, trans. Alastair McEwen (New York: Rizzoli, 2009); Ira Spar, "The Origins of Writing" (October 2004), Heilbrunn Timeline of Art History, Metropolitan Museum of Art, http://www.metmuseum.org/toah/hd/wrtg/hd_wrtg.htm; Allen Guttmann, *From Ritual to Record: The Nature of Modern Sports* (New York: Columbia University Press, 1978), 49–50; N. N. Feltes, *Literary Capital and the Late Victorian Novel* (Madison: University of Wisconsin Press, 1993), 41–52; Katharine Q. Seelye, "Lurid Numbers on Glossy Pages! (Magazines Exploit What Sells)," *New York Times*, February 10, 2006; Fischoff quoted in Mallory Jean Tenore, "The Top 10 Reasons," *Poynter*, November 16, 2011, http://www.poynter.org/2011/the-top-10-reasons-that-top-10-lists-are-so-popular-with-journalists-readers/153289/.

59. Derek Thompson, "The Tyranny of Most-Popular Lists," *Atlantic*, June 17, 2013.

60. Chris Anderson, *The Long Tail: Why the Future of Business Is Selling Less*

of More (New York: Hachette, 2006); Jackson quoted in Nick Bilton, "Focus on Top 10 Stifles Web Choices," *New York Times*, April 2, 2012.

61. Jayson DeMers, "Can We Machine-Learn Google's Machine-Learning Algorithm?," *Search Engine Land*, February 16, 2017, http://searchengine land.com/can-machine-learn-googles-machine-learning-algorithm -267229.

62. Ben H. Bagdikian, *The New Media Monopoly: A Completely Revised and Updated Edition with Seven New Chapters* (Boston: Beacon Press, 2004), 289–90.

63. *Fortune* contributed 15 percent to Time Inc. profits in the mid-1930s, thanks to the prosperity of emerging industries and their executives. See James L. Baughman, *Henry R. Luce and the Rise of the American News Media* (Baltimore: Johns Hopkins University Press, 1987), 66.

64. Art Swift, "Americans Say Social Media Have Little Sway on Purchases," gallup.com, June 23, 2014, http://www.gallup.com/poll/171785/ americans-say-social-media-little-effect-buying-decisions.aspx.

65. Josh Marshall, "A Serf on Google's Farm," *Talking Points Memo*, September 1, 2017, http://talkingpointsmemo.com/edblog/a-serf-on-googles -farm.

66. Matthew Garrahan, "Wall Street Journal Slims Down Amid Slide in Advertising," *Financial Times*, November 15, 2016; Alexandra Bruell and Sharon Terlep, "P&G Cuts More Than $100 Million in 'Largely Ineffective' Digital Ads," *Wall Street Journal* (online), July 27, 2017.

67. Jaime Teevan et al., "Slow Search," *Communications of the ACM* 57, no. 8 (August 2014): 36–38.

68. Jeff Sonderman, "What You Need to Know About StumbleUpon . . . ," *Poynter*, August 23, 2011, http://www.poynter.org/2011/what-you-need-to -know-about-stumbleupon-the-webs-hot-new-referral-source/143686.

69. Peter Thonemann, "The All-Conquering Wikipedia?," *TLS*, May 25, 2016; Dino Flammia, "In a Digital Music World, Jersey Record Shops Are Still Spinning," *NewJersey101.5*, June 7, 2017, http://nj1015.com/ in-a-digital-music-world-jersey-record-shops-are-still-spinning/.

CHAPTER 3

THE MIRAGE OF THE TEACHING MACHINE

1. Thomas D. Snyder, ed., *120 Years of American Education: A Statistical Portrait* (U.S. Department of Education, 1993), http://nces.ed.gov/

pubs93/93442.pdf; National Center for Education Statistics, "Fast Facts: Teacher Trends" (downloaded June 17, 2017), http://nces.ed.gov/fastfacts/display.asp?id=28f; Carolyn Dimitri et al., *The 20th Century Transformation of U.S. Agriculture and Farm Policy* (U.S. Department of Agriculture Economic Information Bulletin EIB-3), June 2005, https://www.ers.usda.gov/webdocs/publications/44197/13566_eib3_1_.pdf; Kentaro Toyama, "Why Technology Alone Won't Fix Schools," *Atlantic*, June 3, 2015 (excerpted from author's book *Geek Heresy: Rescuing Social Change from the Cult of Technology* [New York: PublicAffairs, 2015]).

2. Todd Oppenheimer, "The Flickering Mind" (book excerpt), *New York Times*, January 4, 2004. See also Audrey Watters, "The History of the Future of Education," *hackededucation.com*, February 19, 2015, http://hackeducation.com/2015/02/19/the-history-of-the-future-of-education.

3. Paul Israel, *Edison: A Life of Invention* (New York: Wiley, 1988), 442–43.

4. Ben Singer, "Early Home Cinema and the Edison Home Projecting Kinetoscope," *Film History* 2, no. 1 (Winter 1988): 37–69.

5. Ibid., 53.

6. Charles Musser, *Thomas A. Edison and His Kinetographic Motion Pictures* (New Brunswick, N.J.: Rutgers University Press, 1995), 54.

7. Oppenheimer, "The Flickering Mind."

8. Brian Dear, *The Friendly Orange Glow: The Untold Story of the PLATO System and the Dawn of Cyberculture* (New York: Pantheon, 2017), 14–15, 18–19; B. F. Skinner, "The Shame of American Education," *American Psychologist* 39, no. 9 (September 1984): 947–54; "Skinner Teaching Machine," National Museum of American History (with photograph), http://americanhistory.si.edu/collections/search/object/nmah_690062.

9. Ludy T. Benjamin, Jr., "A History of Teaching Machines," *American Psychologist* 43, no. 9 (September 1988): 711; Elisabeth Van Meer, "PLATO: From Computer-Based Education to Corporate Social Responsibility, *Iterations* (Charles Babbage Institute for the History of Information Technology), November 5, 2003, http://www.cbi.umn.edu/iterations/vanmeer.pdf; Amy Virshup, "The Teachings of Bob Stein," *Wired*, July 1, 1996; Tom Redburn, "He's Finding the Fire, This Time, in Interactive Media," *New York Times*, July 17, 1994; Todd Oppenheimer, *The Flickering Mind: Saving Education from the False Promise of Technology* (New York: Random House, 2004), 45–47.

10. Dear, *Friendly Orange Glow*, 517–22; Eugene Garfield, "The 'Oblitera-

tion Phenomenon' in Science—and the Advantage of Being Obliterated," *Current Contents*, no. 51–52 (December 22, 1975): 5–7; Dennis Schapiro, "Newspaper Challenges CDC Claims on Effectiveness of PLATO Education System," *Computerworld*, August 30, 1982, 12.

11. Cade Metz, "In Two Moves, AlphaGo and Lee Sedol Redefined the Future," *Wired*, March 16, 2016. On complexity theory, see Lance Fortnow, *The Golden Ticket: P, NP, and the Search for the Impossible* (Princeton, N.J.: Princeton University Press, 2013).

12. Dear, *Friendly Orange Glow*, 430–35, 521–22; Van Meer, "PLATO," 8; Josh Schwartz, "Machine Learning Is No Longer Just for Experts," *Harvard Business Review*, October 26, 2016, https://hbr.org/2016/10/machine-learning-is-no-longer-just-for-experts; Earl Hunt, *Will We Be Smart Enough? A Cognitive Analysis of the Coming Workforce* (New York: Russell Sage Foundation, 1995), 263–64.

13. Matt Richtel, "In Classroom of Future, Stagnant Scores," *New York Times*, September 4, 2011.

14. Ben Quinn and Charles Arthur, "PlayStation Network Hackers Access Data of 77 Million Users," *Guardian*, April 26, 2011; "inBloom, Inc.," http://www.gatesfoundation.org/How-We-Work/Quick-Links/Grants-Database/Grants/2012/10/OPP1070519; Valerie Strauss, "$100 Million Gates-Funded Student Data Project Ends in Failure," *Washington Post*, April 21, 2014; "Post-Mortem on inBloom Reignites Data-Sharing Debates," *Education Week* 36, no. 21 (February 15, 2017): n.p.; Valerie Strauss, "The Astonishing Amount of Data Being Collected About Your Children," *Washington Post*, November 12, 2015; "InBloom Sputters as Data Privacy Hits the Spotlight," *Education Week* 33, no. 15 (January 8, 2014): 1.

15. "Technology—an Empowering Tool for Teachers—Or Just a Bit Creepy?," *The Times Educational Supplement*, no. 5082 (February 14, 2014): 12; Valerie Strauss, "Gates Changes Galvanic Bracelet Grant Description," *Washington Post*, June 12, 2012.

16. David F. Labaree, *Someone Has to Fail: The Zero-Sum Game of Public Schooling* (Cambridge, Mass.: Harvard University Press, 2010), 156–62.

17. Carl Wieman, "The 'Curse of Knowledge,' or Why Intuition About Teaching Often Fails," *APS News* 16, no. 10 (November 2007).

18. Natasha Singer, "Tech Billionaires Reinvent Schools, with Students as Beta Testers," *New York Times*, June 7, 2017.

19. Clive Thompson, "How Khan Academy Is Changing the Rules of Education," *Wired*, July 15, 2011; Karim Kai Ani (posted by Valerie Strauss), "Khan Academy: The Revolution That Isn't," https://www.washington post.com/blogs/answer-sheet/post/khan-academy-the-hype-and -the-reality/2012/07/23/gJQAuw4J3W_blog.html; Valerie Straus, "Does the Khan Academy Know How to Teach?," July 27, 2012, https://www .washingtonpost.com/blogs/answer-sheet/post/how-well-does-khan -academy-teach/2012/07/27/gJQA9bWEAX_blog.html.

20. Maria Konnikova, "Will Moocs Be Flukes?," *New Yorker*, November 7, 2014; "The 50 Most Popular MOOCs of All Time," *Online Course Report*, n.d., https://www.onlinecoursereport.com/the-50-most-popular-moocs -of-all-time/.

21. Edward Tenner, "Higher Education's Internet Revolution," *The American*, December 26, 2013, https://www.aei.org/publication/higher-educations -internet-revolution.

22. Matt Richtel, "A Silicon Valley School That Doesn't Compute," *New York Times*, October 23, 2011; Ben Kesling, "Technology in Classrooms Doesn't Always Boost Education Results, OECD Says," *Wall Street Journal*, September 16, 2015; OECD, *Students, Computers and Learning: Making the Connection* (n.p.: PISA, OECD Publishing, 2015), http:// dx.doi.org/10.1787/9789264239555-en; Anders Ericsson and Robert Pool, "Not All Practice Makes Perfect," *Nautilus*, issue 35 (April 21, 2016); "What Is Anthoposophy?" n.d., http://www.waldorfanswers.org/ Anthroposophy.htm.

23. William Doyle, "How Finland Broke Every Rule—and Created a Top School System," *Hechinger Report*, February 18, 2016; Pasi Sahlberg, *Finnish Lessons 2.0: What Can the World Learn from Educational Change in Finland?*, 2nd ed. (New York: Teachers College Press, 2015), 60.

24. Benjamin Herold, "Poor Students Face Digital Divide in How Teachers Learn to Use Tech," *Education Week*, June 12, 2017, https://www .edweek.org/ew/articles/2017/06/14/poor-students-face-digital-divide -in-teacher-technology-training.html.

25. Monica Anderson, "How Having Smartphones (or Not) Shapes the Way Teens Communicate," *Pew Research Fact Tank*, August 20, 2015; Hayley Tsukayama, "Teens Spend Nearly Nine Hours Every Day Consuming Media," *Washington Post*, November 3, 2015; Kate Taylor, "Schools Plan to Lift Ban and Permit Cellphones," *New York Times*, January 7, 2015;

Elizabeth A. Harris, "Bronx Science Bans Cellphones from Wireless System as Students Overwhelm It," *New York Times*, January 14, 2016; Cyrus Farivar, "Seymour Papert, Theorist Behind One Laptop Per Child, Dies at 88," August 1, 2016, https://arstechnica.com/business/2016/08/seymour-papert-theorist-behind-one-laptop-per-child-dies-at-88/.

26. "Signs of Growth in Pen and Pencil Market," *Stationery News*, May 30, 2016; Siri Carpenter, "Must a Paper Trail Be Paper?," *Science*, September 14, 2012.

27. Richard A. Peterson, "Problems in Comparative Research: The Example of Omnivorousness," *Poetics* 33 (2005): 257–82; Lawrence W. Levine, *Highbrow/Lowbrow: The Emergence of Cultural Hierarchy in America* (Cambridge, Mass.: Harvard University Press, 1990).

28. Leslie Reed, "Digital Distraction in Class Is on the Rise, Study Says," phys.org, January 15, 2016, http://phys.org/news/2016-01-digital-distraction-class.html; Bradley Busch, "Fomo, Stress and Sleeplessness: Are Smartphones Bad for Students?," *Guardian*, March 8, 2016.

29. David Sax, "Why Startups Love Moleskines," *New Yorker*, June 15, 2015; Larry Rosen and Alexandra Samuel, "Conquering Digital Distraction," *Harvard Business Review* 93, no. 6 (June 2015): 110–13.

30. Sarah Knapton, "Banning Smartphones from Classrooms Could Damage Education, Warn Researchers," *Telegraph*, August 23, 2016.

31. Tamara Plakins Thornton, *Handwriting in America: A Cultural History* (New Haven: Yale University Press, 1998); Edward Tenner, "Handwriting Is a 21st-Century Skill," *Atlantic*, April 28, 2011; Philip Ball, "Cursive Handwriting and Other Education Myths," *Nautilus*, issue 40 (September 8, 2016).

32. Perri Klass, "Writing to Learn," *New York Times*, June 21, 2016; Robert Lee Hotz, "Can Handwriting Make You Smarter?," *Wall Street Journal*, April 4, 2016; Gwendolyn Bounds, "How Handwriting Trains the Brain," *Wall Street Journal*, October 5, 2010; Joanna Stern, "Handwriting Isn't Dead—Smart Pens and Styluses Are Saving It," *Wall Street Journal*, February 10, 2015. See also Frank R. Wilson, *The Hand: How Its Use Shapes the Brain, Language, and Human Culture* (New York: Pantheon, 1998).

33. Elizabeth L. Bjork and Robert A. Bjork, "Making Things Hard on Yourself, but in a Good Way: Creating Desirable Difficulties to Enhance Learning," in FABBS Foundation et al., eds., *Psychology and the Real World* (New York: Worth Publishers, 2011), 55–64.

34. Pam A. Mueller and Daniel M. Oppenheimer, "The Pen Is Mightier than the Keyboard: Advantages of Longhand over Laptop Note Taking," *Psychological Science* 25, no. 6 (2014): 1159–68.

35. Jan Tschichold, *The New Typography*, trans. Ruari McLean (Berkeley: University of California Press, 1997), 64–66; Connor Diemand-Yauman et al., "Fortune Favors the Bold (and the Italicized): Effects of Disfluency on Educational Outcomes," *Cognition* 118, no. 1 (January 2011): 111–15.

36. Chris Gayomali, "How Typeface Influences the Way We Read and Think," *theweek*, June 4, 2013, http://theweek.com/articles/463196/how-typeface-influences-way-read-think.

37. John Quiggin, "Doing More with Less: The Economic Lesson of Peak Paper," *Aeon*, February 12, 2016, https://aeon.co/ideas/doing-more-with-less-the-economic-lesson-of-peak-paper; Jacob Weisberg, "Book End: How the Kindle Will Change the World," March 21, 2009, http://www.slate.com/articles/news_and_politics/the_big_idea/2009/03/book_end.html; Justin B. Holland, "Long Live Paper!," *New York Times*, October 9, 2012.

38. Michael S. Rosenwald, "Why Digital Natives Prefer Reading in Print. Yes, You Read That Right," *Washington Post*, February 15, 2015.

39. Stephen Heyman, "Reading Literature on Screen: A Price for Convenience?," *International New York Times*, August 14, 2014; Andrea Peterson, "Researchers Say Computer Screens Change How You Think About What You Read," *Washington Post*, May 9, 2016; Anne Mangen and Jean-Luc Velay, "Digitizing Literacy: Reflections on the Haptics of Writing," in Mehrdad Hosseini Zadeh, ed., *Advances in Haptics* (2010), https://www.intechopen.com/books/advances-in-haptics/digitizing-literacy-reflections-on-the-haptics-of-writing; Geoff F. Kaufman and Mary Flanagan, "Lost in Translation: Comparing the Impact of an Analog and Digital Version of a Public Health Game on Players' Perceptions, Attitudes, and Cognitions," *International Journal of Gaming and Computer-Mediated Simulations* 5, no. 3 (July–September 2013): 1–9.

40. Joel J. Brattin, "Dickens & Serial Fiction," n.d., *Project Boz*, http://dickens.wpi.edu/history.html; "Jane Austen > 1831 Pride & Prejudice," n.d., https://exhibitions.cul.columbia.edu/exhibits/show/lit_hum/austen; Ferris Jabr, "Why the Brain Prefers Paper," *Scientific American* 309, no. 5 (November 2013): 48–53.

41. Craig Richardson, "The $250 Econ 101 Textbook," *Wall Street Journal*, January 13, 2015; Joshua Kim, "Why Digital Supplements Drive High-Priced Textbook Adoption," *Inside Higher Ed*, August 30, 2012.

42. Aric Sigman quoted in Liraz Margalit, "What Screen Time Can Really Do to Kids' Brains: Too Much at the Worst Possible Age Can Have Lifetime Consequences," *Psychology Today*, April 17, 2016; Frank R. Wilson, *The Hand: How Its Use Shapes the Brain, Language, and Human Culture* (New York: Pantheon, 1998); Jeff Miller, "Handy Man" [interview with Frank Wilson], *UCSF Magazine*, April 1999, 42–49.

43. Robert Capps, "How Smartphones Have Unleashed Humanity's Creative Potential," *Wired*, July 22, 2014; Jesse Newman, "Hang Up and Shoot," *New York Times*, November 28, 2012; Matthew Sheffield, "Apple's Tim Cook: Trust Me, We Actually Do Care About Desktop Computers," *Salon*, December 21, 2006; David Pierce, "Review: Microsoft Surface Studio," *Wired*, February 23, 2017; Brian Barrett, "With the iMac Pro, Apple Rediscovers the Creative Class," *Wired*, June 6, 2017.

44. Doug Gross, "Have Smartphones Killed Boredom (and Is That Good)?," CNN, September 26, 2012, http://www.cnn.com/2012/09/25/tech/mobile/oms-smartphones-boredom/; "The Desire for Desires: Why Reports of the Death of Boredom Have Been Greatly Exaggerated," http://www.sirc.org/articles/desire_for_desires.shtml; "The Smartphone Difference," Pew Research Center (April, 2015), 9–10, 41–42, http://www.pewinternet.org/2015/04/01/us-smartphone-use-in-2015.

45. Joshua Foer, *Moonwalking with Einstein: The Art and Science of Remembering Everything* (New York: Penguin, 2011), 52–55.

46. Robert McMillan, "About Those Online Password Rules . . . N3v$r M1#d!" *Wall Street Journal*, August 8, 2017.

47. Sophie McBain, "Head in the Cloud," *New Statesman*, February 19, 2016, 38–41.

48. Brendan Nyhan, "Americans Don't Live in Information Cocoons," *New York Times*, October 25, 2014; Joe Keohane, "How Facts Backfire," *Boston Globe*, July 11, 2010.

49. "CZ:Statistics," http://en.citizendium.org/wiki/CZ:Statistics; Timothy B. Lee, "Citizendium Turns Five, but the Wikipedia Fork Is Dead in the Water," *Ars Technica*, October 27, 2011, https://arstechnica.com/tech-policy/2011/10/five-year-old-wikipedia-fork-is-dead-in-the-water/.

50. Helen Georgas, "Google vs. the Library: Student Preferences and Per-

ceptions When Doing Research Using Google and a Federated Search Tool," *Libraries and the Academy* 13, no. 2 (April 2013): 165–85.

51. Helen Georgas, "Google vs. the Library (Part II): Student Search Patterns and Behaviors When Using Google and a Federated Search Tool," *Libraries and the Academy* 14, no. 4 (2014): 503–32; Helen Georgas, "Google vs. the Library (Part III): Assessing the Quality of Sources Found by Undergraduates," *Libraries and the Academy* 15, no. 1 (January 2015): 133–61; Megan O'Neil, "Confronting the Myth of the 'Digital Native,'" *Chronicle of Higher Education*, April 21, 2014; David Pogue, "What Happened to User Manuals?," *Scientific American* 316, no. 4 (April 1, 2017): 30.

52. Edward Tenner, "Infocopia: Edutopia?," *Princeton Alumni Weekly*, December 17, 2003.

53. James R. Chiles, *Inviting Disaster: Lessons from the Edge of Technology* (Harper Business, 2011), is the best-known popular account of the high-reliability idea. See my review, "When Systems Fracture," *Harvard Magazine*, November–December 2001, 26–28.

54. "Google Search Education," https://www.google.com/intl/en-us/insidesearch/searcheducation/.

55. Ben Gose, "Growing Pains Begin to Emerge in Open-Textbook Movement," *Chronicle of Higher Education*, April 9, 2017.

56. Julio Alves, "Unintentional Knowledge: What We Find When We're Not Looking," *Chronicle of Higher Education Review*, June 23, 2013; Robert K. Merton and Elinor Barber, *The Travels and Adventures of Serendipity: A Study in Sociological Semantics and the Sociology of Science* (Princeton, N.J.: Princeton University Press, 2011), 233–42.

57. David A. Bell, "The Bookless Future," *New Republic*, May 2, 2005, 28–33; Ralph Blumenthal, "College Libraries Set Aside Books in a Digital Age," *New York Times*, May 14, 2005; Hector Tobar, "Nation's First Bookless Public Library System Opens," *Los Angeles Times*, January 8, 2014.

CHAPTER 4

MOVING TARGETS

1. See Joshua Foer, *Moonwalking with Einstein: The Art and Science of Remembering Everything* (New York: Penguin, 2011).

2. Mark Sullivan, "A Brief History of GPS," *PCWorld*, August 9, 2012, http://www.pcworld.com/article/2000276/a-brief-history-of-gps.html.

3. Rodolfo Llinás, *I of the Vortex: From Neurons to Self* (Cambridge, Mass.: MIT Press, 2001), 15–17; Eric Hand, "Maverick Scientist Thinks He Has Discovered a Magnetic Sixth Sense in Humans," *Science*, June 23, 2016.

4. May-Britt Moser and Edvard I. Moser, "Where Am I? Where Am I Going," *Scientific American* 314, no. 1 (January 2016): 26–33.

5. David Premack and Ann James Premack, "Why Animals Have Neither Culture Nor History," in Tim Ingold, ed., *Companion Encyclopedia of Anthropology* (London: Routledge, 1994), 350–64.

6. Peter Worsley, *Knowledges* (New York: New Press, 1997), 125–68; Jeff Manaugh, "Slingshots of the Oceanic," *BLDGBLOG*, July 1, 2015, http://www.bldgblog.com/2015/07/slingshots-of-the-oceanic/; Peter Lewis, *We, the Navigators: The Ancient Art of Landfinding in the Pacific*, 2nd ed., Sir Derek Oulton, ed. (Honolulu: University of Hawaii Press, 1994), 298–99; William Grimes, "Ben Finney, Anthropologist, Dies at 83; Thrilled Hawaiians in Voyage to Tahiti," *New York Times*, June 18, 2017.

7. Raymond Mauny, "Trans-Saharan Contacts and the Iron Age in West Africa," in D. Fage, ed., *The Cambridge History of Africa*, vol. 2: *From c. 500 BC to AD 1050* (Cambridge, U.K.: Cambridge University Press, 1977), 296; Claudio Aporta, "The Trail as Home: Inuit and Their Pan-Arctic Network of Routes," *Human Ecology* 37 (2009): 131–46; Stephen C. Jett, "Place Names as the Traditional Navajo's Title-Deeds, Border-Alert System, Remote Sensing, Global Positioning System, Memory Bank, and Monitor Screen," *Journal of Cultural Geography* 31, no. 1 (2014): 106–13; G. Malcolm Lewis, "Maps, Mapmaking, and Map Use by Native North Americans," in David Woodward and G. Malcolm Lewis, eds., *The History of Cartography*, vol. 2, book 3 (Chicago: University of Chicago Press, 1998), 51–182.

8. Claudio Aporta and Eric Higgs, "Satellite Culture: Global Positioning Systems, Inuit Wayfinding, and the Need for a New Account of Technology," *Current Anthropology* 46, no. 5 (December 2005): 729–53.

9. Anna Edwards, "Confused Beatles fans looking for famous Abbey Road zebra crossing turn up ten miles away in West Ham at ANOTHER Abbey Road," *Daily Mail*, October 11, 2012; Brad Plumer, "Have We Become Too Reliant on GPS? This Satellite Expert Thinks So," *Vox*, April 10, 2016, http://www.vox.com/2016/4/10/11379698/gpsnavigation brainproblems.

10. Beth Hale, "Taxi Sat-Nav Bungle," *Daily Mail*, April 4, 2008; "GPS

Causes 300,000 Brits to Crash," *Wired*, July 22, 2008; Ari N. Schulman, "GPS and the End of the Road," *New Atlantis* 31 (Spring 2011): 8–11.

11. Jody Rosen, "The Knowledge, London's Legendary Taxi-Driver Test, Puts Up a Fight in the Age of GPS," *New York Times Magazine*, November 10, 2014; Mark Tran, "London Black Cab 'Knowledge' School Saved from Closure," *Guardian*, January 18, 2016.

12. Ferris Jabr, "Cache Cab: Taxi Drivers' Brains Grow to Navigate London's Streets," *Scientific American*, December 8, 2011; Eleanor A. Maguire et al., "Navigation-Related Structural Change in the Hippocampi of Taxi Drivers," *PNAS* 97, no. 8 (2000): 4398–403.

13. Jed Z. Buchwald and I. Bernard Cohen, "Eloge: Clifford Truesdell, 1919–2000," *Isis* 92, no. 1 (March 2001): 123–25; George Michelsen Foy, "How Using Your GPS Too Much Could Kill You," *Psychology Today*, April 1, 2016; *Global Navigation Space Systems: Reliance and Vulnerabilities* (London: Royal Academy of Engineers, 2011), 44.

14. Leon Neyfakh, "Do Our Brains Pay a Price for GPS?," *Boston Globe*, August 18, 2013.

15. Roger McKinlay, "Use or Lose Our Navigation Skills," *Nature* 531, no. 7596 (March 31, 2016): 573–75.

16. Steven Kurutz, "Real Adventurers Read Maps," *New York Times*, July 19, 2014; William Poundstone, *Head in the Cloud: Why Knowing Things Still Matters When Facts Are So Easy to Look Up* (New York: Little, Brown, 2016), 44; Alex Ward, "Four Out of Five Young Drivers Can't Read a Map as We Become More Reliant on Satnavs," *Daily Mail*, January 21, 2013; Stephen Axon, Janet Speake, and Kevin Crawford, "'At the Next Junction, Turn Left': Attitudes Towards Sat Nav Use," *Area* 44, no. 2 (2012): 170–77.

17. Gavin Raubenheimer, "GPS in the Mountains—the Myth Exposed," http://peakhigh.co.za/blog/gps-in-the-mountains-the-myth-exposed/.

18. Greg Milner, *Pinpoint: How GPS Is Changing Technology, Culture, and Our Minds* (New York: W. W. Norton, 2016), 111–37; Robert Matas, "'No, No, I Am Not Okay. I Need Help,'" *Globe and Mail*, May 10, 2011.

19. David Roberts, "When GPS Leads to SOS," *New York Times*, August 14, 2012; Kathryn Miles, "'When You Find My Body, Please Call My Husband,' Missing Hiker Wrote," *Boston Globe*, May 25, 2016; Jess Bidgood and Richard Pérez-Peña, "'When You Find My Body': Fatal Turn on the Appalachian Trail," *New York Times*, May 27, 2016; Lauren Abbate,

"Hiker Who Died on Appalachian Trail Didn't Know How to Use Compass," *Portland Press-Herald*, May 27, 2016.

20. Ashley Halsey III, "Does Autopilot Dull the Skills of U.S. Airline Pilots?," *Washington Post*, January 14, 2016; Kevin Hartnett, "Humans and Autopilot: A Complicated Relationship," *Boston Globe*, December 8, 2014; Andrew Zolli, "Want to Build Resilience? Kill the Complexity," *Harvard Business Review* blog, September 26, 2012.

21. Charles Perrow, *Normal Accidents: Living with High Risk Technologies*, updated ed. (Princeton, N.J.: Princeton University Press, 1999), 170–231; U.S. National Research Council, Committee on Advances in Pilotage and Navigation, *Minding the Helm: Marine Navigation and Piloting* (Washington, D.C.: National Academies Press, 1994), 268–69; "British, French Nuclear Submarines Collide," February 16, 2009, http://www.cnn.com/2009/WORLD/europe/02/16/british.french.submarine.incident/index.html.

22. "How Large Ships Use Navigation Systems," transcript, *Talk of the Nation*, January 20, 2012, http://www.npr.org/2012/01/20/145525012/how-large-ships-use-navigation-systems.

23. Lt. Col. Jason Wolf, " 'Alive at 25' Teaches Airmen to Drive and Survive," September 11, 2009, http://www.macdill.af.mil/News/Article-Display/Article/232366/alive-at-25-teaches-airmen-to-drive-and-survive.

24. Leonard Evans, *Traffic Safety and the Driver* (New York: Van Nostrand Reinhold, 1991), 315–16.

25. Tudor Van Hampton, "Looking to Cars, Trucks Step Up Safety," *New York Times*, June 29, 2014; Aaron Brown, "8 Reasons That Germany's Autobahn Is So Much Better than US Highways," *Business Insider*, March 30, 2016; Schulman, "GPS and the End of the Road," 6–8.

26. Nicole Perlroth, "Why Automakers Are Hiring Security Experts," *New York Times*, June 8, 2017; Alex Davies, "Google's Self-Driving Car Caused Its First Crash," *Wired*, February 29, 2016; David Gelles, Hiroko Tabuchi, and Matthew Dolan, "The Weak Spot Under the Hood," *New York Times*, September 27, 2015; Francis X. Govers III, "Google Reveals Lessons Learned (and Accident Count) from Self-Driving Car Program," *New Atlas*, May 14, 2015.

27. "Google Reveals How Often Drivers Take Control of Self-Driving Cars: It Won't Pay to Be Distracted," *ACS Information Age*, January 14, 2016.

28. Perlroth, "Why Automakers Are Hiring Security Experts"; Samantha Masunaga and Russ Mitchell, "Tesla Says Jealousy, Not Autopilot Safety Concerns, Caused Breakup with Mobileye," *Los Angeles Times*, September 15, 2016.

29. John Markoff, "Can Robot Cars Trust Us?," *New York Times*, June 8, 2017; Eric A. Taub, "Like a Living Room You Can Take Out on the Freeway," *New York Times*, June 16, 2017.

30. David A. Mindell, *Our Robots, Ourselves: Robotics and the Myths of Autonomy* (New York: Viking, 2015), 198–207.

31. Brian K. Roberts, "Will Traffic Nimbys Ruin Waze?," *Los Angeles Times*, May 4, 2015; Joe Flint, "In L.A., One Way to Beat Traffic Runs into Backlash," *Wall Street Journal*, November 14, 2015.

32. Neal E. Boudette, "Creating a Road Map for the Self-Driving Car," *New York Times*, March 3, 2017; Alex Davies, "Avoiding Squirrels and Other Things Google's Robot Car Can't Do," *Wired*, May 27, 2014.

33. Emma G. Fitzsimmons and Winnie Hu, "Flocking to Uber and Lyft, Commuters Inch Through New York," *New York Times*, March 7, 2017; Joshua Brustein, "Uber and Lyft Want to Replace Public Buses," *Bloomberg*, August 15, 2016; Martine Powers, "This Nightmare Commute on New York's F Train Sounds an Awful Lot Like Metro," *Washington Post*, June 6, 2017; Emily Badger, "More Rides to Hail May Mean More Traffic to Bear," *New York Times*, October 17, 2017.

34. David Hambling, "GPS Chaos: How a $30 Box Can Jam Your Life," *New Scientist*, March 4, 2011; Michael Peck, "The Pentagon Is Worried About Hacked GPS," *The National Interest*, January 14, 2016; Brett Carter and Delores Knipp, "It's Never Been More Important to Keep an Eye on Space Weather," Phys.org, October 3, 2016, http://phys.org/news/2016-10-important-eye-space-weather.html; Alexandra Witze, "US Sharpens Surveillance of Crippling Solar Storms," *Nature* 537 (September 22, 2016): 458–59; United States Department of Transportation, "Federal Automated Vehicles Policy," September 2016, https://www.transportation.gov/sites/dot.gov/files/docs/AV%20policy%20guidance%20PDF.pdf.

35. Hana R. Alberts, "Why a 19th-Century Marble Arch Sits Inside an NYC Auto Shop," Curbed.com, June 4, 2013, http://ny.curbed.com/2013/6/4/10237058/why-a-19th-century-marble-arch-sits-inside-an-nyc-auto-shop; Christopher Gray, "Upper Broadway: Marble Entry to a Vanished Estate," *New York Times*, March 4, 2001.

36. Grady Clay, *Close-Up: How to Read the American City* (Chicago: University of Chicago Press, 1980), 11, 13.

37. Ibid., 117–19, 53–54, 112–13; "This App Was Made for Walking—but Is It Racist?," transcript, *All Things Considered*, January 25, 2012, http://www.npr.org/2012/01/25/145337346/this-app-was-made-for-walking-but-is-it-racist. In 2016 at least one such app, RedZone, was commercially available: Kris Carlon, "This Navigation App Keeps You Out of High-Crime Areas in Real Time," *Apps & Games News*, April 15, 2016, http://www.androidauthority.com/redzone-navigation-app-avoids-high-crime-areas-686894; Mark Monmonier, *No Dig, No Fly, No Go: How Maps Restrict and Control* (Chicago: University of Chicago Press, 2010), 117–24.

38. Rachel Nuwer, "The Last Unmapped Places on Earth," BBC.com, November 28, 2014, http://www.bbc.com/future/story/20141127-the-last-unmapped-places.

39. Kate Losse, "The Art of Failing Upward," *New York Times*, March 6, 2016.

40. Quoted in Matt McGee, "Google's Schmidt: 'Next Great Stage' of Search Is Autonomous, Personal," September 7, 2010, http://searchengineland.com/schmidt-great-stage-search-is-autonomous-personal-50014.

41. Rebecca Solnit, *A Field Guide to Getting Lost* (New York: Penguin, 2006); "Future of Getting Lost" (video), https://www.c-span.org/video/?320447-1/future-getting-lost.

42. "Martin Parr's 'Paris' Photo Exhibit Captures Everyday Life in French Capital," April 5, 2014, http://www.france24.com/en/20140401-france-culture-martin-parr-paris-photo.

43. Schulman, "GPS and the End of the Road," 21.

44. Tim Prudente, "In the Era of GPS, Naval Academy Revives Celestial Navigation Sextant," *Los Angeles Times*, October 15, 2015.

45. Neil Smith, "'Academic War over the Field of Geography': The Elimination of Geography at Harvard, 1947–1951," *Annals of the Association of American Geographers* 77, no. 2 (June 1987): 155–72; Edward Tenner, "Harvard, Bring Back Geography!," *Harvard Magazine*, May–June 1988, 27–30; Christopher Reed, "Hello, Geotech," *Harvard Magazine*, November–December 2006, 44–51.

46. Tenner, "Harvard, Bring Back Geography!," 28–29; Ira Kay, "The Case of Bush II," *Counterpunch*, November 2, 2004, http://www.counterpunch

.org/2004/11/02/the-case-of-bush-ii; Dana Milbank, "Did Trump Know Where He Was?," *Washington Post*, May 24, 2017.

47. Michael Williams, "Sauer and 'Man's Role in Changing the Face of the Earth,'" *Geographical Review* 77, no. 2 (April 1987): 218–31; "About the Committee on Geographical Studies," http://geography.uchicago.edu/.

48. Phuong Le, "Why More Parents Are Seeking to Raise Their Children in the City," *Christian Science Monitor*, March 24, 2015.

49. Guy Hoffman et al., "In-Car Game Design for Children: Child vs. Parent Perspective," Conference Paper, June 2013, https://www.research gate.net/publication/262424622.

50. Patrick Barkham, "HS2: The Human Cost of Britain's Most Expensive Ever Rail Project," *Guardian*, November 17, 2015.

CHAPTER 5

THE MANAGED BODY

1. T. Rees Shapiro, "For When They Can't Heal a Pet, Vets Get Lesson in Loss," *Washington Post*, September 27, 2015; Susan Freinkel, "Rebuilding Our Badly Broken Pets," *New York Times*, January 14, 2014.

2. Thomas C. Leonard, *Illiberal Reformers: Race, Eugenics, and American Economics in the Progressive Era* (Princeton, N.J.: Princeton University Press, 2016), 109–19.

3. James T. Patterson, *The Dread Disease: Cancer and Modern American Culture* (Cambridge, Mass.: Harvard University Press, 1987), 138–40; William Seagle, *Law: The Science of Inefficiency* (New York: Macmillan, 1952), 1–18.

4. Milt Freudenheim, "A Plan to Send Prescriptions Electronically," *New York Times*, February 23, 2001; Milt Freudenheim, "So Much for the Doctor's Bad Handwriting on Drug Prescriptions," *New York Times*, April 9, 2002; Daniel K. Sokol and Samantha Hettige, "Poor Handwriting Remains a Significant Problem in Medicine," *Journal of the Royal Society of Medicine* 99, no. 12 (December 2006): 645–46; F. Javier Rodríguez-Vera et al., "Illegible Handwriting in Medical Records," *Journal of the Royal Society of Medicine* 95, no. 11 (November 2002): 545–46; Philip Aspden et al., *Preventing Medication Errors* (Washington, D.C.: National Academies Press, 2007), 74.

5. Sarah Kliff, "When Squirrels Attack!," *Washington Post*, February 15, 2014.

6. Anna Wilde Mathews, "Walked into a Lamppost? Hurt While Crocheting? Help Is on the Way," *Wall Street Journal*, September 13, 2011.

7. Arthur L. Caplan et al., "Beating Burnout: Are EHRs the Enemy?" (conference video), October 19, 2016, http://www.medscape.com/view article/869437; Christine Sinsky et al., "Allocation of Physician Time in Ambulatory Practice: A Time and Motion Study in 4 Specialties," *Annals of Internal Medicine* online, September 6, 2016 (I am grateful to Dr. Russell Maulitz for calling this paper to my attention); Robert M. Wachter, "How Measurement Fails Us," *New York Times*, January 17, 2016; Michael Geruso and Timothy Layton, "Upcoding: Evidence from Medicare on Squishy Risk Adjustment," National Bureau of Economic Research Working Paper 21222, http://www.nber.org/papers/w21222; Elisabeth Rosenthal, "The Code Rush," *New York Times Magazine*, April 2, 2017, 42ff.

8. Rick Mullin, "Cost to Develop New Pharmaceutical Drug Now Exceeds $2.5B," *Chemical & Engineering News*, November 24, 2014, republished in *Scientific American*, https://www.scientificamerican.com/article/cost-to -develop-new-pharmaceutical-drug-now-exceeds-2-5b; Jason Millman, "Does It Really Cost $2.6 Billion to Develop a New Drug?," *Washington Post*, November 19, 2014.

9. U.S. Department of Health and Human Services, Food and Drug Administration, Center for Evaluation and Research, "The History of Drug Regulation in the United States," http://www.fda.gov/downloads/ AboutFDA/WhatWeDo/History/ProductRegulation/PromotingSafe andEffectiveDrugsfor100Years/UCM114468.pdf.

10. "An Incurable Disease," *Economist*, September 29, 2012.

11. Ashutosh Jogalekar, "Why Drugs Are Expensive: It's the Science, Stupid," *Scientific American*, January 6, 2014. Jogalekar also explains why the apparently hyperefficient techniques for screening natural substances yield so few successes: "Why Drug Discovery Is Hard—Part 2: Easter Island, Pit Vipers; Where Do Drugs Come From?," *Scientific American*, January 7, 2014.

12. Stephen M. Strittmatter, "Old Drugs Learn New Tricks," *Nature Medicine* 20, no. 6 (June 2014): 590–91; Andrew Pollack, "Viagra Gains Some Advocates as Treatment for Lung Disease," *New York Times*, April 10, 2004; Aaron S. Kesselheim et al., "The Roles of Academia, Rare Diseases, and Repurposing in the Development of the Most Transformative Drugs," *Health Affairs* 34, no. 2 (February 2015), 286–93.

13. Statistics from Kesselheim et al., "Roles of Academia," 287.

14. John P. A. Ioannidis, "How to Make More Published Research True," *PLOS Medicine*, October 21, 2014, http://dx.doi.org/10.1371/journal.pmed.1001747.

15. Des Spence, "Evidence Based Medicine Is Broken," *BMJ* online, BMJ 2014;348:g22, doi: 10.1136/bmj.g22 (published January 3, 2014).

16. John P. A. Ioannidis, "The Mass Production of Redundant, Misleading, and Conflicted Systematic Reviews and Meta-analyses," *Milbank Quarterly* 94, no. 3 (September 2016): 485–514.

17. David Bornstein, "Helping New Drugs out of Research's 'Valley of Death,'" "Opinionator" blog, *New York Times*, May 2, 2011; "The Cost of Salami Slicing" (editorial), *Nature Materials* 4, no.1 (January 2005): 1; Whitney J. Owen, "In Defense of the Least Publishable Unit," *Chronicle of Higher Education*, February 9, 2004.

18. "OA by the Numbers," http://oad.simmons.edu/oadwiki/OA_by_the_numbers; Declan Butler, "The Dark Side of Publishing," *Nature* 495, no. 7,442 (March 28, 2013): 433–35; Andrew Silver, "Controversial Website That Lists 'Predatory' Publishers Shuts Down," *Nature*, January 18, 2017; Carl Straumsheim, "Academic Terrorist," *Inside Higher Ed*, June 2, 2017, https://www.insidehighered.com/news/2017/06/02/librarian-behind-list-predatory-publishers-still-faces-harassment-online; Jeffrey Beall, "What I Learned from Predatory Publishers," *Biochemia Medica* 27, no. 2 (2017): 273–79, http://www.biochemia-medica.com/2017/27/273.

19. Esmé E. Deprez and Caroline Chen, "Medical Journals Have a Fake News Problem," *Bloomberg Businessweek*, September 4, 2017, 52–57.

20. Gina Kolata, "So Many Research Scientists, So Few Professorships," *New York Times*, July 14, 2016.

21. "Scientists Discover Multitude of Drug Side Effects, Interactions Using New Computer Algorithm," *Stanford Medicine News Center*, March 14, 2012, https://med.stanford.edu/news/all-news/2012/03/scientists-discover-multitude-of-drug-side-effects-interactions-using-new-computer-algorithm.html.

22. Amber Dance, "Medical Histories," *Nature* 537, no. 7,619 (September 8, 2016): S52–S53; David Cyranoski, "The Sequencing Superpower," *Nature* 534, no. 2,607 (June 23, 2016): 462–63.

23. Stephen S. Hall, "Revolution Postponed," *Scientific American* 303, no. 4 (October 2010): 64–65.

24. Alison Abbott, "Scientists Bust Myth That Our Bodies Have More Bacteria than Human Cells," *Nature*, January 8, 2016; Knvul Sheikh, "The Breast Has Its Own Microbiome—and the Mix of Bacteria Could Prevent or Encourage Cancer," *Scientific American* 315, no. 4 (October 2016): 21; Vinay Prasad, "The Precision-Oncology Illusion," *Nature* 537, no. 7619 (September 8, 2016): S52–S53; Abigail Zuger, "Genes Tell Only Part of Story," *New York Times*, February 17, 2015.

25. Xiao-Li Meng, "Statistical Paradises and Paradoxes in Big Data," Royal Statistical Society Annual Conference, October 3, 2016, https://www.youtube.com/watch?v=8YLdIDOMEZs; Xiao-Li Meng to author, September 6, 2017.

26. Siddhartha Mukherjee, *The Gene: An Intimate History* (New York: Simon & Schuster, 2016), 408; Gina Kolata, "Project Sheds Light on What Drives Genes," *New York Times*, February 19, 2015.

27. See the critique of Mukherjee's *The Gene* as "whiggish" by the astrobiologist and historian of science Nathaniel Comfort, "Genes Are Overrated," *Atlantic*, June 2016, 42–44; Abigail Zuger, "Genes Tell Only Part of Story," *New York Times*, February 17, 2015.

28. "Fact Sheet," https://mediacenter.23andme.com/fact-sheet/; "What Is the Difference Between Genotyping and Sequencing," https://customercare.23andme.com/hc/en-us/articles/202904600-What-is-the-difference-between-genotyping-and-sequencing-; Gina Kolata, "Consumer Genetic Tests Win F.D.A. Approval," *New York Times*, April 7, 2017; Malcolm Ritter, "Science Says: DNA Test Results May Not Change Health Habits," *U.S. News*, August 17, 2017.

29. Jon Fingas, "Fitbit's Lead in the Wearable World Shrinks Due to Newcomers," *Engadget*, May 16, 2016, https://www.engadget.com/2016/05/16/wearable-market-share-q1-2016/; http://www.idc.com/getdoc.jsp?containerId=prUS41530816; PwC, "The Wearable Life 2.0" (2016), https://www.pwc.com/us/en/industry/entertainment-media/assets/pwc-cis-wearables.pdf, 5.

30. PwC, "The Wearable Life 2.0," 7–8, 14.

31. Ibid., 21–22; Rachel Bachman, "To Add Steps, Fitbit Cheats Use Pets, Ceiling Fans, Power Tools," *Wall Street Journal*, June 10, 2016; Thomas Heath, "This Employee ID Badge Monitors and Listens to You at Work—Except in the Bathroom," *Washington Post*, September 7, 2016.

32. Jordan Etkin, "The Hidden Cost of Personal Quantification," *Journal of*

Consumer Research 42, no. 6 (April 2016): 967–83; Alfie Kohn, *Punished by Rewards* (Boston: Houghton Mifflin, 1993).

33. Cari Romm, "The Nihilistic Angst of Quitting Your Fitbit," *New York* magazine (blog), August 26, 2016, nymag.com/scienceofus/2016/08/i-quit-fitbit-and-fell-into-nihilistic-despair.html; Paul Ford, "I Tried to Build My Perfect Quantified Self," *New Republic*, Fall 2015, 4–5.

34. Gretchen Reynolds, "The False Hope of Activity Trackers," *New York Times*, September 27, 2016; John M. Jakicic et al., "Effect of Wearable Technology Combined with a Lifestyle Intervention on Long-term Weight Loss: The IDEA Randomized Clinical Trial," *JAMA* 316, no. 11 (September 20, 2016): 1161–71; Aaron E. Carroll, "Don't Expect to Lose Weight with Fitness Devices," *New York Times*, February 21, 2017.

35. "Pokemon Go Increased U.S. Activity Levels by 144 Billion Steps in Just 30 Days," *Technology Review*, October 21, 2016, https://www.technology review.com/s/602706/pokemon-go-increased-us-activity-levels-by-144 -billion-steps-in-just-30-days/.

36. National Institutes of Health, Office of Dietary Supplements, "Multi-vitamin/Mineral Supplements: Fact Sheet for Health Professionals, https://ods.od.nih.gov/factsheets/MVMS-HealthProfessional/ (down-loaded October 17, 2016); Jared Newman, "FDA Wants to Regulate Some Wearables, but Fitbit's Fine," *PCWorld*, January 20, 2015; Andrea Bartz and Brenna Ehrlich, "Be Careful When Diagnosing Your Ailments Online," *CNN*, August 8, 2012, http://www.cnn.com/2012/08/08/tech/socialmedia/netiquetteonlinediagnoses/; Katherine Boehret, "Google Will Help Your Self-Diagnosis with New Symptom Search," *The Verge*, June 20, 2016, http://www.theverge.com/2016/6/20/11978338/google -symptom-search-app-web-md-health-doctor; Jane E. Brody, "Studies Show Little Benefit in Supplements," *New York Times*, November 15, 2016.

37. Jan Van den Bulck, "Sleep Apps and the Quantified Self: Blessing or Curse?," *Journal of Sleep Research* 24, no. 2 (April 2015): 121–23.

38. Deborah Lupton, "Quantified Sex: A Critical Analysis of Sexual and Reproductive Self-Tracking Using Apps," *Culture, Health & Sexuality* 17, no. 4 (2015): 440–53.

39. Deborah Lupton, "Understanding the Human Machine," *IEEE Technology and Society Magazine*, Winter 2013, 25–30.

40. David Brown, "Diagnostic Errors Are Leading Cause of Successful

Malpractice Claims," *Washington Post*, April 23, 2013; Ali S. Saber Tehrani et al., "25-Year Summary of US Malpractice Claims for Diagnostic Errors, 1986–2010," *BMJ Quality and Safety*, published online April 22, 2013.

41. "Artificial Intelligence Positioned to Be a Game-Changer," transcript, CBS News, *60 Minutes*, http://www.cbsnews.com/news/60-minutes -artificial-intelligence-charlie-rose-robot-sophia/.

42. M. Mitchell Waldrop, "More than Moore," *Nature* 530 (February 11, 2016): 143–47; Larry Greenemeier, "Will IBM's Watson Usher in a New Era of Cognitive Computing?," *Scientific American*, November 13, 2013; Judy Stone, "Have Pain? Are You Crazy? Rare Diseases Pt. 2," *Scientific American*, February 18, 2014.

43. Casey Ross and Ike Swetlitz, "IBM Pitched Its Watson Supercomputer as Revolution in Cancer Care. It's Nowhere Close," STAT, September 5, 2017, https://www.statnews.com/2017/09/05/watson-ibm-cancer/.

44. Katherine Igoe, "Head-to-Head Comparison Reveals Human Physicians Vastly Outperform Virtual Ones," October 11, 2016, https://hms .harvard.edu/news/doc-versus-machine-0; Hannah L. Semigran et al., "Comparison of Physician and Computer Diagnostic Accuracy," *JAMA Internal Medicine* 176, no. 12 (2016): 1860–61.

45. Edward Tenner, *Why Things Bite Back: Technology and the Revenge of Unintended Consequences* (New York: Alfred A. Knopf, 1996), 7; Paul Sullivan, "Weighing the Value of a Home Security System," *New York Times*, May 1, 2010; Alexander George, "Why the Hell Do They Still Make Car Alarms?," *Popular Mechanics*, September 24, 2015.

46. Robert M. Wachter, *The Digital Doctor: Hope, Hype, and Harm at the Dawn of Medicine's Computer Age* (New York: McGraw-Hill, 2015), 143–46.

47. Ibid., 146–49.

48. Ibid.; Lesley McClurg, "Don't Look Now! How Your Devices Hurt Your Productivity," NPR, October 19, 2016, http://www.npr.org/ sections/health-shots/2016/10/19/498450445/dont-look-now-how -your-devices-hurt-your-productivity.

49. Abha Agrawal, "Medication Errors: Prevention Using Information Technology Systems," *British Journal of Clinical Pharmacology* 67, no. 6 (2009): 681–86; Wachter, *The Digital Doctor*, 131–42.

50. Elena Conis, "When Bleeding Was a Treatment," *Los Angeles Times*, June 26, 2006; Ray Moynihan et al., "Preventing Overdiagnosis: How

to Stop Harming the Healthy," *BMJ* 2012;344:e3502, doi: 10.1136/bmj .e3502 (published May 29, 2012).

51. Aviva Rutkin, "Medicine by Machine," *New Scientist* 231, no. 3089 (September 6, 2016): 20–21; Moynihan, "Preventing Overdiagnosis"; Tara Parker-Pope, "Overtreatment Is Taking a Harmful Toll," *New York Times*, August 28, 2012.

52. Charles Siebert, "The DNA We've Been Dealt," *New York Times Magazine*, September 17, 1995, 50ff; Shari Roan, "Cancer's Legacy: Haunted by Their Family History, Women and Men Are Opting for Genetic Testing. The Results Can Bring New Agony," *Los Angeles Times*, October 1, 2007; Gina Kolata, "Doubt Is Raised on Quick Surgery on Breast Lesion," *New York Times*, August 21, 2015; Patricia Fall, "Waiting for Cancer," *New York Times*, September 1, 2016.

53. Jacalyn Duffin, *To See with a Better Eye: A Life of R. T. H. Laennec* (Princeton, N.J.: Princeton University Press, 1998), 152–55; Ron Winslow, "Some Doctors Aren't Skilled with Stethoscopes, Study Says," *Wall Street Journal*, September 3, 1997; Laura H. Kahn, "Stethoscopes Belong in Museums," *Bulletin of the Atomic Scientists*, February 3, 2008, http://www .thebulletin.org/node/162.

54. Vikas Saini, "Improving Health Care with the Simple Act of Listening," *STAT*, October 17, 2016; Abigail Zuger, "Are Doctors Losing Touch with Hands On Medicine?," *New York Times*, July 13, 1999; Deborah Lupton, *The Quantified Self : A Sociology of Self-Tracking* (Cambridge, U.K.: Polity, 2016).

55. Gerd Gigerenzer, *Gut Feelings: The Intelligence of the Unconscious* (New York: Viking, 2007), 167–78.

56. Ibid., 165.

57. James Colgrove, "The McKeown Thesis: A Historical Controversy and Its Enduring Influence," *American Journal of Public Health* 92, no. 5 (May 2002): 725–29; John P. Bunker, "The Role of Medical Care in Contributing to Health Improvements Within Societies," *International Journal of Epidemiology* 30, no. 6 (2001): 1260–63; Celine Gounder, "Who Is Responsible for the Pain-Pill Epidemic?," *New Yorker*, November 8, 2013; Abby Goodnough, "Treating Pain Without Feeding the Epidemic of Opioid Addiction," *New York Times*, May 23, 2016; Art Van Zee, "The Promotion and Marketing of OxyContin: Commercial Triumph, Public Health Tragedy," *American Journal of Public Health* 99, no. 2 (February 2009): 221–27.

58. Gillian Mohney, "Looking for Answers in Places Where People Live the Longest," *ABC News*, April 1, 2013, http://abcnews.go.com/Health/answers-places-people-live-longest/story?id=18838734; Rock Positano, "The Mystery of the Rosetan People," *Huffington Post*, March 28, 2008.

CONCLUSION

INSPIRED INEFFICIENCY

1. Alex Hern, "'Partnership on AI' formed by Google, Facebook, Amazon, IBM and Microsoft," *Guardian*, September 28, 2016; Sewell Chan, "Fearful of Hacking, Dutch Will Count Ballots by Hand," *New York Times*, February 2, 2017.

2. Elroy Dimson et al., *Triumph of the Optimists: 101 Years of Global Investment Returns* (Princeton, N.J.: Princeton University Press, 2009), 23; William Herman Rau et al., *Traveling the Pennsylvania Railroad: Photographs of William H. Rau* (Philadelphia: University of Pennsylvania Press, 2002), 20; Andrew Ross Sorkin, "To Mark Its Territory, Uber Fattens Its Bankroll," *New York Times*, June 21, 2016; Mike Isaac, "Expedia Leader Emerges as Pick for Uber's Chief," *New York Times*, August 28, 2017; "Uber (Company)," https://en.wikipedia.org/wiki/Uber_(company); "Pennsylvania's Dividend," *New York Times*, November 2, 1900.

3. Evgeny Morozov, "Rockefeller Gave Away Money for No Return. Can We Say the Same of Today's Tech Barons?," *Guardian*, October 15, 2016.

4. Valerie Strauss, "Gates Changes Galvanic Bracelet Grant Description," *Washington Post*, June 12, 2012; Alexi Mostrous and David Brown, "Microsoft Seeks Patent for Office 'Spy' Software," *Times* (London), January 16, 2008.

5. Alex Hern, "Why Data Is the New Coal," *Guardian*, September 27, 2016; Jack Clark, "Google Cuts Its Giant Electricity Bill with DeepMind-Powered AI," *Bloomberg*, July 19, 2016; Quentin Hardy, "Google Says Its Data Centers Will Run Entirely on Renewable Energy by 2017," *New York Times*, December 7, 2016; Yevgeniy Sverdlik, "Here's How Much Energy All US Data Centers Consume," *Data Center Knowledge*, June 27, 2016.

6. Daniel J. Boorstin, *Democracy and Its Discontents: Reflections on Everyday America* (New York: Vintage, 1975), 26–27, 49; William O'Reilly, "Conceptualizing America in Early Modern Central Europe," *Pennsylvania History: A Journal of Mid-Atlantic Studies* 65, Explorations in Early American Culture (1998): 101–21.

7. Georgia Wells, "Facebook's 'Trending' Feature Exhibits Flaws Under New Algorithm," *Wall Street Journal*, September 6, 2016.

8. Christopher Hawthorne, "Apple's Retrograde Cocoon; The Proposed Headquarters Wraps Workers in a Suburban Setting, Removing the Feeling of a Collective Metropolitan Realm," *Los Angeles Times*, September 11, 2011, cited in Steven Levy, "One More Thing: Inside Apple's Insanely Great (or Just Insane) New Mothership," *Wired*, May 16, 2017; John Simons, "IBM Says No to Home Work," *Wall Street Journal*, May 19, 2017.

9. Mike Murphy, "Ford CEO Mark Fields on Self-Driving Cars, Buying Things from Amazon While We Drive, and Mustangs," January 14, 2016, http://qz.com/593820/ford-ceo-mark-fields-on-self-driving-cars-buying-things-from-amazon-while-we-drive-and-mustangs/.

10. David A. Mindell, *Our Robots, Ourselves: Robotics and the Myths of Autonomy* (New York: Viking, 2015), 37–39; David A. Mindell, "Driverless Cars and the Myths of Autonomy," *Huffington Post*, October 14, 2015.

11. Harry Collins, *Artificial Experts: Social Knowledge and Intelligent Machines* (Cambridge, Mass.: MIT Press, 1990), 7–8; Gerd Gigerenzer, *Gut Feelings: The Intelligence of the Unconscious* (New York: Viking, 2007), 103.

12. Whitehead quoted in Jason Zweig, "Mindless Robots, Overblown Worries," *Wall Street Journal*, February 25, 2017.

13. Lynnell Hancock, "A+ for Finland," *Smithsonian*, September 2011, 94–102.

14. Jonah Weiner, "In Stitches," *New York Times Magazine*, April 19, 2013, 38ff.

15. Chess websites run many discussions on this question, but I defer to the chess columnist Shelby Lyman: "Checkmate," *Salt Lake Tribune*, October 19, 2003.

16. Brett Scott, "In Praise of Cash," *Aeon*, March 1, 2017, https://aeon.co/essays/if-plastic-replaces-cash-much-that-is-good-will-be-lost.

17. Grant McCracken, "Spielberg: 1, Harvard: 0," *Cultureby.com*, September 8, 2016, http://cultureby.com/2016/09/spielberg-1-harvard-0.html; Brooks Barnes, "A Summer Full of Superflops: Is It the Films or Ticket Buyers?," *New York Times*, September 5, 2016.

18. "The New York Public Library Reopens Its Historic Rose Main Reading Room and Bill Blass Public Catalog Room" (press release), October 5, 2016, https://www.nypl.org/press/press-release/october-5-2016/

new-york-public-library-reopens-its-historic-rose-main-reading; Ann E. Michael, "It's Not Too Late to Save the Stacks," *Chronicle of Higher Education*, October 19, 2016.

19. Alex Soojung-Kim Pang, *The Distraction Addiction* (New York: Little, Brown, 2013); Nicholas Jackson, "Foursquare and Facebook Try to Force Serendipity," *Atlantic*, December 20, 2010; Schmidt quoted in Evgeny Morozov, *To Save Everything, Click Here* (New York: PublicAffairs, 2013), 257–58.

20. Sophie McBain, "Head in the Cloud," *New Statesman*, February 19, 2016, 40; Leslie Nguyen-Okwu, "The Revenge of Dial-Up Internet," *Ozy*, February 13, 2017, http://www.ozy.com/fast-forward/the-revenge-of-dial-up-internet/75471. For Adrian Ward's dissertation, referenced by Nguyen-Okwu, see Adrian Frank Ward, "One with the Cloud: Why People Mistake the Internet's Knowledge for Their Own" (PhD diss., Harvard University, 2013), http://nrs.harvard.edu/urn-3:HUL.InstRepos:11004901.

21. Mihret Yohannes, "German Rallying Cry Is 'Cash Only,'" *USA Today*, July 17, 2015; Kathleen D. Vohs et al., "Rituals Enhance Consumption," *Psychological Science* 24, no. 9 (2013): 1714–21; Stephen M. Nowlis et al., "The Effect of a Delay Between Choice and Consumption on Consumption Enjoyment," *Journal of Consumer Research* 31, no. 3 (December 2004): 502–10.

22. Paul Hoffman, "Why Are Smart People Some of the Most Gullible People Around?," *Discover*, October 2010, 40–41; Stephen Greenspan, "Fooled by Ponzi (and Madoff)," *eSkeptic*, December 23, 2008, http://www.skeptic.com/eskeptic/08-12-23.

INDEX

A NOTE ABOUT THE AUTHOR

Edward Tenner is a distinguished scholar of the Smithsonian's Lemelson Center for the Study of Invention and Innovation and a visiting scholar in the Rutgers University Department of History. He was a visiting lecturer in the Humanities Council at Princeton, teaching one of the first courses on the history of information, and has held visiting research positions at the Institute for Advanced Study, the Woodrow Wilson International Center for Scholars, and the University of Pennsylvania. His essays and reviews have appeared in *The New York Times, The Washington Post, The Wall Street Journal, The Atlantic, The Wilson Quarterly,* and on Forbes.com, and he has spoken to researchers and designers at Microsoft, Intel, AT&T, and IDEO and at venture capital entrepreneur summits and TED conferences. His *Why Things Bite Back: Technology and the Revenge of Unintended Consequences,* written in part with support from a Guggenheim Fellowship, has been translated into German, Japanese, Chinese, Italian, Portuguese, and Czech. His most recent book, *Our Own Devices: How Technology Remakes Humanity,* was named one of 100 Notable Books of 2003 by *The New York Times Book Review.*

Edward Tenner received the AB from Princeton and the PhD in European history from the University of Chicago and was a German Academic Exchange Service scholar at the University of Heidelberg and a junior fellow of the Harvard Society of Fellows. Before becoming a full-time writer, he was executive editor for physical science and history at Princeton University Press.

A NOTE ON THE TYPE

This book was set in Janson, a typeface long thought to have been made by the Dutchman Anton Janson, who was a practicing typefounder in Leipzig during the years 1668–1687. However, it has been conclusively demonstrated that these types are actually the work of Nicholas Kis (1650–1702), a Hungarian, who most probably learned his trade from the master Dutch typefounder Dirk Voskens. The type is an excellent example of the influential and sturdy Dutch types that prevailed in England up to the time William Caslon (1692–1766) developed his own incomparable designs from them.

Composed by North Market Street Graphics,
Lancaster, Pennsylvania

Printed and bound by Berryville Graphics,
Berryville, Virginia

Designed by Soonyoung Kwon